in the Country

ROSIES EGG'S SOLD HERE

52 Weekends in the Country

Brigid Benson & Craig Easton

Virgin BOOKS

10 9 8 7 6 5 4 3 2 1

First published in the UK in 2012 by Virgin Books, an imprint of Ebury Publishing

A Random House Group Company

Designed by David Rowley
www.davidrowleydesign.com

Maps © Michael Hill 2012
www.michaelahill.com

'The Whack of the Stone' by Elspeth Wills reprinted by kind permission of Elspeth Wills.

'*Fratri Dilectissimo*' by John Buchan and quote from *Memory Hold the Door* by John Buchan reprinted by kind permission of the 4th Lord Tweedsmuir.

Extract from *A Coast to Coast Walk* by Alfred Wainwright reprinted by kind permission of Francis Lincoln Publishers.

'*Idyll*' by Siegfried Sassoon reprinted by kind permission of the Estate of George Sassoon.

'*Wind*' by Ted Hughes and '*Morning Song*' by Sylvia Plath reprinted by kind permission of Faber and Faber Ltd.

Extract from *Coot Club* by Arthur Ransome reprinted by kind permission of The Random House Group Ltd.

Extract from *A Room with a View* by EM Forster reprinted by kind permission of The Provost and Scholars of King's College, Cambridge and The Society of Authors as the Literary Representative of The Estate of EM Forster.

Extract from *Feet in Chains* by Kate Roberts translated into English by John Idris Jones reprinted by kind permission of John Jones Publishing Ltd.

Extract from '*The South Country*' by Hilaire Belloc reprinted by kind permission of Peters, Fraser & Dunlop

'*Cofio*' (Remembering) by Waldo Williams translated by Tony Conran reprinted by kind permission of Gomer Press.

www.randomhouse.co.uk

Addresses for companies within The Random House Group Limited can be found at www.randomhouse.co.uk/offices.htm

The Random House Group Limited Reg. No. 954009
A CIP catalogue record for this book is available from the British Library

ISBN: 9780753522172

MIX
Paper from responsible sources
FSC® C008047

The Random House Group Limited supports The Forest Stewardship Council® (FSC®), the leading international forest certification organisation. Our books carrying the FSC label are printed on FSC® certified paper. FSC is the only forest certification scheme endorsed by the leading environmental organisations, including Greenpeace. Our paper procurement policy can be found at www.randomhouse.co.uk/environment

Printed and bound in China by C&C Offset Printing Co., Ltd

To buy books by your favourite authors and register for offers, visit www.randomhouse.co.uk

Rhiannon, Ella, Jamie, Felix, Millie, Hattie
Molly & James
For your own special journeys and amazing adventures

Contents

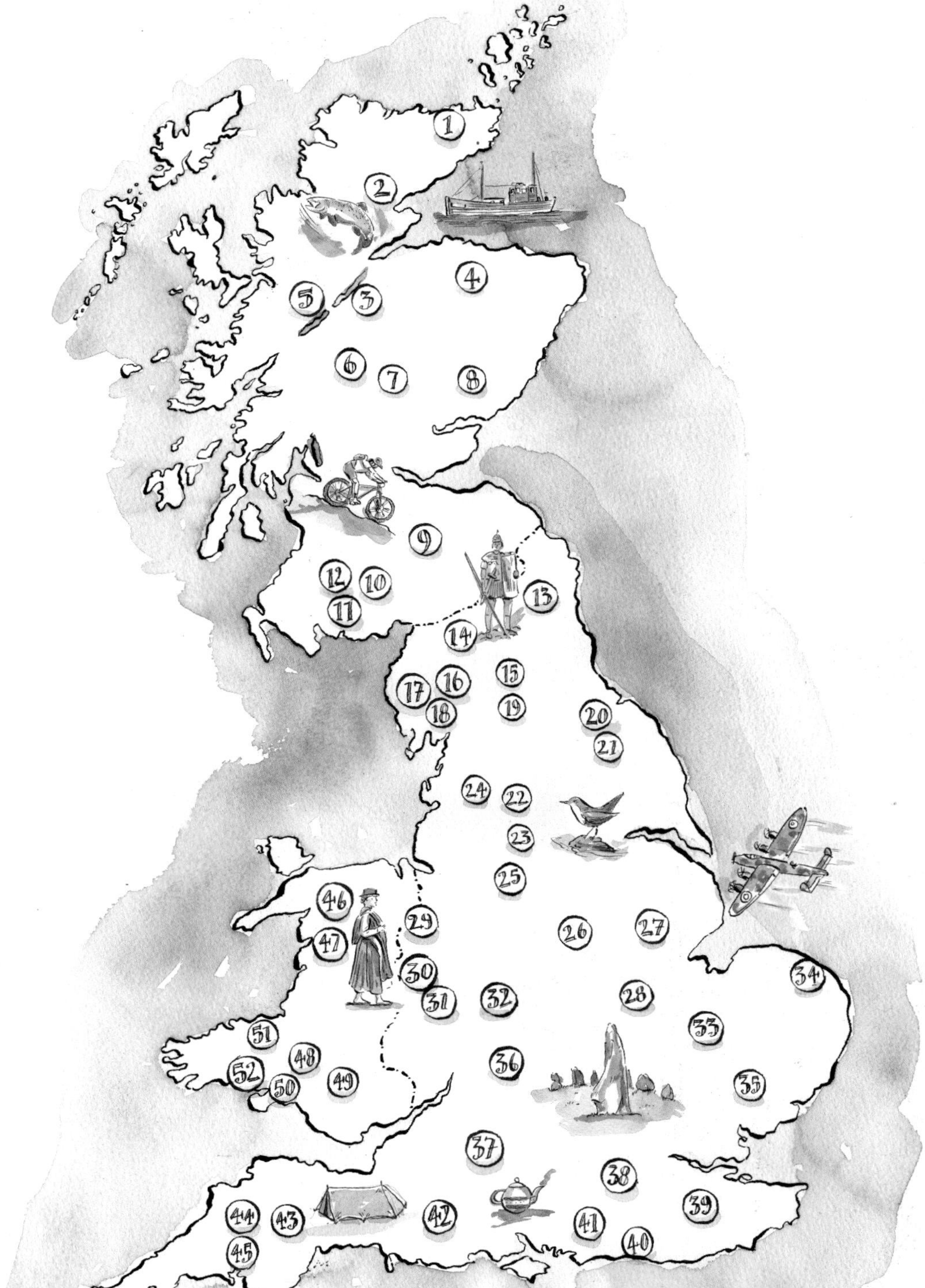
1
2
3
4
5
6
7
8
9
10
11
12
13
14
15
16
17
18
19
20
21
22
23
24
25
26
27
28
29
30
31
32
33
34
35
36
37
38
39
40
41
42
43
44
45
46
47
48
49
50
51
52

Introduction

WELCOME TO *52 Weekends in the Country*, the companion book to the award-winning *52 Weekends by the Sea*. The mission continues to create fascinating short break experiences throughout Britain for travellers on all budgets.

I write from personal experience because it's very important to me that every one of the 52 weekends is original and special: each has been thoroughly road tested. A huge part of the pleasure of travel for me is meeting local people and understanding how their environment shapes their lives.

Craig Easton's photography captures the feel of the landscape and his portraits reveal many of the people we met along the way. I hope you will find inspiration here to make your own adventures and discoveries.

Just as with *52 Weekends by the Sea*, some of the destinations are well known, others are unsung delights. I am not a fair weather traveller, so there is something for every season.

I am passionate about the distinctive qualities of Britain's regions. Together we can help keep that character alive by supporting local producers and services; shop local, stay local, eat local. Before making your trip, please do check the opening hours of places mentioned, some are subject to seasonal change.

Be sure to have a good map and compass with you, especially

if you are going off road, and please follow the Countryside Code and the Moorland Visitor's Code:

* Be safe: plan ahead and follow any signs
* Leave gates and property as you find them
* Protect plants and animals: take your litter home
* Keep dogs under close control
* Consider other people
* Prevent uncontrolled moorland fires, which spread quickly once ignited by smouldering cigarette ends, discarded bottlesand dropped matches

For outdoor adventures in Scotland, please know the access code before you set off. You'll find it at www.outdooraccess-scotland.com.

So that's it. Here's to amazing adventures in Britain! If you'd like to follow more of our work and travels, please visit www.52hq.co.uk and tweets at @52HQ.

See you there!

The scale of this wild territory is breathtaking, covering

Go with the Flow

Peatlands Fishing Burnings

lmost one million acres, 50 per cent of Caithness and Sutherland

Welcome to a far-flung weekend in the extraordinary landscape of the Forsinard Flows National Nature Reserve. Here you'll find the largest expanse of blanketbog in the world and the largest UK nature reserve managed by the Royal Society for the Protection of Birds (RSPB), in association with the local crofting community. The scale of this wild territory is breathtaking, covering almost one million acres, 50 per cent of Caithness and Sutherland

The Forsinard Flows visitor centre is splendidly situated on the isolated platform of Forsinard Station near a level crossing on a lonely single-track road. This unstaffed outpost on the Far North Line, known as Frozen'ard by World War One troops en route to London, is one of my favourite stations. A platform information board sets the scene: passengers disembarking from the train will discover that there is no bus stop nearby, there are no taxis in the vicinity, and there are no more than three spaces in the station car park. There is, however, a warm welcome in the visitor centre where a cosy cinema screens a forty-minute film showing the Flows' extraordinary landscape through the seasons.

The Vikings roamed, and named, the Flows, which are as close to Iceland and the Arctic as they are to London. In the cool moist climate created by the Atlantic Ocean the peatland of Forsinard has developed over thousands of years, gathering fragments of a changing world in slowly deepening layers; on average, less than one millimetre of peat forms each year. Peculiar rare species thrive in this habitat, including rare dwarf birches just fifteen centimetres

...tired, hungry and thirsty?

In this unspoiled remote landscape, tourist facilities are few yet all offer great experiences. Who could resist a remote lochside campsite twenty-five miles from the nearest shops with a shingle beach and sheep grazing the pitches? The Caravan Club's Grummore site is very special.

Discuss the size of your catch with fishing parties in the bar of the Forsinard Hotel, which is also the local Post Office. The hotel has its own river beats and hill lochs. Hole up in a converted cornmeal mill on the Bighouse Estate, where up to fourteen people can sleep in two bunkhouse rooms. There are reels, rods and antlers in the doorway of the lovely Altnaharra Hotel, a former drovers' inn that offers fishing on Loch Naver and Loch Hope and on the Borgie, Strathmore and Mudale rivers. Tackle and equipment are available to buy or hire; ghillies and casting tuition are on hand too. There's a warm welcome at The Bed and Breakfast in the village, a great favourite with cyclists.

high and spongy mounds of moss that grow slowly over hundreds of years and hold up to eight times their weight in water. Deer savour the fleshy leaves of bogbean; Vikings brewed and drank the liquor of shrubby bog myrtle.

Writer Neil Gunn describes Caithness as 'the northland, the land of exquisite light' in his 1937 novel *Highland River*. There's almost perpetual daylight in June while winter brings the mesmerising northern lights. Bird activity peaks between April and September when merlins, greenshanks, dunlins, golden plovers, common scoters, red-throated divers and hen harriers all breed here. There are buzzards, golden eagles, red deer and otters too. Dubh lochans, or watery black hollows around the peat hummocks, are reflecting pools, mirroring the drama of fast-moving clouds. They provide the perfect habitat for diving beetles, whirligig beetles, water boatmen, dragonflies, frogs, newts and pond skaters, all good nourishment for birds. The unique Dubh Lochan stepping-stone trail over one mile through the ridges and hollows created by peat cutting takes about an hour. Trains took peat from Forsinard to distilleries all over Scotland, where it was used to malt barley for whisky.

The train tracks and the road travel south through Strath Halladale towards Knockfin Heights where the Halladale River rises. Between 12 January and 30 September the spate river is the haunt of fishing parties in pursuit of salmon, the king of fish. At Kinbrace the Helmsdale River performs a highland fling, sashaying across a vast open landscape. Just a handful of children populate the tiny school near the station. A lichen-clad rowan stands guard over the windswept burial ground and throughout the strath, or valley, stone-built circular sheepfolds and drying peat stacks are rural works of art.

The lightly used B871 road from Kinbrace is extraordinary; bales of compressed recycled tyres form the base of a road that floats over deep and weak peat to Syre. Here the red and white corrugated-iron mission church, built in 1891 by the Free Church of Scotland, has oil lamps along the walls and glass windows in boiled-sweet colours. Among the church's flock are shepherds, gamekeepers and ghillies. On the shores of Loch Naver, the geography and geology of Altnaharra create extreme conditions throughout the year. Extraordinary weather reports make national headline news and this isolated village is a familiar name to many.

THE YEAR OF THE BURNINGS

In Strathnaver the Donald Macleod monument recalls the horror of Highland Clearances in 1814. Under estate owners' schemes to introduce sheep farms, thousands of people were displaced from the fertile strath to poorer land by the sea. Some left voluntarily, some emigrated and some were evicted. Lives were lost and villages destroyed when thatched homes and byres were set alight under the supervision of Patrick Sellar, who was later charged with culpable homicide. Sellar was brought to trial but not convicted by a jury of landowners. In *Gloomy Memories in the Highlands of Scotland*, stonemason Donald Macleod described the burning of his village, Rosal: 'The cries of the women and children, the roaring of the affrighted cattle, hunted at the same time by the yelping dogs of shepherds around the smoke and fire, altogether presented a scene that completely baffles description.'

The Strathnaver Trail interprets twenty-nine archaeological sites. Many, like the ruins of the crofting community at Grumbeg, are associated with the clearances. Trail leaflets are available from Strathnaver Museum at Bettyhill.

2

Leap of Faith

Sheep Salmon Raven

The crossroads of the north at Lairg, or An Luirg, on Loch Shin have been an important meeting place for centuries; Neolithic people, Gaels and Vikings have left their marks and names here. This weekend explores the heritage of one of the oldest communities in Scotland

Drovers' roads and all major routes to the towns and villages of Sutherland pass through Lairg, bringing estate owners, farmers and crofters of the north to seasonal livestock sales in August, September and October. On approach to the market, close by the station two miles out of the village, a sign announces the 'Historic home of Europe's largest one day lamb sales'.

Until the Beeching closures of the 1960s, much livestock was transported to and from the sales by special trains. Before the arrival of the railway in 1895, drovers and their dogs herded sheep and small black Highland cattle along green roads and through Highland rivers, resting at farmsteads and remote inns along the way. Today hardy North Country Cheviot ewes, wedder lambs, gimmers and rams from Caithness, Ross-shire and Sutherland arrive in vehicles large and small. Shepherded into the mass of interlocked pens sprawling across the hillside, each lot awaits a turn in the sales ring.

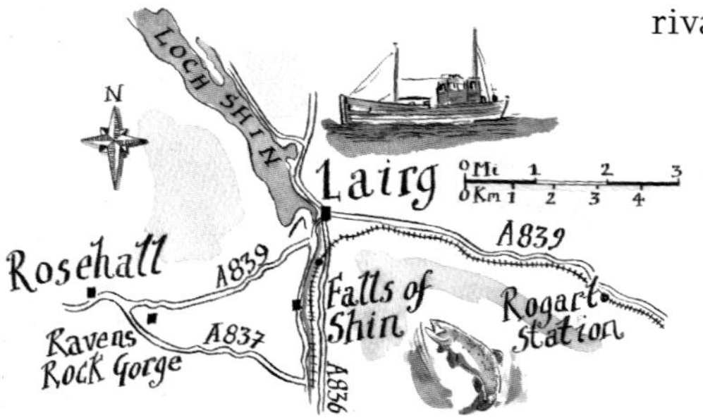

Allow an hour to follow the archaeological trail from Ferrycroft car park up Ord Hill. See hut circles and stone burial tombs, evidence of a Neolithic community that cleared wooded slopes to grow oats and barley and keep livestock. The summit of the Ord offers panoramic views over central Sutherland, Ben Kilbreck and Loch Shin. At the mouth of the Tirry River, Dalchork Wildlife Hide is the perfect spot to observe fishing ospreys, black-throated divers, hen harriers and passing migrants.

...hungry and thirsty?

Fish and chips from Shin Fry always taste good when eaten by the shore of Loch Shin. Tuck into home-made cakes at the Pier Café with fine views of boats and ducks. Campers will find everything from wellies to curry sauce and oatmeal in the Lairg Spar shop. Beyond Lairg, the Overscaig hotel, restaurant and bar is open to non-residents. Rosehall craft shop is a quirky eating place offering home cooking in the woods; venison burgers with braised red cabbage are a local favourite. Walkers and cyclists are welcome at The Falls of Shin restaurant, a great place to refuel after the watching the exertions of leaping salmon. You'll find fine food and drink and exclusive gifts from Harrods in the shop.

Built by the Scottish Hydro Electric Company in 1954 to provide electricity for communities in the far north, the Lairg Dam across Loch Shin created Little Loch Shin. Migrating Atlantic salmon require a 66-foot-high Borland lift to pass through it. To fish on the loch contact Lairg Angling Club, which has nine boats for hire. Permits are available from the club and the Sutherland Sporting Company, Lairg's supreme highland outfitters, who can satisfy all your tweed needs with resplendent breeks, plus twos and plus fours.

Between June and September the spectacle of wild Atlantic salmon leaping at the foaming Falls of Shin is thrilling. Find yourself willing the brave fish on, oohing and aahing at their sheer determination to make progress upstream and spawn at their place of birth. Having

survived the dangers and predators of the open sea and rivers it seems cruel that nature should impose this final assault course upon them. The sound of rushing water enables the salmon to select the best spot for their leap. Ready for take-off, they develop 'burst speed' to hurl themselves forward like gleaming arrows fired by an unseen archer in the peaty pools below. It seems a miraculous achievement. The sad sound of those that fail is haunting; slapping and slithering heavily against the rock, it may take weeks before they are able to summon the strength to try again.

Raven's Rock Gorge is a magical, mossy place; visit in late afternoon and you may have this dappled, pine-scented forest to yourself. Wear stout shoes and allow 45 minutes to follow the trail from the car park to the steep-sided gorge where wooden staircases lead to a cola-coloured burn rushing to a cascade.

...tired?

One of my favourite overnight stops anywhere is Rogart Station sidings, where Kate and Frank have amassed a curious collection of vehicles to transport you to the land of Nod. There's a Bedford bus, converted train carriages and, my favourite, a showman's wagon. Roll up! Roll up! Smell the grease-paint and dream of life on the road. In Lairg, Park House bed and breakfast is popular with fishing and field sports enthusiasts. For camping and caravanning, there's Woodend, with panoramic views over Loch Shin, and Dunroamin in Lairg.

The whack
of stone axe on wood as farmers cleared the forest
The songs
of drovers walking the green road down Loch Shin
The hiss
of steam from the Duke's railway
The tramp
of summer walkers and pedlars
The gossip
of shoppers boarding the Tongue bus
The rumble
of lorries taking timber from the forest
The baaing of lambs
on their way to the sales
These are the sounds of Lairg's crossroads

ELSPETH WILLS

3

A Road Less Travelled

Forest Falls Grebes

Slip away to the secret side of Loch Ness

Slip away to the secret side of Loch Ness. Walk through ancient woods to the spectacular Eas na Smudh (waterfall of smoke), seek out rare Slavonian grebe and try a spot of monster hunting

Elusive Nessie, the Loch Ness Monster, has yet to be found despite highly commercialised beast-hunt activities on the A82 side of Loch Ness. There's much less mention of the monster along the back roads of the opposite shore but on a winter's day, when bare trees afford a clear view of the water, it's hard not to be mesmerised by any unusual disturbance on the surface of the Great Glen's deep, long and narrow loch. If anyone here has seen her, they're not telling.

Victorian tourists sailed by steamboat from Inverness to see the thrilling Falls of Foyers, which thunder 165 feet over 400-million-year-old rocks into a deep dark pool below. Today a network of woodland paths leads to viewpoints over the falls and a tantalising verse by Robert Burns on the hillside at Upper Foyers warns of 'the horrid cauldron' ahead. The creamy, peaty cascade is a magnificent

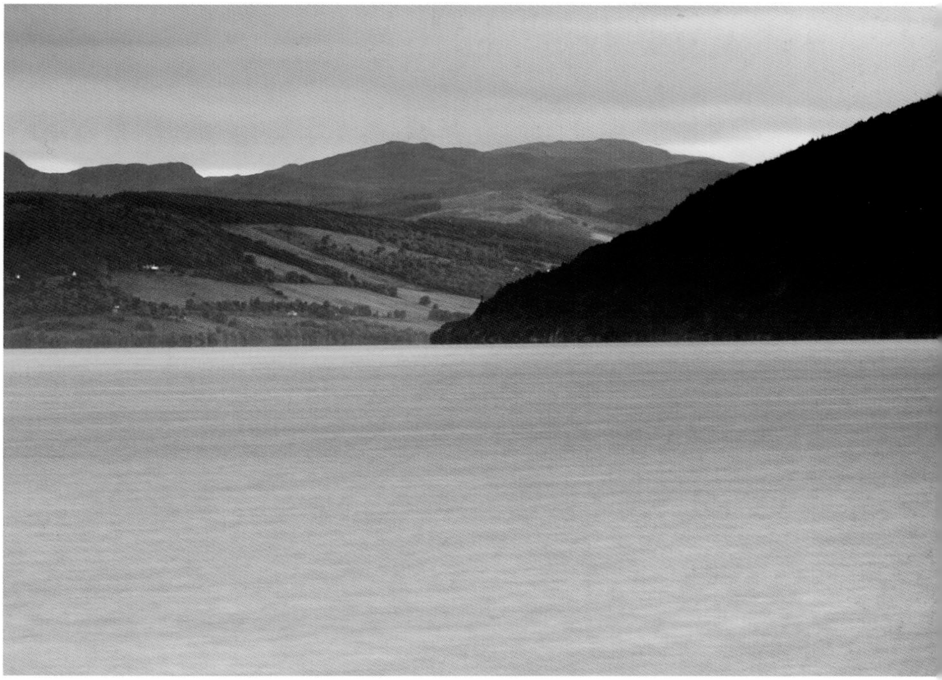

sight, especially when the Foyers River is in full spate and the sound of raging water so loud you can barely hear yourself speak.

Inverfarigaig village is on the road between Loch Ness and Farigaig Forest; nearby is Boleskine House, where the infamous Aleister Crowley practised black magic rituals. Inspired by the occultist, the lyrics of Ozzy Osbourne's single 'Mr Crowley' enquire whether mysterious

...hungry and thirsty?

Book well ahead for supper at the Dores Inn, where good food, friendly service and a happy atmosphere make this a favourite place. Telescopes on the terrace are great for spotting wildlife (or Nessie). Foyers village grew up around the now defunct aluminium smelter. The village stores is still going strong although the butcher's shop became a café some hundred years ago– look out for the meat hooks on the walls. Now known as the Waterfall Café, full breakfasts are a treat. There's brunch on Sundays and fish and chip specials on Thursday, Friday and Saturday evenings. Take a seat on the deck to observe red squirrels at feeders in the woods opposite.

Combine plants and lunch at the Schoolroom café of Brin Herb Nursery in Flichity, where you are welcome to leave your car or bike while you wander for a day in the hills. Hire fly rods, tackle and the services of a ghillie for the day from the Whitebridge Inn, a popular fishing hotel. The Steadings at the Grouse and Trout is popular with regulars who enjoy watching hares on the lawn and ospreys on Loch Flichity.

Aleister communed with the dead. After Crowley the next resident of Boleskine House was Jimmy Page of Led Zeppelin, though he rarely visited during the twenty years he owned it.

In contrast to the dark mysteries of Boleskine, there are more earthly delights in Farigaig Forest, where pine martens, badgers, wild goats, otters and sika deer live among ash, oak, hazel and Scots pine trees. Their tracks are especially clear on snowy winter days. Look out for curious rope bridges that hang high across the road, allowing red squirrels to cross safely from one side to another. From the Forestry Commission car park there are waymarked paths; take a ten-minute stroll along the river, or walk an hour uphill to Lochan Torr an Tuill, a scenic pond with waterlillies.

There are spectacular views sweeping twenty miles down Loch Ness from Dores village, which is beautifully situated on the shore. Here you'll find the caravan of professional monster hunter Steve. From the shingle beach a few brave souls swim in the deep cold water of the loch, though most are happy to gather around barbecues at the water's edge. The backdrop of Urquhart Castle and the Great Glen is spectacular.

Visit Loch Ruthven in spring to see rare Slavonian grebes; they prefer breeding here to anywhere else in Britain. Ospreys scour the loch for fish, capturing them in their talons, while red-throated divers and black-throated divers put in comically clumsy performances waddling around the shore.

RIDE, RUN AND WATCH

The largely undiscovered side of Loch Ness may be rural but there's still plenty going on. For highland horse-riding and walking follow the Trail of the Seven Lochs, a fifty-mile circular route. Experienced riders can saddle up for the two-day adventure at Loch Ness Riding in Dores, though horses cannot be provided. The increasingly popular Loch Ness marathon takes place in autumn when a swarm of enthusiasts competes in one of the most scenic running events in Britain. RockNess is among Britain's best small summer festivals and the Loch Ness Film Festival screens amateur and professional short films from around the world.

...tired?

There are woodland walks from the door of Evergreen bed and breakfast at Inverfarigaig, big country views from Rohan at Gorthleck and picnic-basket lunches for guests at the Pottery House. Log fires and Loch Ness views are a big draw at Craigdarroch House restaurant with rooms. Morgan car owners and members of the Charles Rennie Mackintosh Society may claim a discounted rate when staying at South Gate House in Farr, on the estate where Mackintosh designed the Artist's Cottage.

4

The Angels' Share

Cask strength   Mitherless bairns   Whisky galore

Ready for a long weekend in Speyside? Brooding hills, heather moorland and peaty rivers tell the story of a simple drink that became a worldwide phenomenon. Discover the history of uisge beatha, water of life, or whisky, Scotland's signature tipple.

Speyside is the home of malt whisky; Highland glens are dotted with the distinctive pagoda roofs of Speyside distilleries, designed by architect Charles Doig. Using barley, water, yeast and heat, each ingredient and every stage of the whisky-making process contribute flavour; through malting, milling, mashing, fermentation, distilling and ageing. The process can't be rushed; to be known as whisky the spirit must be matured in casks for at least three years and contain a minimum of 40 per cent alcohol by volume. Malt whisky is considered mature at eight years, although many casks remain untouched until they are between ten and fifteen years old, and some for even longer. The spirit teaches the art of patience; maturing silently in the cask, it develops flavour and aroma, becoming creamier with age and breathing out alcoholic fumes known as 'the angels' share'.

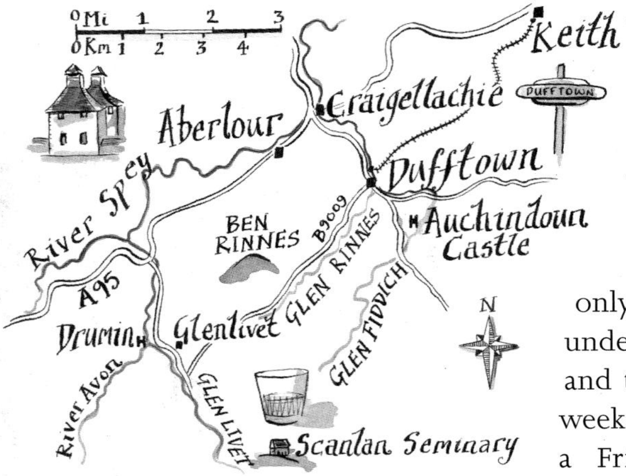

Speyside Cooperage at Craigellachie is the only cooperage in Britain with a visitor centre. To understand the critical relationship between whisky and the casks in which it matures, make this a long weekend and begin with a visit to the cooperage on a Friday (it's not open on Saturday and Sunday). The Acorn to Cask exhibition traces the historic importance of oak casks around the world and there's the opportunity to observe skilled coopers and apprentices in the workshop. Because new oak casks don't do the flavour of whisky any favours, distillers commission the cooperage to repair and renovate casks previously used for sherry or bourbon. The skilled workers labour with traditional hand tools in a process unchanged for centuries.

Rolling casks around the shop floor with ease, the coopers' hand–eye co-ordination is extraordinary. Mere mortals would be crushed under runaway casks. Appearing powerfully balletic, the coopers treat staves and casks as if they were simply an extension of their own bodies. The wood of each worker's hammer becomes shaped by the grip of his hand. There's a fug of alcohol from spirit-soaked oak and the workshop resounds to the rhythm of hammers dealing precise blows. Sparks fly,

fires flare and steam rises, yet the coopers work on unperturbed. Gary, who learned his craft from a herring cooper, explained that every stave is shaped in six different ways to create a cask. The process is fiendishly difficult, calculations are by eye and by the feel of the wood alone, a learning curve which takes an apprentice four years. Melding the staves together – close isn't good enough – each cask is tested and must hold water. The expert coopers are piece workers achieving flawless results.

Between 60 and 80 per cent of the flavour of whisky is imparted by the cask in which it matures. Every cask is an individual and the eventual flavour of the whisky is influenced by the species of oak and the

...hungry and thirsty?

A favourite Highland foodie haunt is the Spey Larder in Aberlour. In a beautiful 1867 grocer's shop you'll find tasty treats, homewares and whisky. Allow owner David Catto to prepare your picnic or river lunch or simply pop in for fresh coffee and try resisting the home-made soups, sandwiches and tarts. Founded in Aberlour in 1898, Walkers Shortbread produces 20,000 tonnes of this delicious biscuit annually. The village shop sells every item in the range and the factory shop has bargains. The Mash Tun whisky bar in Aberlour was built as a station bar by a former seaman who wanted his pub to look like a ship. Find an extraordinary collection of rare Glenfarclas whisky, which you can buy by the dram. The Buffer Stop restaurant is in railway carriages at Dufftown Station and there are cafés at the cooperage and most distilleries.

region where it grew. Smaller casks create more intense flavour. In fearsome flames casks are subjected to toasting and charring to open the grain of the wood and to impart colour and flavour to the whisky. The charcoal acts as a filter to remove impurities, and the intensity of the burn, from light, through medium and heavy to alligator skin, depends on a distiller's requirements.

Structurally a cask may have a lifespan of up to fifty years; decharring and then recharring them is part of the renewal process. Master Distillers create different tastes by 'marrying' single malts from a range of casks and Gary believes that we each bring our own life experience to whisky tasting, detecting flavours reminiscent of tastes and smells we've experienced previously. Acutely aware of a multitude of forces at work to create flavour, Gary never takes his whisky with water – why dilute it?

From the cooperage it's a short trip to the Macallan Distillery overlooking the River Spey. Join a small tour group led by a knowledgeable guide to discover the distillery; a tutored tasting or nosing is also possible. Booking is essential for both events. Railway enthusiasts will be tempted by a ride on the Keith and Dufftown Railway, known as the whisky line. Dufftown Station is surrounded by distilleries and adjacent to the Glenfiddich Distillery. In Keith Strathmill Distillery welcomes visitors who book in advance, while guided tours at pretty Strathisla Distillery introduce single malts and premium-blended scotch including Chivas Regal.

Away from the whisky there is gentle walk along the leafy banks of the River Avon (pronounced A'an) a tributary of the Spey; explore the romantic ruins of Drumin Castle, perched above the confluence of the Avon and Livet rivers; a lovely three-kilometre circular walk starts here. To visit the ruins of fifteenth-century Auchindoun Castle, park at the side of the A941 and walk two kilometres up a rough track. The fortress

was the stronghold of Adam Gordon, known as the Herod of the North. He burned to death Margaret Campbell, wife of Forbes of Towie, and twenty-seven of her family and servants at Corgarff castle in 1571.

After a day of casks and castles, there are further distilleries to discover around Aberlour, but first explore the country town on the banks of the Spey. The Speyside Way visitor centre is situated in the former railway station, with information about the long-distance route that links the east coast with Aviemore and Tomintoul. Reservations are essential for tours of Aberlour Distillery, which take around two hours and give you the opportunity to nose and taste new distillate and five single malts. The Gothic St Margaret's Church was designed by leading

Scottish architect Alexander Ross for the children of Aberlour orphanage, founded in 1875. The orphanage was funded entirely by voluntary contributions, and at its height 1,000 'mitherless bairns' were on the register; fortunately Reverend Charles Jupp was a formidable fundraiser. The orphanage closed in 1967 and the site is marked by the statue of a young girl reading a fairy tale on a bed of heather.

At the foot of Ben Rinnes, the Glenfarclas Distillery is a rare independent family-run business. You are invited to take a tour and sample a wee dram in the splendid Ship's Room with elegant oak-carved panels and furniture from the *Empress of Australia*, a Canadian–Pacific liner. There are further tours at Cardhu Distillery, which produces a silky malt whisky used in some of the award-winning Johnnie Walker blended range of Scotch whiskies.

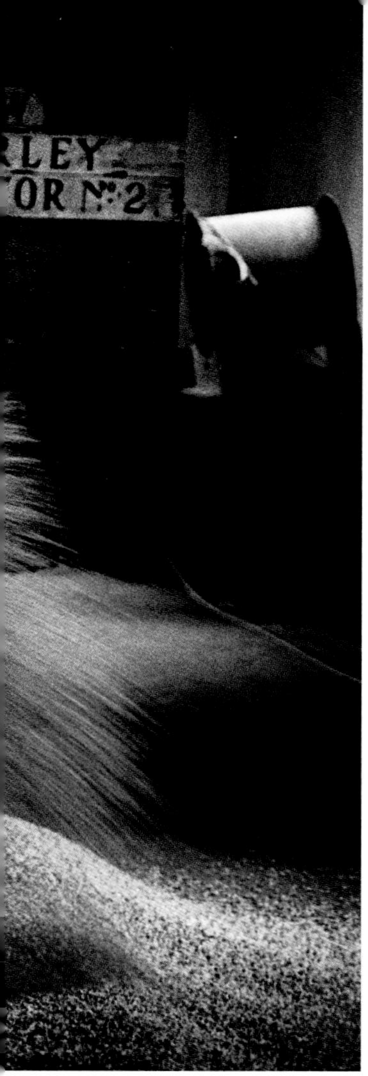

...tired?

There's a huge range of accommodation over this large area. Aberlour makes a great base, whether you seek the comfort of a sporting retreat like Dowans Hotel or the whisky-imbued character of the stylish Mash Tun bar with rooms. There's friendly bed and breakfast at Castleview and Laggan Farmhouse, camping at Aberlour Gardens and in the grounds of Glenlivet Public Hall, or enjoy sweet dreams in the highest village in the Highlands; Tomintoul Youth Hostel is in the refurbished village school.

When customs and excise men came to call, Cardhu's co-founder Helen Cumming raised a flag to warn bootleggers in the hills of their presence. Avoiding taxes in the eighteenth century, smugglers trafficked whisky across remote Speyside hills hotly pursued by excise men. Discover three waymarked trails across the Crown Estate in the footsteps of renowned whisky characters: smugglers George Smith and Robbie MacPherson, and excise man Malcolm Gillespie. The walking routes, available from the Glenlivet Distillery, are to be used with Ordnance Survey Landranger maps sheets 36 and 37. In the heyday of bootleg whisky there were 200 illicit stills in Glenlivet; you can learn more about them at the distillery where tours are free – the whisky-flavoured ice cream in the coffee shop is sumptuous! Age is important at Glenlivet; the minimum age of any whisky in the range is twelve years.

The Speyside hills sheltered not only illicit stills but also the isolated college of Scanlan, the seat of Catholic teaching in Scotland. Here the faith was kept alive throughout the challenges of the eighteenth century, following the Reformation of 1560 and the persecution of the Catholic Church. Around a hundred Scottish priests were trained at Scanlan, some completing their courses abroad, many ordained at the college. Young students lived in Spartan conditions, embracing the wilderness to make fresh air and exercise part of a regime founded on prayer and study. They learned French, Irish and Gaelic, and lived by thirty-one rules drawn up by Bishop George Gordon, regarded as one of the greatest Scottish bishops. By 1799 Scanlan (meaning 'turf-roofed shelter' in Gaelic) had served its purpose and the students moved to Inverurie. Visiting the lonely buildings of the windswept outpost is intriguing; it's hard to believe that important letters were sent to Rome from here.

In 1769 Scanlan saw the consecration of Bishop George Hay, Vicar Apostolic of the Lowland District. In turn he consecrated Bishop Alexander MacDonald, Vicar Apostolic of the Highland District at Scanlan in 1780.

5

John Anderson, My Jo

John Anderson, my jo, John,
When we were first acquent;
Your locks were like the raven,
Your bonie brow was brent;
But now your brow is beld, John,
Your locks are like the snaw;
But blessings on your frosty pow,
John Anderson, my jo.

John Anderson, my jo, John,
We clamb the hill thegither;
And mony a cantie day, John,
We've had wi' ane anither:
Now we maun totter down, John,
And hand in hand we'll go,
And sleep thegither at the foot,
John Anderson, my jo.

ROBERT BURNS

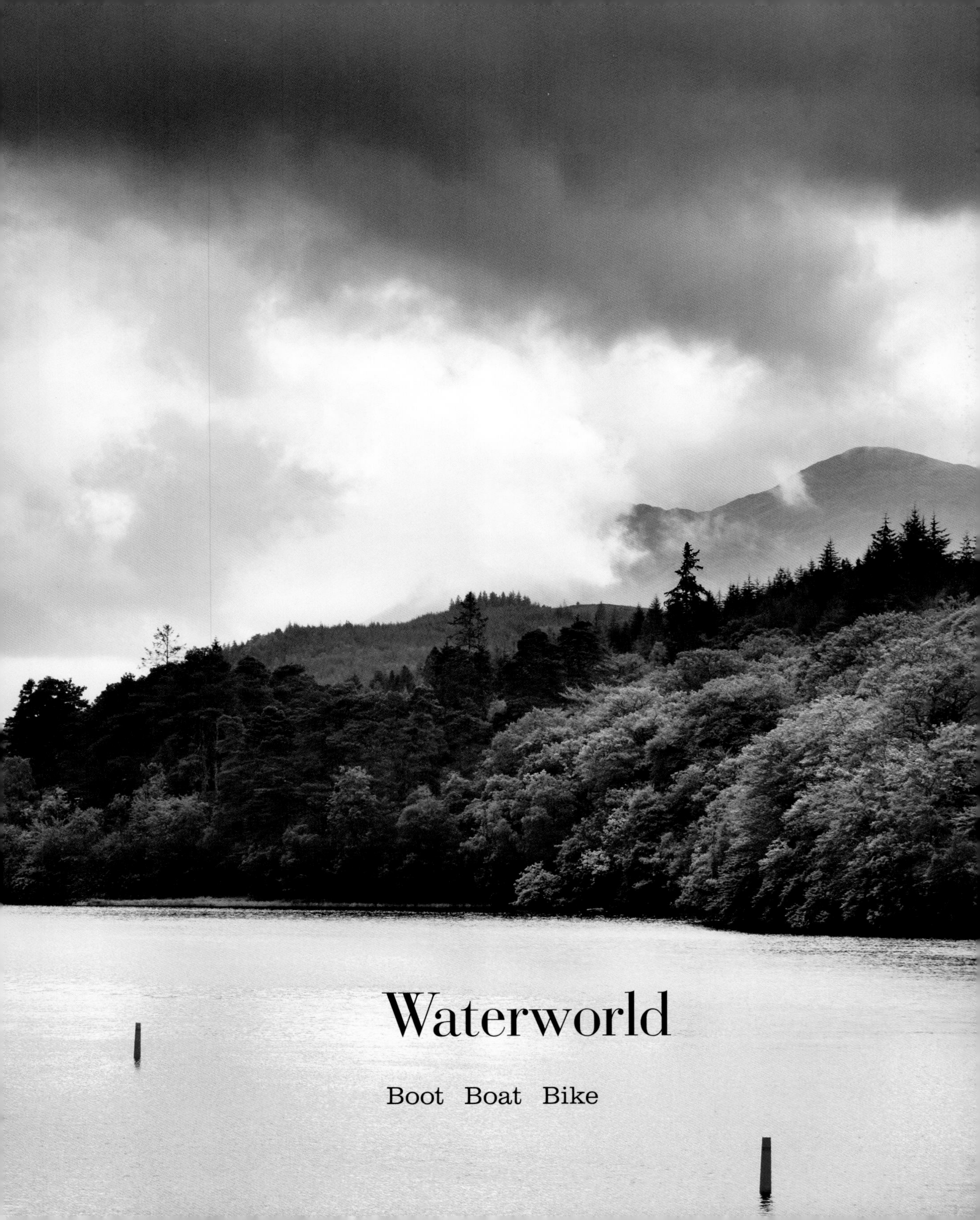

Waterworld

Boot Boat Bike

Following the natural geological fault line of Scotland's Great Glen, the Caledonian Canal is a Scheduled Ancient Monument and an extraordinary short-cut. Designed by Thomas Telford, the waterway between the Atlantic Ocean and the North Sea links four natural lochs – Lochy, Oich, Ness and Dochfour – and granted the herring fleet and sailing ships a new safe passage to the Baltic and West Indies without threat of shipwreck on the fierce and remote coasts of Cape Wrath and the Pentland Firth. The project, begun in 1803, took twenty years to complete; twenty-two miles of canal were dug out by hand.

While few fishing boats still use the canal, outstanding scenery makes the route between Corpach sea lock near Fort William in the southwest and Clachnaharry sea lock near Inverness in the northeast popular with cruisers, sailboats, kayaks, canoes and occasional naval vessels. The canal is one of four ways to explore the Great Glen, alongside the Great Glen Long Distance Footpath, the Great Glen Mountain Bike Trails and the new Great Glen Canoe Trail.

Fort Augustus is situated at the midpoint of the canal's length. Built by General Wade in the eighteenth century, it was named after Prince William Augustus. Scots know the Prince as 'Butcher Cumberland' for his cruel role in the Battle of Culloden.

A busy hub of five locks links the canal with Loch Ness and provides great entertainment to onlookers observing captains and crew at work under the strict instruction of efficient lock-keepers. In a converted lock-keeper's cottage the Caledonian Canal Visitor Centre is a small yet informative British Waterways Museum.

...hungry and thirsty?

Buy a drink from the Lock Inn at Fort Augustus and enjoy the canal action from bench seats at the water's edge. The Lock Inn boasts a handsome oak bar made from local wood by local craftsmen and an impressive selection of whiskies to savour by the log fire. The Boathouse restaurant offers outdoor seating on the shore of Loch Ness. The Eagle Barge Inn and restaurant is a quirky converted Dutch barge moored at South Laggan locks. Fish suppers from the canalside chip shop at Fort Augustus are a big hit with ravenous paddlers from canoes and kayaks.

Visit the grave of John Anderson, carpenter friend of Robert Burns at Kilchuimen burial ground. Planning ahead, Burns is believed to have commissioned his coffin from his Ayrshire chum who inspired the celebrated song 'John Anderson, My Jo'.

For an easy two-hour walk along the towpath and back follow the Great Glen Way out of Fort Augustus to pretty Kytra Lock. Here stand Mingulay and Vatersay, a pair of charming canalside cottages surrounded by picket fences and country gardens. Named after Hebridean islands, they were formerly lock-keepers' homes. At the water's edge there's a picnic bench and a teeny camping spot under a clump of Scots pines where small groups of canoeists and kayakers are permitted to pull up their boats and put up their tents to wild-camp for one night only due to limited space and high demand. It is possible to extend this walk to the swing bridge carrying the A82 road over the canal at Aberchalder. There's great excitement when large boats arrive at the bridge; a warning blast sounds, flashing lights halt the traffic and the roadway bridge sweeps open to allow vessels to pass by.

Should you fancy taking to the water, there are many hire companies along the canal. Take your pick from motor cruisers, floating hotels, luxury yachts large and small, and even a floating bunkhouse and pub.

...tired?

The locks at Fort Augustus have long been a tourist attraction. Accommodation includes The Lovat Hotel on the site of General Wade's fort where the west curtain wall remains. Nearby, the small Caledonian Hotel boasts a bowling and putting green. Lady Andorina, a 70-foot wooden ketch, is now a floating bunkhouse. The Great Glen Canoe Trail offers informal campsites with open-side shelters, fire pits and composting toilets.

Skimming the moor, the tracks of the West Highland Line lie on layer:

6

Night Train

Mountains Moor Wilderness

f earth and ashes, brushwood and ancient pine tree roots.

Take the train this weekend for an unforgettable journey through scenic Scottish landscape. Moody mountains, soggy bog, ancient forests and outstanding feats of engineering are all part of this magnificent trip.

For me, one of the most thrilling British train journeys is the night-time adventure of the Caledonian Sleeper. Board the train in London, Crewe or at other stations along the way, snuggle into a wee berth and wake to find yourself in breathtaking highland scenery. From Crianlarich to Fort William, the northbound fork of the world-famous West Highland Line climbs to Upper Tyndrum, snakes around the lower slopes of Beinn Odhar and crosses the waters of the Allt Coralan on the extraordinary Horseshoe Curve viaduct. Onward to the Bridge of Orchy, built by King George's troops in 1751 to carry the military road over the River Orchy, and past the ruined tower of Achallader Castle. The railway rattles through the ancient Caledonian Forest, once the realm of wolves and wild boar, before reaching flat and boggy Crannoch Moor. Ahead lies the high and lonely amphitheatre of Great Rannoch Moor. That anyone in the 1890s considered building a railway across a deep peat bog, approximately fifty square miles across, is astonishing, and yet the engineers triumphed. Skimming the moor, the tracks of the West Highland Line lie on layers of earth and ashes, brushwood and ancient pine tree roots.

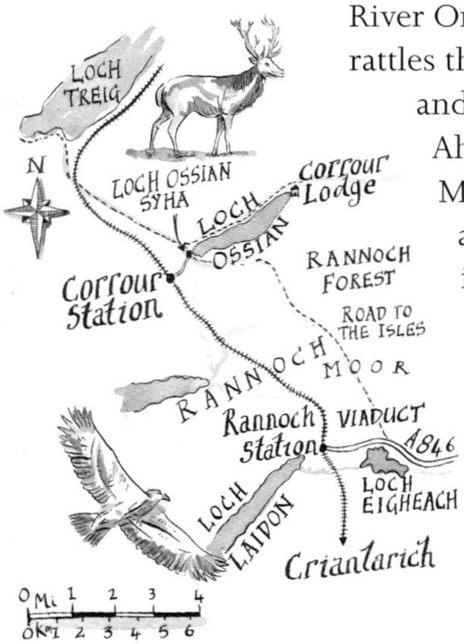

Depending on the season, the heathery landscape is shades of rust and brown, ice-white or purple. Weather conditions change wildly; a serene day may whip up a fierce blizzard and close with an ethereal sunset. The drama of Rannoch inspired the trials of David Balfour and Jacobite Alan Breck in Robert Louis Stevenson's *Kidnapped*. Fleeing from redcoat troops and false accusations of murder, they reach the moor: 'a bald, naked, flat place' that offers little cover.

Exploring the moor is a serious challenge; in the past even the most knowledgeable local shepherds respected the terrain, aware that they might perish if they lost their way. It may appear to be a great flat plain encircled by mountains, but close up it is a lumpy combination of earthy sods, granite boulders, lochans and deep hags or ditches. Dug in 1745 after the Jacobite Rebellion, the Soldier's Trenches were an attempt to drain the moor for defence and pasture. The ditches soon flooded with rainwater and were abandoned.

Stevenson's hero, Balfour, is lucky to escape from the moor, scrambling to safety on the slopes of Beinn Eallair.

As the train travels on, the mountains of Glencoe, Glen Lyon, Glen Ogle and Glen Etive begin to crowd the distant scene. The railway goes undercover at Cruach cutting where the corrugated-iron roof of Britain's only snow shed protects the West Highland Line from avalanche. There's brief contact with civilisation at Rannoch Station where a dinky green wooden chalet stands on an island platform. It's the kind of place you romance about living in until you remember the harsh environment. Railway sidings are littered with paraphernalia, including abandoned coaches used by railway workers for social gatherings. Thousands of navvies constructed this stretch of line and when the moor presented technical challenges funds ran critically low. The head of financier James Renton was carved on a granite boulder by workers who

...hungry and thirsty?

There's tasty bar food and Isle of Colonsay beer at the Crianlarich Hotel. In season there are tearooms at Crianlarich and Rannoch stations.

depended on his continued support and investment in the project; you can still find it on the north end of the platform.

From Rannoch viaduct the train travels towards Corrour Forest and locations from recent film history. Scenes from *Harry Potter* and *Trainspotting* were filmed around here. Alight at Corrour, one of the shortest station platforms in Britain for a great weekend of high- or low-level adventures, but be sure to come prepared. Walking boots, warm clothes, wet-weather gear, maps and compass are essential at any time of year. Along with a cheery welcome you'll find detailed weather reports for the area. On my last winter trip the forecast read, 'Even at fairly low level you could be blown over and higher up the transition to storm force or above will take place very suddenly.' Beware!

Early nineteenth-century visitors to the Corrour Estate had an enviable journey; taking a pony and trap from the train station they trotted to Loch Ossian boathouse where they boarded an elegant steam yacht by the name of Cailleach, or the witch, to sail four miles down the loch to Corrour Lodge. In Scottish folk tales Cailleach is the giant hag who ruled the winter months and created a mountainous landscape by dropping rocks from her apron.

In 1931 the Scottish Youth Hostel Association (SYHA) opened the former Loch Ossian boathouse for hillwalkers. Recent refurbishment has made it an outstanding example of eco-friendly accommodation in the wilderness. Wind and solar power provide energy, 'grey' water is recycled and a dry toilet system provides fertiliser for newly planted native trees. From the tranquil shore of the lonely loch, visitors can observe red deer and red squirrels, otters, pine martens, white mountain hares, black-throated divers and golden eagles.

Whether you are inclined to walk a circuit of the loch, climb mountains, or follow the old drovers' road to the isles, the feeling of escape is unforgettable.

SIDE ORDERS

Besides the magnificent walking, Corrour Estate offers fishing permits and the opportunity to hire a Canadian canoe for a day on Loch Treig. Or hire a bike, take a picnic and allow three leisurely hours to cycle around Loch Ossian. Alternatively take the train from Corrour to Rannoch and allow five hours to walk safely back over the moor.

...tired?

For overnight accommodation before taking the train from Crianlarich, there's the local youth hostel and the friendly Crianlarich Hotel. Alternatively take the 'Deerstalker' or Caledonian Sleeper direct from London to Corrour. Stay at the eco-friendly Loch Ossian hostel or in Corrour Estate cottages. For something completely different, step into the steel, glass and granite dream world of Corrour Lodge, a mind-blowing example of extraordinary modern architecture on the shore of Loch Ossian.

7

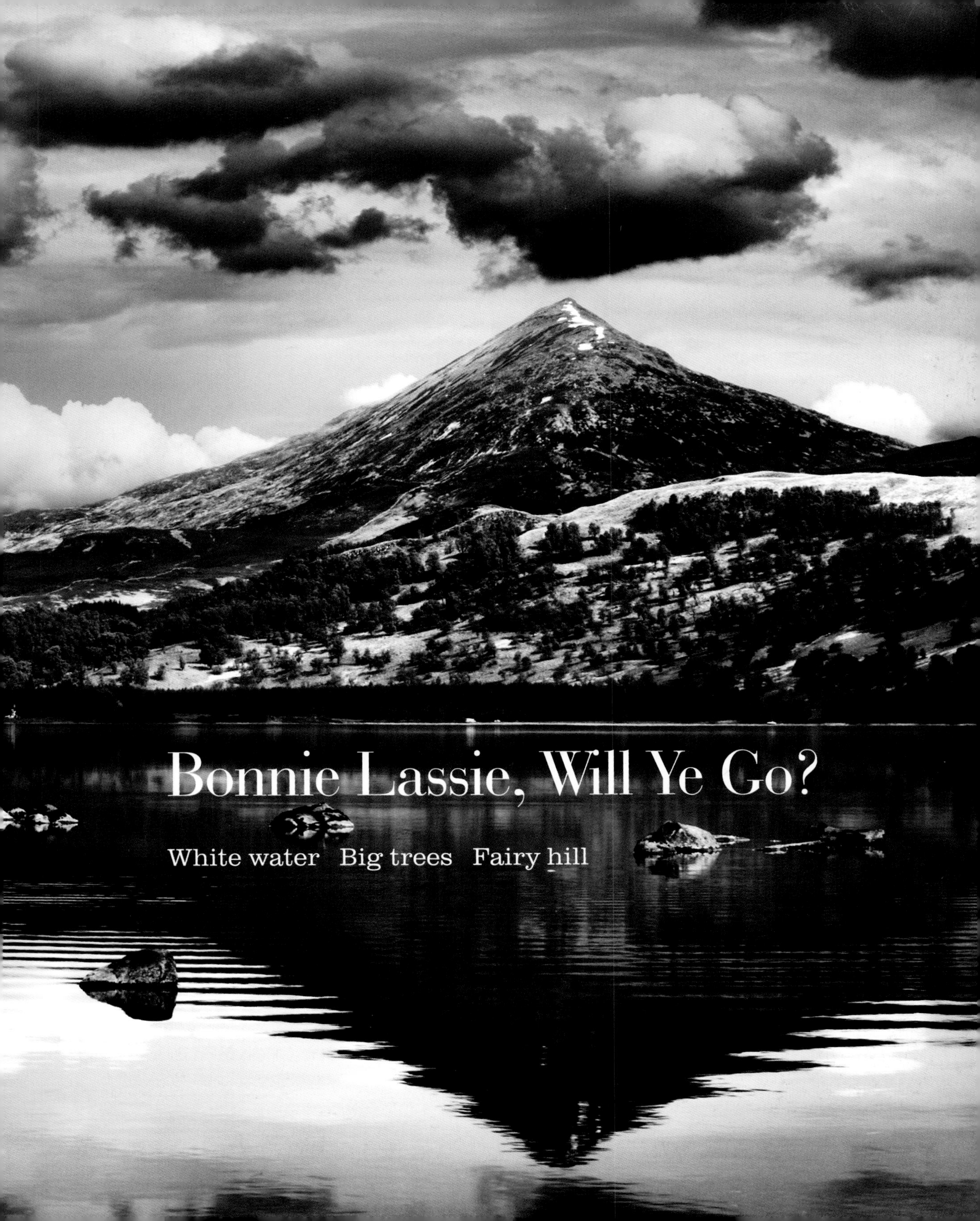

Bonnie Lassie, Will Ye Go?

White water   Big trees   Fairy hill

Entranced by birch trees in a lush woodland gorge, Robert Burns was inspired to write one of his most famous songs, 'The Birks of Aberfeldy'. This weekend takes you to the poetic birks and the small town at the geographic centre of Scotland where the rapids on the Tay, Scotland's longest river, provide white-water thrills for adrenaline junkies.

Surrounded by peaks, lochs and fast-flowing water, Aberfeldy makes a great base for an active weekend. Before the town existed, General Wade, leader of the King's army in Scotland, constructed a military road through the area in a bid to control unruly highland clans. In 1733 William Adam, one of Scotland's finest architects, was commissioned to design a road crossing of the Tay at Aberfeldy. Still in use, Adam's elegant five-arch bridge is one of the loveliest in Scotland and testament to the skill of the master masons.

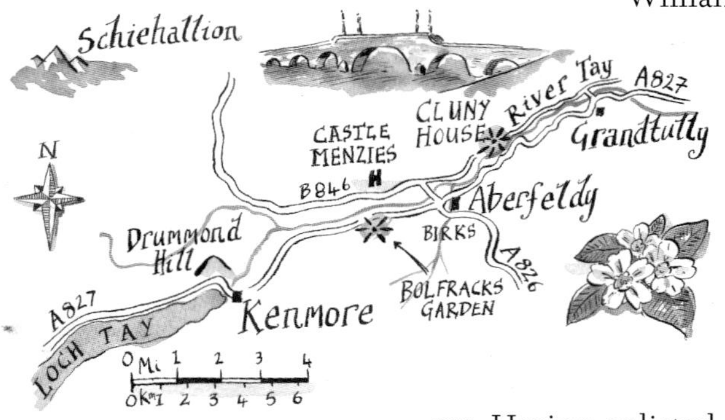

Beside the bridge a statue of Private Farquhar Shaw, in kilted military uniform, stands high on the Black Watch monument commemorating the 1740 muster in fields nearby of the regiment that later became the 42nd Royal Highlanders. Having enlisted to serve in Scotland, many were surprised by their summons to England in 1743. Fearing they were to be shipped to the American plantations, they mutinied. Private Shaw and two others were accused of desertion and shot.

Robert Burns' beloved birks, or birches, are easily reached by footpath from Aberfeldy. Allow two hours for the woodland walk alongside the splashy Moness Burn, especially lovely on a spring morning when,

...hungry and thirsty?

No visit to Aberfeldy is complete without calling at The Watermill, an outstanding destination in itself whether you are looking for music, art, books, good food, great coffee or fine tea. Made all the more intriguing because owners Jayne and Kevin Rammage have kept the industrial guts of the building *in situ*, The Watermill is a must. Check out exciting design at Homer, the lifestyle shop in the barn next door.

Dine on the deck of the family-run Ailean Chraggan hotel in Weem, choose picnic treats from the deli and New World wine shop at the House of Menzies or the Courtyard at Kenmore; both have cafés too. Try a wee dram at the Weem Hotel next to the house where General Wade stayed while his bridge was being built. Connoisseurs and the curious are invited to tour Dewar's World of Whisky at the Aberfeldy Distillery, home of the award-winning White Label single malt. Hot chocolate and exquisite hand-made truffles are hard to resist at Legends of Grandtully.

as Burns wrote, 'the little birdies blithely sing' and the air is heavy with the scent of wild garlic and mint, primroses and dog violets. While the birks enchanted Burns, Perthshire is also Big Tree Country. In the late eighteenth century, estate owners 'enhanced' the countryside with exotic trees from distant countries. To see red squirrels and Britain's widest sequoia explore the woodland at Cluny House. There's a 3,000-year-old yew tree in the kirk yard at Fortingall and rare plants and views over Loch Tay at Bolfracks Garden.

There's great weekend walking around Aberfeldy and Loch Tay, which is fifteen miles long. Take the four-mile riverside stroll from Aberfeldy to Grandtully (pronounced Grantly) where canoeists ride white water on the Tay, or a longer walk of fifteen miles along the riverside path to Kenmore. Return to Aberfeldy via Newhall, Croftmoraig, Bolfracks Hill and Dunskaig. Climb Drummond Hill near Kenmore for a bird's-eye view of Loch Tay, allowing two hours for the round trip; a steep forestry footpath leads to the viewpoint. If you'd prefer to be on the water, a variety of boats, and

Bonnie lassie, will ye go,
Will ye go, will ye go,
Bonnie lassie, will ye go
To the birks of Aberfeldy!

ROBERT BURNS

mountain bikes, may be hired from Loch Tay Boating Centre.

In the deep waters of Loch Tay there were once eighteen crannogs – Iron Age homes that stood on stilts and were connected to the shore by a walkway. The Scottish Crannog Centre at Kenmore offers the opportunity to explore a crannog and learn about the lives of the lake dwellers. From Iron Age crannogs fast-forward to sixteenth-century Menzies Castle. Once a fortress, now a family home, the ancestral seat of the Chief of the Clan Menzies welcomes visitors.

Ask children to draw a mountain and it's likely they'll come up with a symmetrical peak just like Schiehallion, the Fairy Hill of the Caledonians. Cup-marked rocks surrounding the mystical mountain and caves suggest ancient rituals. From the Braes of Foss car park at East Schiehallion there's a path to the summit; allow six hours for the journey there and back by the same route.

This highland landscape is perfect for an active weekend; simply choose your sport.

CLIMBING

The crags and boulders of Weem are popular with climbers and a steep 45-minute walking trail through the ancient wood reveals mysterious sculptures before reaching St David's Well and a panoramic view over Aberfeldy.

CYCLING

The scenic national cycle route number 7 travels along Loch Tay for fifteen miles between Killin and Kenmore.

CANOEING AND RAFTING

White water entices canoeists and rafters to the Tay. Absolute beginners and advanced enthusiasts are all welcome at the National Kayak School and hostel, Freespirits, Splash Whitewater Rafting or Beyond Adventure.

SWIMMING

If you prefer to enter the water without a paddle, try swimming in Loch Tay from shingly Kenmore beach. For safety, use a swimming wetsuit, a brightly coloured swim hat and goggles. Take a friend and have warm clothes and a hot drink ready for your exit.

GOLF

Boasting the world's longest composite bridge, Aberfeldy Golf Club is beautifully situated on both banks of the Tay. Golfing visitors are most welcome to bounce their way across it.

...tired?

Robert Burns left his mark on Scotland's oldest inn by writing a poem in pencil on the fireplace of the Kenmore Hotel. You can still see it in the Poet's Bar.

For chic rooms and riverside views stay at the family-run Inn on the Tay at Grandtully, or for bed and breakfast with reflexology try Fernbank House in Aberfeldy. Enjoy an evening dram of Aberfeldy malt on the house at Rose Cottage bed and breakfast, a handsome Victorian villa. There's camping by the Tay with the Scottish Canoe Association at Grandtully and accommodation for groups at The Bunkhouse and Glassie Farm.

8

Neverland

Angus Glens Captain Scott JM Barrie

This weekend in the northeast of Scotland combines the remote Angus Glens with a sprinkling of the South Pole and a handful of pixie dust; discover the wild landscape of Glen Clova, Glen Doll and Glen Prosen, beloved by Captain Scott, and rekindle childhood magic in Kirriemuir, birthplace of Sir JM Barrie, author of *Peter Pan*.

Lonely Glen Clova is an instant geography lesson; the smooth steep slopes of the valley shaped by glaciers, the flat floor strewn with boulders and moraine heaps deposited as huge ice flows melted and, up in the hills, spectacular corries where glaciers formed in the Ice Age. Visit by car and you should be aware that, traditionally, the west branch of the narrow B955 is the road into the glen while the east branch is the exit route.

Clova's isolated kirk is surrounded by the graves of shepherds from scattered farmsteads. In hills all round there's magnificent walking; some routes are easy, most are strenuous and it pays, as ever, to respect rapidly changing weather conditions. Every year the local community organises a walk from neighbouring Glen Prosen over the mountain to Glen Clova to celebrate the Minister's Path, a wilderness route taken by missionary ministers serving congregations in both glens since 1814. Depending on the season, the minister's four-mile journey on horseback or with pony and cart was frequently perilous. The annual celebration begins with a morning service at Glen Prosen followed by a hike over the hills and a service at Clova kirk. There's also a thanksgiving service for the lambs in May, at the end of lambing season. In the 1840s, Jock's Road from Braemar to Glen Doll was a mountain highway used by drovers and caterans (cattle rustlers). Thousands of sheep were taken to Cullow Market, now a walkers' car park, in lower Glen Clova for spring and autumn lamb sales.

Glen Clova gives way to a minor road leading to Glen Doll car park and the Corrie Fee National Nature Reserve. Call into the visitor centre on the banks of the River South Esk to discover exhibitions of rare wildlife that inhabit this landscape, including pine marten, mountain hares, red squirrels, golden eagles and Scottish wildcats. The cliffs and crags create hideaway places for rare low-growing plants: alpine blue-sow-thistles, yellow milk vetch and woolly willows. From here experienced hill walkers follow the Corrie Fee trail, a challenging route of six miles there and back. Deerstalking takes place in late summer and autumn, so be sure to confirm the access situation before you set out.

PETER PAN

Kirriemuir, or Kirrie, is a magical place; there's much charm about the wee red sandstone town on a hill. Visit the birthplace of Sir James Matthew Barrie in Brechin Road. This small cottage, in the care of the National Trust for Scotland, reveals the humble origins and sorrows of the gifted novelist, dramatist and creator of the world's favourite dream-child, Peter Pan. In a cramped weaver's home the family lived upstairs while Barrie's father worked at his loom.

Barrie was one of eleven children, although two died before Barrie's birth. At night the kitchen became the children's bedroom; little wonder that Barrie and his older brother David escaped to play in the detached washhouse, which served as their theatre. When David was killed in a skating accident on the eve of his fourteenth birthday, Barrie's world changed. Hoping to relieve his grieving mother's pain, six-year-old Barrie would dress up as David, mimicking him in the hope of making her smile. Private agony and public success are laid bare in this fascinating home. Obsessed with his mother, Barrie's childless marriage failed and, following the tragic deaths of his dear friends Arthur and Sylvia, he became the legal guardian to their five children, the lost boys. Tragically, he outlived all but one of them. In creating Neverland, he made a world where the young are carefree, wise and never grow up. Peter Pan tells Wendy, 'Come with me where you'll never, never have to worry about grown-up things again.'

Captain Scott and JM Barrie were good friends; in one of his final letters from the South Pole, Scott beseeched the writer to 'think well of me and of my end and more practically I want you to help my widow and my boy/your Godson.' Barrie's affection for Kirriemuir was unstinting; upon his death in 1937 he could have been buried in Poets' Corner, Westminster Abbey, but his clear instruction was for a simple burial in Kirrie. Visit his grave in the cemetery where poet and suffragette Helen Cruickshank (1886–1975) is also buried. She too was proud of her origins and wrote in her distinctive Lowland Scots dialect.

Near the graveyard is Kirrie's handsome cricket pavilion, a gift from Barrie in 1930. In a turret above the pavilion is another of his gifts, a magnificent camera obscura, one of just three in Scotland. Climb the staircase to a darkened room where panoramic views appear as if by magic; how the townsfolk must have been amazed to see their glens, hills and tattie farms conjured up in this way. Before leaving magical Kirrie, visit the Gateway to the Glens museum and the Peter Pan statue in the town square. But most importantly, make plenty of time for children to romp around the magnificent pirate ship and Lost Boys'

...hungry and thirsty?

There are several inns in Kirriemuir, including the Airlie Arms and the Thrums Hotel. The 88 Degrees café serves great coffee and good food, while the shabby chic Auld Surgery is a friendly place for home-made soup and carrot cake. There's art with tea at the Angus Gallery and the Steeple serves traditional fish suppers. The Star Rock sweetie shop opened in 1833 and must have been one of Barrie's haunts – locals go for Horehounds, aniseed humbugs, and rock hand-made on the premises. McLaren's bakers opened in 1893; call in for a macaroni pie, one of Scotland's bakery delicacies, or a Forfar bridie, a horseshoe-shaped pastry filled with meat (the man in the queue ahead of me requested 'an ingin een an aw' – one with onion in as well). Since the 1930s Visocchi's Café has served home-made ice cream (try Peter Pan flavour!). There are picnic benches at Gella Bridge, once a freshwater pearl fishery, and beside the South Esk in Glen Doll car park.

Hideout in the wonderful Neverland play area near the cricket pavilion on Kirrie Hill.

CURIOUS

In January 1959 a party of five experienced walkers encountered extreme weather conditions on Jock's Road and the entire group disappeared. Rescuers, including shepherds and gamekeepers, set out to search for them but tragically it took four desperate months before all bodies were found. Davy Glen was so moved by the experience that he built a rough shelter, Davy's Bourach, on the path.

Fierce mountain conditions were well known to explorer Captain Robert Falcon Scott. With his friend Edward Adrian Wilson, artistic scientist and expedition doctor, he visited Glen Prosen to prepare for his South Pole mission. Near one of Scott's favourite viewpoints at Dykehead a roadside cairn recalls how in Antarctica in 1912 they 'died together on the great ice barrier'. The inscription, from Robert Browning's poem 'Prospice', reads: 'For the journey is done and the summit attained, and the barriers fall.'

...tired?

Why not be Barrie's neighbour for a while? Stay at Thrums Cottage, owned by the National Trust for Scotland. Thrums is the pen name Barrie gave to Kirriemuir. Glen Clova hotel provides welcome comfort for walkers and shooting parties returning from the hills; its luxury lodges have saunas and hot tubs. The Bothy at Clach Na Brain is a stone-built cottage. There's bed and breakfast at Cortachy House next to Cortachy Castle and at Muirhouse Farm. Drumshademuir is a popular caravan and camping park. From Prosen Hostel there's a footpath along the river Prosen to Colmuir, Glenisla and the Cateran Trail.

When we were little, wandering boys,
And every hill was blue and high,
On ballad ways and martial joys
We fed our fancies, you and I.
With Bruce we crouched in bracken shade,
With Douglas charged the Paynim foes;
And oft in moorland noons I played
Colkitto to your grave Montrose.

FROM 'FRATRI DILECTISSIMO' BY JOHN BUCHAN

9

Walk This Way

Writer's haunts   Country pursuits   Hidden treasures

Dedicated to the memory of his younger brother, Willie, 'Fratri Dilectissimo' recalls John Buchan's childhood on the banks and braes of the River Tweed.

Here the Minister's son delighted in the country pursuits of hunting, shooting, and fishing and while his later achievements as a writer, politician, lawyer, soldier, historian, biographer and the Governor General of Canada took him far from the Scottish Borders, the valley of the River Tweed remained his first love.

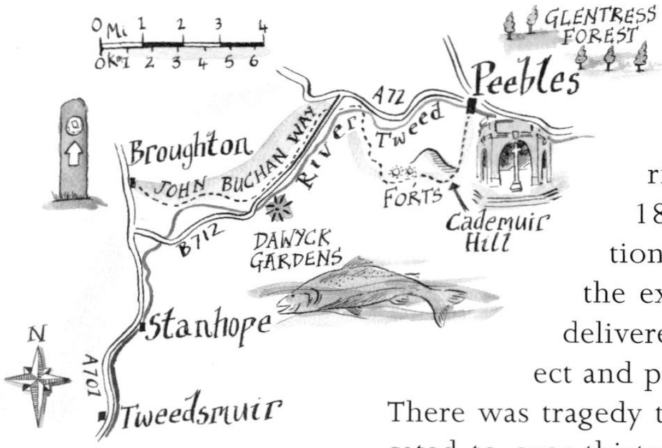

Elected to the House of Lords in 1935 John Buchan chose to be the first Lord of Tweedsmuir, paying homage to the village closest to the source of the famous salmon river. All's quiet in Tweedsmuir now, but between 1895–1905 the hills resounded to the construction of the Talla reservoir, built to supply water to the expanding city of Edinburgh. A new railway line delivered hundreds of men and materials to the project and payday evenings at the Crook Inn were legendary. There was tragedy too; a memorial in the village kirk yard is dedicated to over thirty men who died during the construction of the water works.

Upon his grandmother's death in 1901, Buchan reflected 'Since ever I was a very little boy I have liked Broughton better than any other place in the world.' Summer holidays at his grandfather's farmhouse house encouraged Buchan and his brother Willie to become great adventurers in an imaginary world. Broughton inspired Woodilee, the setting of his 1927 novel *Witch Wood*. Among his many works, this tale of a young minister who discovers witchcraft in his parish was Buchan's personal favourite.

There's a wonderfully quirky collection of literary memorabilia at the John Buchan Story, in Peebles' Chambers Institution from late summer 2012. The exhibition celebrates the author's connection with the town and reveals the extraordinary achievements of his life. Family heirlooms on display include photographs revealing Buchan's sense of fun: the dashing fellow beams from under a floppy hat on his honeymoon and puffs his pipe while wearing his bathing suit in the middle of a South African river. His kilt is alongside bookcases stuffed with assorted editions of *The Thirty-Nine Steps* and if you are in luck you may meet his granddaughter Deborah at the reception desk.

...hungry and thirsty?

There's a friendly welcome at Broughton's Laurel Bank tearoom and bistro, open seven days a week all year round. Famous for home baking, the cosy Oven Door tearoom in Peebles is a favourite. For fresh local food, visit Peebles Farmers' Market, held on the second Saturday of every month and after a walk through the historic trees of Scrape Glen at Dawyck Botanic Garden, visit the café for seasonal dishes.

...tired?

The stylish Tontine Hotel in the heart of Peebles makes a great base for an active break. Popular with mountain bikers exploring challenging routes in Glentress Forest, the Tontine offers lockable bike storage racks, pressure washers and a drying room. Not far away lies the rare Adam and Eve gravestone in Lyne Kirk. The beautifully carved 1712 memorial to farmer's daughter Janet Veitch, 'aged 16 years and 6 weiks' is a unique example of Scottish folk-art sculpture. Observe wildlife at large from the windows of peaceful Castlehill Knowe bed and breakfast in the lovely Manor Valley or eat and sleep in Arts and Crafts style at Skirling House, designed by Ramsey Traquar for Sir Gibson Carmichael, Governor of Bengal.

Elegant Peebles is beautifully situated on the River Tweed; salmon and trout fishing is world class and the independent shops are among the best in Scotland but, for me, further delights include the extraordinary war memorial and an astonishing plasterwork frieze.

Inspired by the colours of Palermo cathedral and enriched with Saracenic mosaics, the magnificent Peeblesshire War Memorial stands in the quadrangle of the Chambers Institution. The shrine combines Renaissance architecture with Moorish influences. Beneath a domed copper roof, a dazzling Celtic cross leaves no doubt that architect Burnett Orphoot achieved his ambition 'to get a bright note of colour' in the surroundings; the vibrant flowerbeds can barely compete.

Across the quad find the Chambers Room and sculptor Bertil Throvaldsen's plaster cast of significant sections of the Parthenon Frieze – or Elgin Marbles – extending 62 foot (16 metres) along one wall. Opposite is his complete facsimile of the Triumph of Alexander. To be surrounded by Ancient Greeks and Babylonians in the country museum's hideaway room is an unusual experience, especially when figures lean out of the plaster because the relief is cut deeper at the top of the frieze. From the Chambers Room it is a short walk to the Scottish Museum of Ornamental Plasterwork in the workshop of L.Grandison & Son, traditional lime and ornamental plasterwork specialists. The Grandison collection of historic patterns or 'originals' as they are known in the trade, is well worth a visit.

THE JOHN BUCHAN WAY

Paying homage to the writer and diplomat who loved to walk in the Peeblesshire countryside, the John Buchan Way is a 22-kilometre (13 mile) waymarked route between Peebles and Broughton. Strong walkers can complete it in a day. Close to Peebles the route climbs Cademuir Hill, which boasts two prehistoric hill forts. The larger of the pair enclosed at least 35 circular dwellings.

10

Tents are pitched by the bur

nd groups gather to pan for gold or chatter into the night.

Treasure Hunt

Silver Gold Gloves

Scottish gold is among the purest in the world and in the late eighteenth century there was high demand for flakes and nuggets of the precious metal found in the burns and rivers of the Lowther Hills. Known as 'God's Treasure House', the Southern Uplands were also mined for rich deposits of lead, zinc, copper and silver. This weekend is a treasure hunt, exploring the rich heritage of Leadhills, Wanlockhead and Sanquhar.

From the A74(M) the road to Leadhills travels through rounded windswept hills where red grouse are raised for the shooting season between August and December. There are few trees but plenty of heather. At Leadhills a cluster of low miners' cottages are seemingly stitched together for shelter against the elements. Following the closure of the last mine in 1930, the village faced dereliction but in recent years newcomers have restored abandoned homes. Here you'll find the oldest subscription library in Scotland (founded in 1741), the highest nine-hole golf course and the highest narrow-gauge adhesion railway in Britain. The graveyard is the final resting place of John Taylor, a hardy miner whose tombstone records his death 'at the remarkable age of 137 years'; a diet of oatmeal porridge, meat, broth and malt liquor seems to account for his longevity.

At 1,500 feet above sea level Wanlockhead is the highest village in Scotland. Here the first miners lived in tented villages and worked only in summer because winter conditions were too severe. As the mines expanded so too did the community, and permanent homes were built. What remains today is only half of that which existed at the peak.

While exploiting deposits of lead, zinc and gold on his land, the Duke of Buccleuch and Queensbury showed some concern for the welfare of his workers thanks to the influence of Robert Owen and the Quakers. Sports and education were promoted and by 1740 every man and boy in the village was able to read and write...though not the women and girls. The first female member of the subscription library was Isabella Rutherford, who joined in 1784.

The Wanlockhead Museum of Lead Mining tells the story of the miners and their village. Visit the library and workers' cottages, explore Lochnell Mine and see how the UK's only remaining example of a waterbucket pumping engine was used to drain Straitsteps Mine.

Provided you have a licence, you can take part in the new Scottish goldrush, panning for flakes and nuggets in fast-flowing burns around

...tired?

Good friends might like to cosy up in wooden wigwams at the Wanlockhead Inn. There's quiet rural camping at Lettershaws Farm and Craigend bed and breakfast in Westoun welcomes cyclists and walkers on the Southern Upland Way. Blackaddie House Hotel in Sanquhar has accommodation and fine dining.

the village – don't expect to make your fortune, though. The museum has gold-panning equipment for hire and sells licences for the day, week or year. It also offers gold-panning courses.

The magnificent Mennock Pass connects Wanlockhead to the Royal Burgh of Sanquhar. Weaving through hills shaped by glaciers, the country road travels alongside Mennock Water. On hot summer days careless lambs doze on tarmac, defeated by the heat, and the valley becomes a popular wild camping site. Tents are pitched by the burn and groups gather to pan for gold or chatter into the night. If you are inclined to join them, be sure to take bin bags and clear all your waste from this beautiful natural landscape.

Sanquhar's handsome Tolbooth Museum is a quirky gem. Call in to discover historic knitting patterns for highly prized Sanquhar gloves. Geometric designs with names like 'the midge and fly' are worked in black and white yarn on fine needles and the wearer's initials are knitted into the cuff. The museum sells a selection of the fiendishly challenging patterns, much appreciated by Japanese tourists and knitters with the patience of a saint. Look out for an extraordinary handbill published in 1580 by a local genius known as 'The Admirable Crichton'. Polymath James Crichton entered St Andrews University at the age of eleven and graduated at the age of fourteen. Promoting himself in Italy, his brazen handbill declares him to be 'a prodigy of prodigies… in a body so gracefully formed'. Unfortunately others did not share James' high opinion of himself. The Duke of Mantua's son so detested the egotist that he killed him in a brawl.

Recalling high drama in June 1680, the obelisk in Sanquhar High Street marks the site where Scottish Presbyterian Reverend Richard Cameron read the Sanquhar Declaration. Cameron, a leading Covenanter, supported the National Covenant of 1638, which pledged opposition to the English Episcopalian interference in their worship. His defiant statement disowned King Charles II as the spiritual head of the church and was interpreted as a declaration of war. This led to further religious conflict and 'killing times' across the Southern Uplands.

'Out of the world and into Crawfordjohn' is the motto of the Crawfordjohn Heritage Venture Museum, situated in the only village or town in Scotland to have the surname precede the first name. The former parish church is a cabinet of curiosities: mole traps, lanterns and shepherds' snowshoes are part of a hotchpotch display celebrating country life.

…hungry and thirsty?

If a proper fry-up is your thing, refuel at Harvey's Café in Sanquhar. The 'Designer Breakfast' offers a choice of eight items including haggis, tattie scones and fried bread. When I was there a regular demolished the lot spread over two plates.

CURIOUS

Sanquhar Tolbooth was one of the most lenient lock-ups in Scotland; prisoners would clamber out of the skylight to join their gaolers for an evening in the local pub and a night at home before returning to their cell by morning.

Siege Mentality

Island castle Ospreys Food town

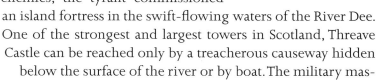

Travel to Galloway in southwest Scotland to discover a masterpiece of military architecture, the lively market town of Castle Douglas and the colourful gardens of Threave Estate.

Sir Archibald Douglas, the fourteenth-century Lord of Galloway, was an unpopular man, despised by local Gallovidians, who distrusted the Bruce dynasty he supported, and loathed by the English, who called him Archibald the Grim. To protect himself from enemies, the tyrant commissioned an island fortress in the swift-flowing waters of the River Dee. One of the strongest and largest towers in Scotland, Threave Castle can be reached only by a treacherous causeway hidden below the surface of the river or by boat. The military masterpiece resisted two terrible sieges, one of two months in 1455 and another of thirteen weeks in 1640.

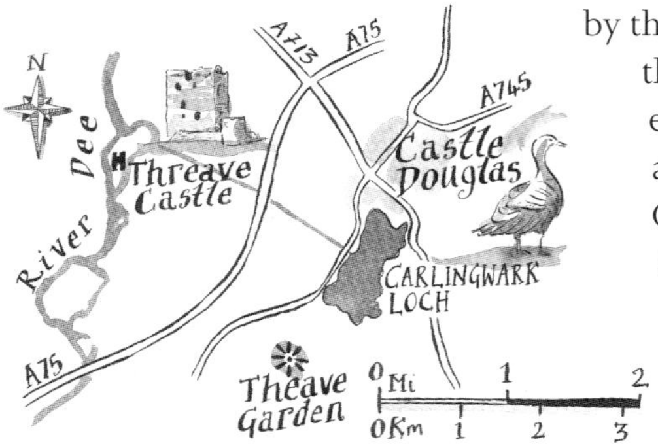

Now managed by Historic Scotland, the castle extends a warm welcome. In summer a small boat ferries visitors to the island across the Dee; just ring the bell to call the boatman. The lovely crossing takes just a few minutes. All is peaceful in the five-storey tower where the garrison gathered to defend Archibald's house-

...tired?

A favourite bed and breakfast in Castle Douglas is Albion House; the King Suite comes with private lounge, bedroom and pantry. Lochside Caravan Park at Carlingwark Loch is in a great location; regulars have been returning here since childhood.

hold. Barn owls and ravens nest in the walls and there's a good view of Threave Estate's distant osprey nest; you may be lucky to catch sight of the male bird swooping to feed his family with fish captured in his talons from the River Dee. A viewing platform on the riverbank opposite the eyrie makes it possible to observe the comings and goings of these highly protected birds at a safe legal distance. The woodlands, farmland, wetland and marshes of Threave Estate are managed sensitively to encourage birds and wildlife. Pink-footed geese, Greenland white-fronted geese and whooper swans are seasonal visitors; observe them from hides in the woods and on the riverbank. The estate's dedicated bat reserve is a first for Scotland; seven species roost on the estate.

Proud of its independent shops and local producers, Castle Douglas hosts the annual Food Town Day in May; cookery demonstrations and tastings offer a flavour of Dumfries and Galloway. After a busy day, a gentle stroll around lovely Carlingwark Loch, situated at the edge of town, will take about an hour and a half and is highly recommended. Alternatively take to the water and hire a boat in season or simply savour the pleasure of watching the birds on the loch from the boardwalk. Iron Age crannogs (lake dwellings) have been discovered here and in the 1860s two fishermen netted a large bronze cooking pot, which is now on display at the Scottish National Museum in Edinburgh.

In late spring the technicolour display of rhododendrons at Threave Garden is outstanding.

...hungry and thirsty?

Castle Douglas has cafés for all tastes. For colour therapy and artistic influences my favourite is Designs, showcasing contemporary art and design-led craft. The sunny walled garden is a great spot to enjoy a bowl of home-made soup or to read the papers over coffee. The town's good food shops make it fun to create a picnic of local flavours to be savoured on the grassy banks of Threave Island. Close by Carlingwark Loch, Moore's Chippy in Castle Douglas is a big hit with locals and families on holiday. The Sulwath Brewery, named after a crossing place in the Solway Estuary, named Black Galloway porter in honour of the region's native cattle. The microbrewery welcomes visitors and tours reveal how real ales are crafted from only natural ingredients.

12

There's magic in the heavens above the Galloway Hills of southwest Scotland. Far from the artificial light pollution of our densely populated cities, a stargazing weekend in the UK's first Dark Sky Park is awe-inspiring and life-affirming.

Starstruck

Dark skies   Ancient woods   Mountain bikes

On a clear night a breathtaking 2,000 glittering stars can be seen in the dark skies above Galloway Forest Park, while just 200 are visible over Glasgow. To behold this extraordinary sight, plan your visit with care. The long dark months from October to March offer maximum opportunity. Avoid dates when the moon is up – its glow competes with the twinkling stars – and keep a close eye on the weather, as clear, dry nights are best.

Glentrool Visitor Centre has plenty of information for would-be stargazers; clear skies bring chilly nights so cosy clothes and hot drinks are essential, and a sleeping bag or blanket is a bonus. You won't need a telescope; binoculars will do the job, although photographers should take a tripod. Pack a torch with a red filter for the dark and, as unlikely as it sounds, take a deckchair too – then you can lie back and gaze upwards without straining your neck. This may not be a good look but with rewards as big as the cosmos, who cares? Wrap up warm, pick a spot and prepare for the greatest show on earth.

Between Glentrool village and Newton Stewart it is possible to combine stargazing with the earthly delights of ancient woodland, hill walking, mountain biking and bird watching in the company of golden eagles, black grouse, red squirrels, red deer, pine martens and otters. Glentrool is one of the '7stanes' world-class mountain biking centres across the south of Scotland, each with a specially commissioned 'stane', or stone sculpture, reflecting local legends. There are waymarked trails for experienced riders, children, families and beginners. Bike hire is available from thebreakpad at Kirroughtree and HDI in Newton Stewart.

...hungry and thirsty?

For great local food and a good night's sleep there's the House O'Hill hotel in Glentrool. The attractions of wild venison casserole, home-made pie of the day and beer from microbreweries make reservations essential. The friendly Café Cree in Newton Stewart serves Galloway Breakfast all day, and Cinammon is a colourful community arts and crafts café.

Kirroughtree, the second of the '7stanes' in the Galloway Forest Park, offers some of the best single-track bike trails in the world. The red trail is for experienced riders and the black for experts. One of the UK's best mountain bike events, 10@Kirroughtree, tests the endurance of solo riders and teams. Only the strong survive this ten-hour mountain bike marathon.

A little further into the forest, Bruce's Stone stands high above Loch Trool in the glen known as 'the cradle of independence'. The stone commemorates the battle of 1307 in which Robert Bruce, King of the Scots, defeated the English. Adopting guerrilla warfare tactics, Bruce's army used their hilltop position to bombard the enemy below with rocks and boulders. So began the fierce campaign of independence that raged until 1314 when Bruce won the Battle of Bannockburn. It was a further ten years before the English fully recognised Scottish independence.

From the car park at the western end of Loch Trool there's a scenic circular walk of three hours. Experienced hill walkers will relish a four-mile route up the Merrick, the highest of twenty-four named peaks in the Galloway Hills. At 2,764 feet, the Merrick is just short of a Munro

(any Scottish mountain over 3,000 feet). Views from the summit are among the finest in Scotland; on a clear day you'll see the Isle of Man, the Lake District and Northern Ireland.

On the approach to the Wood of Cree RSPB Nature Reserve a sign reads 'Quiet please, there may be otters about'; wait patiently a few hours before dusk, or at dawn, and you might be rewarded. Dumfries and Galloway has the largest density of otters of any mainland region of Britain. The atmospheric Wood of Cree is the largest remaining ancient woodland in the south of Scotland. The Bridge of Cree connects the burgh of Newton Stewart and the smaller settlement of Minnigaff. Drovers with Galloway cattle crossed the peaty Black Ford here on their long journey south to market in Carlisle. In May hikers of all abilities descend on Newton Stewart for Walkfest, the biggest annual walking festival in the south of Scotland. The friendly riverside town boasts a charming one-screen cinema, an historic gem with a modern digital projection system. Running the gauntlet of hungry deer, Elmlea Plants in Old Minnigaff is a small and pretty nursery specialising in herbaceous perennials and grasses.

HEAVENS ABOVE

The Galloway Forest Observatory Astronomical Society meets at Glenamour on the fourth Friday of every month when the skies are clear.

...tired?

In 1815 American author Edgar Allan Poe enjoyed a childhood holiday in Dumfries and Galloway. He stayed at Flowerbank, now a guesthouse with a pretty garden alongside the River Cree. Kirroughtree House Hotel offers Stargazers Breaks and Newton Stewart Youth Hostel in Minnigaff welcomes travellers on a budget. Responsible wild camping is permitted in Galloway Forest Park, in accordance with the Scottish Outdoor Access Code. Campers should be aware that barbecues and campfires are not allowed due to the high risk of fire.

13

In a weird time warp, Space Age and Bronze Age meet o

Theatre of War

Soldiers Smugglers Sausages

he moors and in the hay meadows of Upper Coquetdale.

Now for something completely different. Covering over ninety square miles, Otterburn Range in Northumberland National Park is the second largest live firing range in the country. This extraordinary weekend is an invitation to discover the dramatic remote landscape where British and NATO soldiers train with infantry weapons, artillery and helicopters.

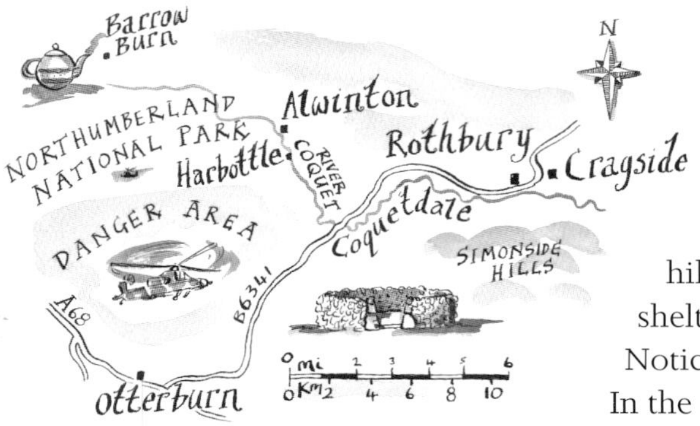

In a weird time warp, Space Age and Bronze Age meet on the moors and in the hay meadows of Upper Coquetdale. There are traces of the Romans too in this unusual environment where archaeological sites and military targets are landmarks. Scattered across the flanks of the exposed, rounded hills, magnificent stells (circular stone pens) offer shelter to flocks of Cheviot and Scottish Blackface sheep. Notices warn that they are out of bounds to troops.

In the early 1800s, when tax on spirits was increased fourfold in England, the fast-flowing water and inaccessible hills of Coquetdale made a perfect hideaway for the production of illicit duty-free whisky. Remains of secret stills like Black Rory's can be found in the undergrowth. Smugglers loaded disguised kegs onto packhorses and called at farms in the valley with their popular and potent 'new milk'.

...hungry and thirsty?

Barrowburn Tea Room is a cheery refreshment stop in the heart of the valley. There's a community craft shop at Harbottle's Star Inn; after admiring the work of skilled locals, take a walk up the fellside to the Drake Stone, a mysterious boulder that appears to have been an important vantage point over Coquetdale through the ages. Harbottle Lake lies a little further on.

There's no shortage of cafés in Rothbury. Favourites include Tomlinson's for tasty wholesome food, Harley's Tearoom with a pretty garden, and inspirational art at The Congregational, an airy café-cum-gallery in a former chapel. For picnic feasts pop into Tully's deli and tearoom, where hand-made Northumberland cheese is on sale alongside the red-squirrel feeders that locals are urged to use in their gardens. Foodies flock to the Rothbury Family Butchers for champion sausages, the most popular being the Cragside Cracker and the peppery Rothbury Sausage.

Explore on foot, by bike or on horseback, but it is essential to familiarise yourself with the rules of engagement. The training area has two zones: the Open Access Area, which can be explored all year round, and the Controlled Access Area, which is closed when red warning flags are flying. When no red flags are flying you must keep to the road or waymarked paths. The sound of hovering helicopters and distant booming explosions can be alarming; in the Open Access Area troops use blank rounds and pyrotechnics. In the Controlled Access Area they may be

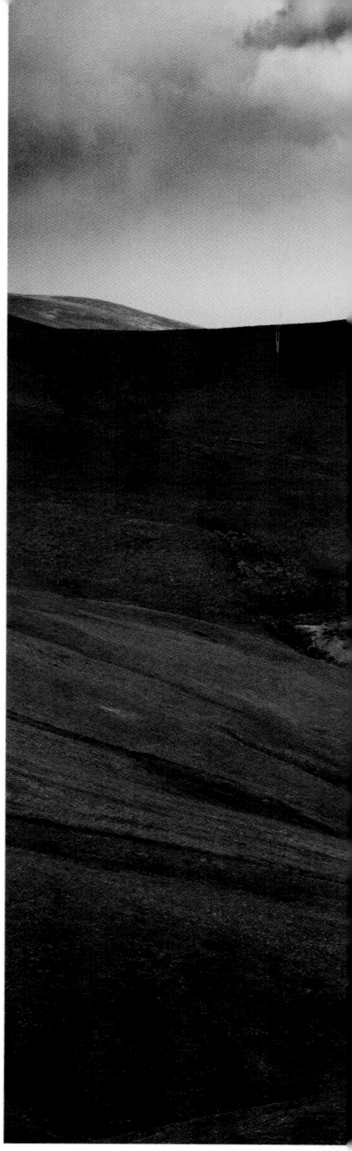

firing with live ammunition. Do not touch or pick up any object lying on the ground. At the weekend the military tend to melt away, but visit in the week and you may find yourself on the fringes of an unseen operation, with troops at lookout posts on hilltops, or driving along the narrow, winding country roads pursued rather bizarrely by tractors from the local farms.

Outer Golden Pot, or OP Tactical Viewpoint 12, is a windswept lookout to three Bronze Age cairns on Thirl Moor and the all-arms range where modern soldiers train for operational deployment across the world. Targets abound; some for machine-gun training, some for field artillery and others for air-to-ground training for aircraft. Long before any firing begins, sheep and cattle are cleared from the area and the ranges are closed to the public. Nearby a poignant Falklands Memorial commemorates Royal Marines who died on active service in 1982.

For information about walks, cycle routes and bridleways, visit the Northumberland National Park information centre in Rothbury, the capital of Coquetdale. This attractive village is situated around a sloping green on the banks of the River Coquet. From Beggars Rigg car park and picnic site there's an easy half-hour riverbank stroll into the village, following the lovely Coquet on part of its journey to the sea at Amble. One mile to the east of Rothbury is Cragside, the first house in the world to be lit by hydro-electricity. Now owned by the National Trust, it was formerly the home of Lord Armstrong, Victorian inventor and engineer. Further afield there's more good walking and mountain biking in Simonside Hills.

...tired?

To see the wildflowers of Barrowburn hay meadows at their peak in May and June is an uplifting experience. Stay in their midst at Barrowburn farmhouse, which offers a camping barn in the former valley school. The Deer Hut Lodge is perfectly situated for an early morning start on the Cheviot Hills, or try bed and breakfast in the farmhouse. Sir Walter Scott stayed at the historic Rose and Thistle Inn at Alwinton, and this charming country pub still offers bed and breakfast. The Potting Shed in Harbottle is a cosy retreat for two in a former walled kitchen garden close by the ruins of hilltop Harbottle Castle. In Great Tosson, Tosson Tower Farm offers award-winning bed and breakfast plus holiday cottages to let. There's a wide range of accommodation in Rothbury, including Tomlinson's bunkhouse; hire bikes from here or bring your own. Storage is provided. The Orchard House offers bed and breakfast in an elegant Georgian residence.

14

Empire Building

Forts Pre-Raphaelites Countrymen

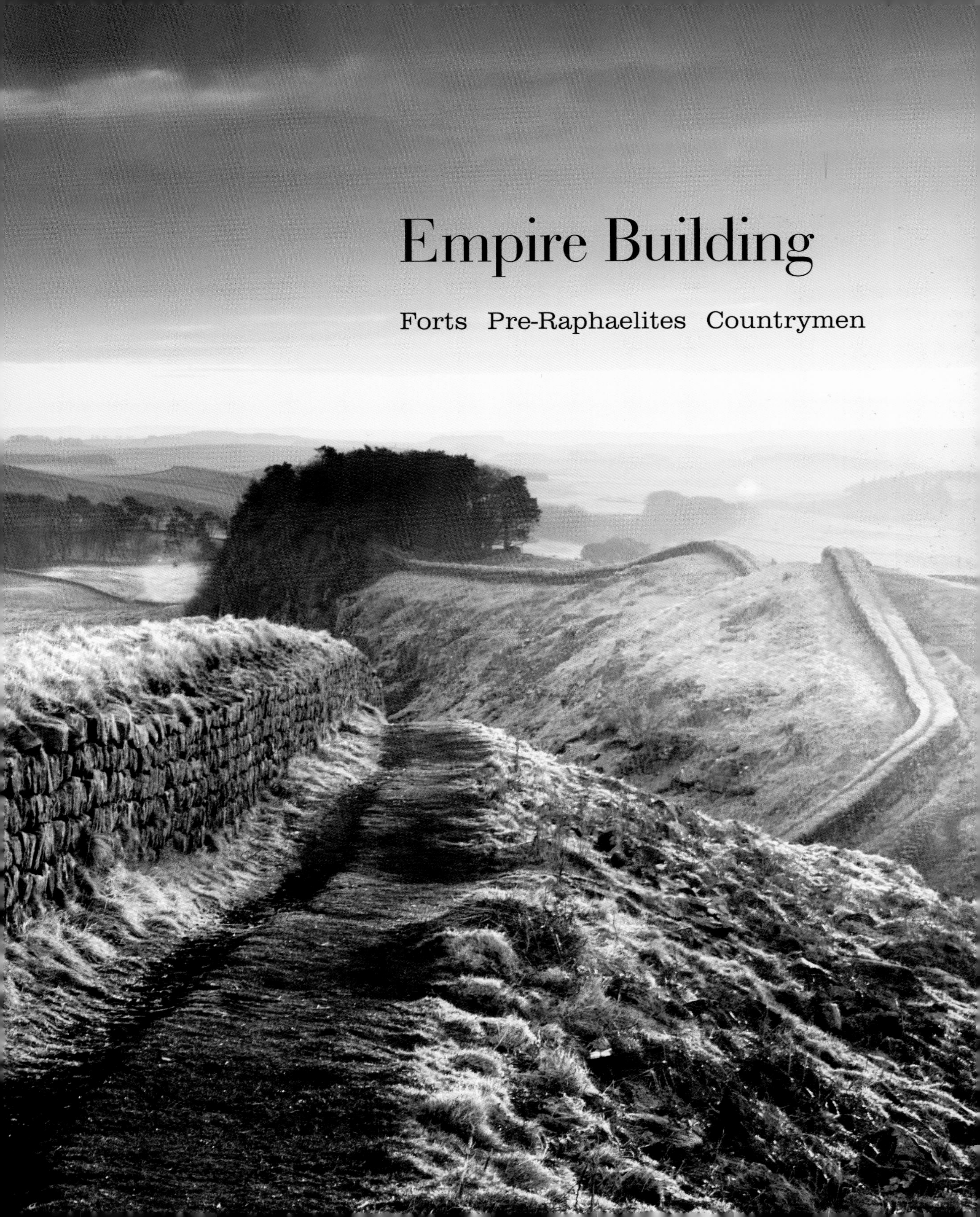

When Hadrian commissioned a mighty structure 80 Roman miles in length along the northern frontier of his empire, little did he know that his project, instigated around AD122, would be declared a World Heritage Site in 1987 due to its outstanding importance to mankind. To explore the full extent of the emperor's wall, forts, milecastles and turrets in a couple of days is impossible. This weekend of history and culture in outstanding natural landscape should whet the appetite for more.

The journey begins in Brampton where Emperor Hadrian's statue stands high on a sandstone plinth. You wouldn't know it at first glance, but this modest country town conceals extraordinary art. Within St Martin's Church is a series of awe-inspiring Pre-Raphaelite stained-glass windows, designed by Edward Burne-Jones and made by William Morris's firm. The east window features fifteen subjects in glowing colours: red, purple, blue, crimson and copper. Burne-Jones described it as 'a masterpiece of style' and a 'Herculean labour'.

The ruins of medieval Lanercost Priory are romantically situated on the banks of the River Irthing. Built with stones from Hadrian's Wall, the priory was founded by Augustinian canons in 1169 and dissolved by Henry VIII in 1537. Look out for the exquisite tomb of young Elizabeth Dacre Howard, known as Bessie, in the thirteenth-century priory church of St Mary Magdalene. In spring the graveyard is strewn with snowdrops and daffodils, there are cattle and lambs in the meadow and birdsong on the breeze.

...hungry and thirsty?

Among my favourite places to eat is The Garden Station at Langley on Tyne. A few miles from the wall, the cheery painted café on the platform of a former railway station is well worth a visit. The gardens are special too. On Sundays you can watch Diane and Eric making Birdoswald organic cheese by hand at Slack House Farm near Birdoswald Fort. They have a Fairtrade café, the Scypen, in the farmyard. The elegant Lanercost Tearoom and Restaurant is ideally situated next to the priory, and there's an attractive farm shop too. Enjoy home-made cakes at Ye Olde Forge Tea Rooms in Greenhead and real ale by the fire at the Greenhead Hotel. Try Twice Brewed Bitter at the Twice Brewed Inn on the military road. Do enquire about the extraordinary wetland sewage system; they are justifiably proud of their Green Tourism credentials.

Near Lanercost, Banks East Turret is one of the finest vantage points on Hadrian's Wall. Spy Cold Fell and Talkin Fell in the North Pennines from here and the summits of Helvellyn, Blencathra and Skiddaw in the Lake District. From here the Hadrian's Wall Path leads to Birdoswald Roman fort, where long straight stretches of the wall march impressively across the countryside.

The B6318 Military Road travels through rugged country landscape divided by many stone walls, not just Hadrian's. There's great walking from Once Brewed; get maps and routes from the National Park Centre next to the youth hostel. A favourite is the scenic circular walk to Roman forts at Housesteads and Vindolanda, which takes about five hours.

Among the earliest examples of the written word in Britain found at Vindolanda were extraordinary 'postcards' written on thin leaves of wood. They provide clues to domestic life in a Roman camp; one is a birthday invitation, another speaks of socks and underwear required for the harsh northern weather.

The exposed volcanic rock of the Great Whin Sill challenged Hadrian's builders and the spectacularly writhing section at Walltown Crags

is testament to their skill. With panoramic views, this is a great picnic spot – if a little windswept!

Close by the Roman Army Museum at Greenhead, Walltown Quarry recreation site is a wildlife haven; likewise Greenlee Lough National Nature Reserve where whooper swans, greylag, white-fronted, pink-footed and barnacle geese are winter visitors.

The glades of Allen Banks and Staward Gorge feature in the paintings of Victorian artist John Martin. Follow National Trust waymarked trails along the River Allen as it tumbles to the Tyne. From Plankey Mill a path climbs through steep Staward Gorge to a ruined medieval peel tower high above the trees.

WHEN TO GO?

An international army of tourists swarms over Hadrian's Wall in high season, making it a crowded experience. A visit at quieter times is highly recommended, though check travel arrangements and opening hours first. The Hadrian's Wall bus – the AD122 – visits all the sites along the wall from April to October. Hadrian's Wall Path from Tyne to Solway is 84 miles long and Hadrian's Cycleway from Ravensglass to South Shields is 174 miles long.

...tired?

There's plenty of accommodation for the many visitors to this World Heritage Site. Among B&Bs with a difference there's the Reading Rooms at Haydon Bridge, where men read the Bible and newspapers in the 1850s, and the Old Repeater Station near Grindon. There are youth hostels at Once Brewed and Greenhead and a campsite and bunkhouse at Windshields Farm.

15

Tranquillity

Starry skies   Hay meadows   Waterfalls

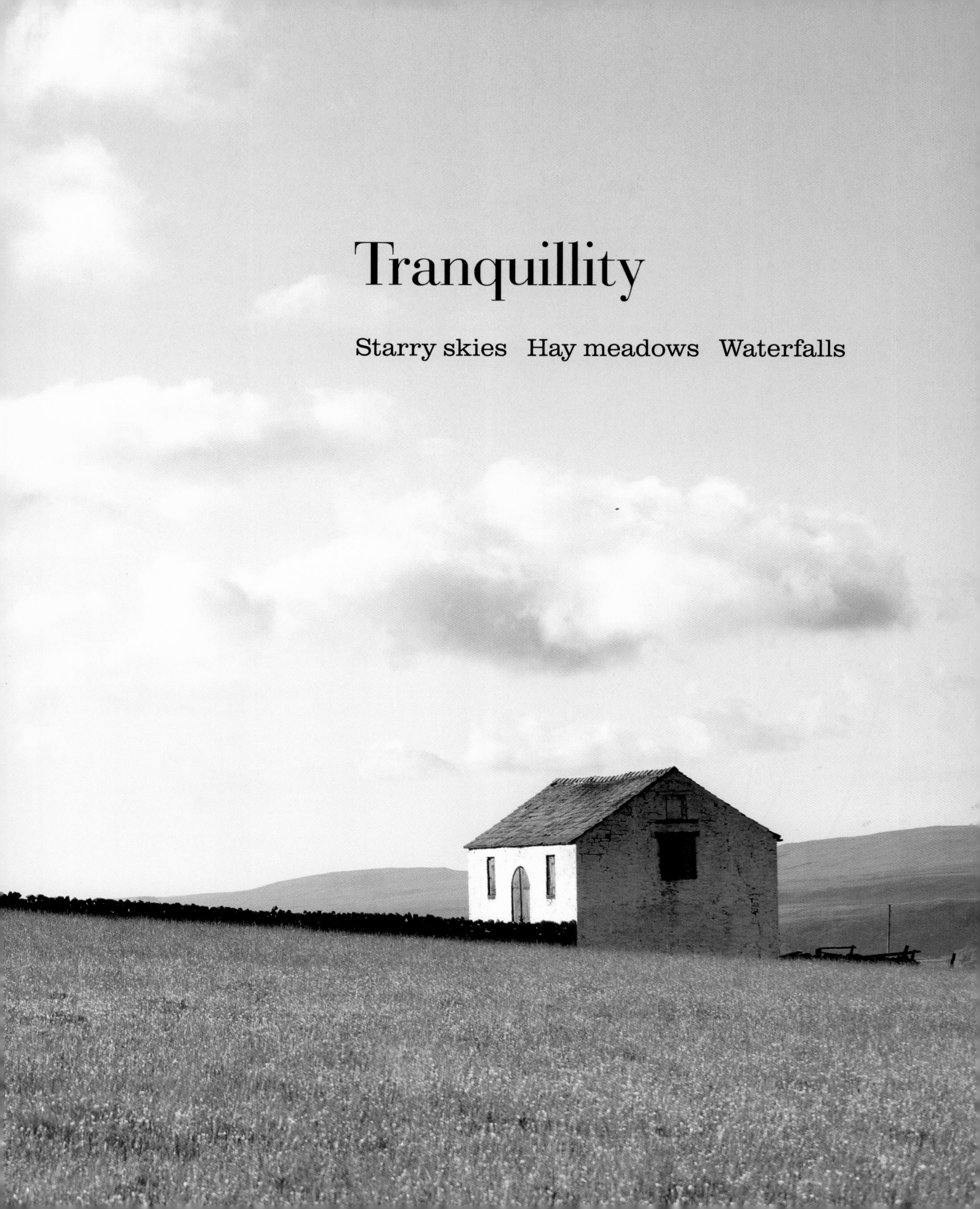

Teesdale, the most southerly of the Durham dales, is one of England's most tranquil places. Escape the hurly-burly and spend a weekend discovering remote moors, powerful waterfalls and clear, starry skies.

The geology and geography of Teesdale created a lead-mining boom in the eighteenth and nineteenth centuries. Men who cared for livestock and cultivated small family plots of land also laboured in scattered mines across the remote upland valleys; Teesdale became one of the most productive lead-mining areas in the world. Middleton-in-Teesdale flourished when the headquarters of the London Lead Mining Company came to town. Although the mines declined, unable to compete with cheaper imports, traces of the industry remain across the North Pennines landscape, which fascinated Anglo-American poet WH Auden. Inspired by the grief and isolation of derelict mine workings, he referred to them often in his verse.

One of my favourite minor roads in Upper Teesdale is the narrow lane that slips out of Middleton-in-Teesdale to scramble up the valley and over the moors to Westgate in Weardale. Running parallel with the main road, this elevated route offers a bird's-eye view of the landscape. See the Tees weaving through the broad upland dale past quarry workings, miners' cottages, forbidding barns, cliffs of igneous rock and stone-walled fields. The lane dips into Newbiggin, a hamlet of close-knit country cottages largely unchanged since the early nineteenth century.

At the height of the lead-mining boom Newbiggin was a busy community with a smelt mill, post office, inn, library, school, shop and hearse house. The decline of lead mining forced many families to move

...hungry and thirsty?

In Middleton-in-Teesdale there's stylish dining at the Forresters Hotel and restaurant. Try local Cotherstone cheese at the farmers' market on the last Sunday of every month, it goes well with a slice of fruitcake. Cheery Café 1618, the bikers' rendezvous, is also a bistro and bed and breakfast. Nearby Café Caramel is renowned for home-made cakes; on taking over the café, new owner David was presented with the establishment's long-standing recipe book (ginger drizzle cake is the local favourite). Muddy boots and dogs are welcome at the Conduit Tea Rooms. There's bed and breakfast, fine ale and home-made food at the Strathmore Arms, a favourite with walkers on the Pennine Way. Take an evening stroll along the river from Langdon Beck Youth Hostel to Langdon Beck pub where there's a quirky geology room full of glittering crystal and a black grouse lekking site just beyond the garden.

away and village life was transformed; buildings on Shiney Row which housed twenty-one people in six flats are three terraced houses today. Newbiggin Methodist Chapel claims to be the world's oldest chapel in continuous use, having been a centre of worship since 1760. To visit when the chapel is closed, collect a key from Middleton Tourist Information Centre. Lead miners built the place of worship for themselves, working by candlelight after their shifts at the mine. Tiered pews face the pulpit where John Wesley preached; a wall-hanging depicts him travelling on horseback through the Pennine hills and a quote from his journal dated 2 June 1772 reads, 'We rode to Newbiggin in Teesdale. The people were deeply attentive but I think not deeply affected.'

From Newbiggin there's a gentle riverside walk to High Force waterfall, where the Tees plummets nearly seventy feet over a lip of exposed hard Whin Sill rock, about 295 million years old, into a peaty plunge pool below. There is an admission charge to see the magnificent torrent, which attracted Victorian tourists, including JMW Turner. The keen angler was commissioned to paint High Force in 1816 and his watercolour features two fishermen casting and netting in the plunge pool. Beyond the coach parties at High Force, the upper dale is more sparsely populated and wild.

Forest of Teesdale Primary School is an educational outpost of fewer than twenty pupils in an isolated white cottage. Stop at Hanging

Shaw lay-by to admire the pupils' creativity; working with artist Phil Townsend they made tiles for a stone sculpture which attempts to make sense of the ocean of time that has washed over their valley. Featuring life forms from each period, the large stone has a recessed geological time line with *Homo sapiens* at the top. Peer through a hole in the sculpture to spy a smaller stone, representing how far we are from the beginnings of fossil life. The smaller stone, about 60 yards away, marks the start of the Cambrian period on earth 570 million years ago. On the same line of sight, a smaller pillar a quarter of a mile away represents the Pre-Cambrian era when earth was thought to have come into being. It's all mind-boggling stuff. The fact that this reminder of our place in the grand scheme of things is sited next to a bus stop delights me.

Nowhere in Britain has the diverse uplands habitats of the Moor House Nature Reserve; low-lying hay meadows, rough grazing, juniper woods, limestone grassland, blanket bog and summit heaths on high fells. This is wonderful walking country; routes are available from Natural England and Middleton-in-Teesdale Tourist Information Centre. The mood of the landscape changes constantly as light shifts across green pastures, illuminating scattered whitewashed cottages and black-painted barns. Farming is harsh; summers are short and unpredictable with drought or downpours and winters are long. Grass for grazing livestock is the only profitable crop.

In colder months beef cattle retreat to sheds while hardy Swaledale sheep remain outdoors. Springtime comes as welcome relief; shy blue gentians, the symbol of Teesdale, unfurl to greet the sunshine and wading birds seek high pastures to breed. The dale is a rare stronghold of black grouse; rise early to catch sight of males gathering to 'lek' at regular haunts. Their strutting display of fancy white tail feathers encourages females to choose their hot favourite. By summer the hay meadows are awash with colourful flowers including purple melancholy thistles, which were traditionally used to treat sadness.

GETTING AROUND

Many footpaths and two long-distance routes, the Pennine Way and the Teesdale Way, traverse the dale. Allow two and a half hours in total for the popular walk from Newbiggin across the Wynch Bridge and along the banks of the Tees to High Force waterfall, returning by the same route. From Cow Green follow the Widdybank Fell Nature Trail for three miles to Cauldron Snout Waterfall. Wheels to the Wild is a three-day cycling tour of the North Pennines; the exhilarating route is available from Tourist Information Centres.

...tired?

With eco-friendly credentials Langdon Beck Youth Hostel is a great place to observe clear starry skies. In Middleton in Teesdale the Old Barn bed and breakfast is stylish and friendly. For centuries travellers have rested at the Teesdale Hotel, and the eighteenth-century coaching inn has a great mural in the cobbled yard. Find thick stone walls, low oak beams and cosy log fires at Brunswick House guesthouse. At Low Way Farm, Holwick camping barn is conveniently situated next to the Farmhouse Kitchen.

16

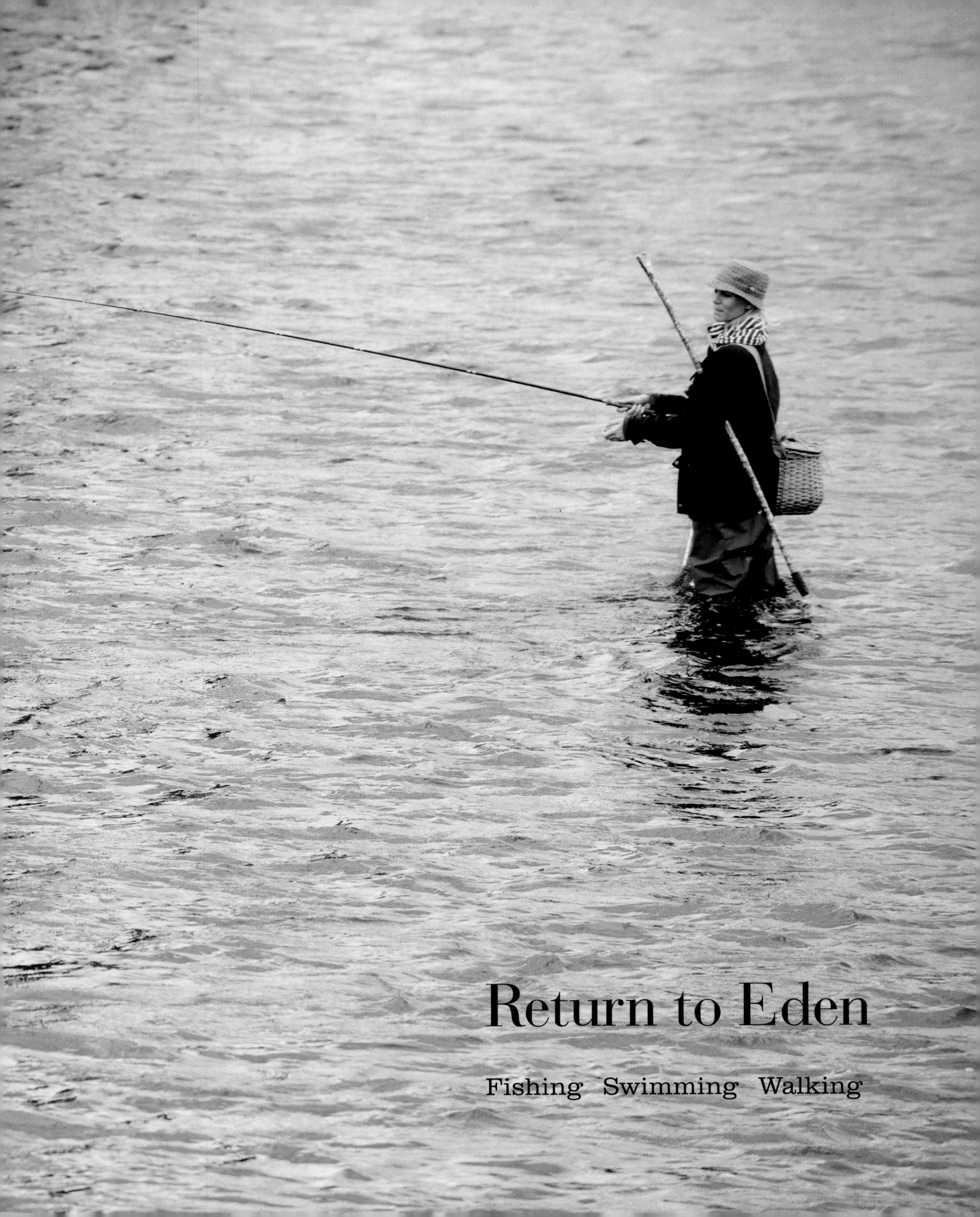

Return to Eden

Fishing Swimming Walking

Nestling between the Pennines to the east and the Lake District to the west is the heavenly Eden Valley. Discover just a pocket of this unspoiled paradise and it's likely to whet your appetite for more.

The River Eden, one of the finest salmon and trout rivers in England, journeys north from its source above the Mallerstang Valley to the Solway Firth, and along the way a series of ten riverbank sculptures invite visitors to sit, rest and absorb uplifting scenery. With a fine view of the sweeping arched bridge that connects the villages of Lazonby and Kirkoswald, sculptor Frances Perry's Cypher Piece is a favourite.

Lazonby and Kirkoswald Station on the Leeds–Settle–Carlisle railway line takes the names of both villages, although it is actually situated in Lazonby. The picture-book platform with colourful flowerbeds is adjacent to a historic auction mart renowned for sales of the hardy North of England Mule sheep and the annual sale of working and unbroken

Speak, Giant-mother! Tell it to the Morn
While she dispels the cumbrous shades of Night;
Let the Moon hear, emerging from a cloud;
At whose behest uprose on British ground
That sisterhood in hieroglyphic round...

FROM 'A WEIGHT OF AWE, NOT EASY TO BE BORNE'
BY WILLIAM WORDSWORTH

...hungry and thirsty?

There's delicious organic, vegetarian food on the menu at Salkeld Watermill tearoom. Bread is made from biodynamic and organic flours milled in the traditional way and a tour of the working watermill on Sunny Gill Beck makes the visit extra special. Should you get the baking bug, the watermill team offer a great range of courses to hone your skills. Join Lazonby locals at Bells Bakery on Saturday mornings when the staff coffee bar becomes a friendly village café serving great bread and cakes at discounted prices. Hot drinks and snacks are available from Lazonby swimming pool and the village Co-op is superbly stocked for picnic feasts and camping essentials.

The Highland Drove Inn at Great Salkeld is renowned for real ale and good food, with accommodation too; other friendly country pubs are the Fetherston Arms and Crown Inn at Kirkoswald and the Midland Hotel in Lazonby where Cumberland sausages go down a treat on auction day.

sheepdogs and puppies, which attracts buyers from all over Britain. The handsome church of St Nicholas watches over auction action while, across the tracks, former station buildings now house Bells Bakery.

Lazonby's open-air heated swimming pool on the riverbank makes the village a great family destination. Alongside the pool, which is open in summer only, there's a splendid community garden with playground area, picnic benches, willow tunnels and young native trees. Beyond this a quiet ten-pitch camping and caravanning site at the water's edge; a fisherman's dream. You might try your luck against the local otter; fishing permits are available from the Midland Hotel in the village.

From the village there are walks along the river into surrounding countryside. A favourite is to Lacy's Caves, an extraordinary five-chambered grotto commissioned in the 1700s by Colonel Lacy of Salkeld Hall. Extravagant dinner parties took place in the sandstone hideaway concealed by the laburnum and rhododendrons that still put on a gaudy show in spring. To visit from Lazonby, cross the Eden bridge and follow the riverside footpath through the meadows, or cross the bridge, turn right and follow the road to a parking place and fingerpost indicating the footpath to Little Salkeld and the caves on the riverbank.

Local lore tells of Colonel's Lacy's attempt to blow up one of Britain's most impressive prehistoric standing-stone circles, Long Meg and Her Daughters, at Little Salkeld. Fortunately adverse weather conditions prevented his gunpowder plot and the large circle stands resolute in a sloping field shared by grazing cattle. The tall red sandstone block of Long Meg is set apart from her daughters. Their history is largely unknown and so a tingling sense of mystery surrounds this magnificent monument. Awestruck William Wordsworth was inspired to write a verse demanding to know of their origins.

CURIOUS

Four churches in the villages of Lazonby, Kirkoswald, Renwick and Great Salkeld form the Trail of Saints in Eden, a fifteen-mile route around the valley. A trail leaflet is available from any of them. Don't miss St Cuthbert's in Great Salkeld. Two centuries after the death of the Celtic saint in 687, devoted monks carried his remains around northern England to prevent his body being desecrated by Viking invaders. For a while they sought shelter in Great Salkeld. A stained-glass window depicts the saint with an eider duck at his feet, recalling his time on the Farne Islands where he communed with the seabirds now known commonly as Cuddy (or St Cuthbert's) ducks.

...tired?

Lazonby's riverside camping and caravan site has just ten pitches so be sure to reserve yours; bookings are made with the Midland Hotel. Across the river Mains Farm offers a further twelve pitches for caravans and a bunkhouse. For a Cumbrian country house retreat, there are eight luxury apartments at Staffield Hall in Kirkoswald.

17

From High Fell to Gentle Shore

Skiddaw   Ospreys   Musical stones

'If I were asked by a stranger to the district to recommend a single climb that would give him a superb panorama I would send him up Skiddaw.'

ALFRED WAINWRIGHT

Travel to the shores of Bassenthwaite Lake for a weekend in the company of fishing ospreys and majestic Skiddaw, England's fourth highest mountain. Whether you retreat to the luxury of a lakeside country house or more rustic accommodation on the fell, the breathtaking north Lakeland will soon have you under its spell.

The village of Bassenthwaite is an idyllic cluster of farms and cottages; ducks dabble in the gurgling beck, free-range chickens peck at hedgerows, children aim for goalposts on the village green and a handsome avenue of mature lime trees commemorates the jubilee of Queen Victoria. From the village magnificent hiking routes explore the mountain massif of Skiddaw.

There's something about Skiddaw, pronounced 'Skidda' locally, that has secured its place in the affections of artists, writers, geologists and walkers for centuries. Stacked upon Skiddaw slate, the domed peak presides over the country town of Keswick. Steep, smooth fells bear many scars: prehistoric and Roman remains, the tips, hushes and entrances of mineral workings, and erosion caused by recreational activities. Valleys are narrow and vast open moorland is windswept; buildings are few. Merlin, buzzard and grouse patrol heather and bilberry heath with roe deer and reptiles too. Approach routes to the summit are many, including the well-trodden tourist track over Jenkin Hill taken by Victorian ladies on horseback. The panoramic views are breathtaking; on a clear day Derwent Water and Bassenthwaite's lake glint in the sunlight and beyond lie the Pennines, the Solway coast and the southern uplands of Scotland.

From Dodd Wood car park a strenuous but well-surfaced path leads up the Dodd, a small fell in the Skiddaw range. However, many spring and summer visitors head not for the summit but to an open-air viewing platform bristling with powerful telescopes. This is one of the best places to legally observe the ospreys that nest in woodland below. The thrill of watching parents and chicks on a king-size bed of sticks is addictive; prepare to spend hours spying from afar. Shouts go up as an adult returns from a fishing trip, gripping prey in its talons, and all heads duck to the telescopes, observing the delivery of perch and pike to the chicks.

Known as sea eagles, ospreys spot fish from up to 130 feet in the air; hitting the water with wings folded back and feet pushed forward they seize prey with their talons. Fish are turned head first to reduce

...hungry and thirsty?

Refuel after osprey watching at the Old Sawmill tearoom where traditional local food is served, including Cumberland sausage and sticky gingerbread.

Take afternoon tea with lemon posset at Armathwaite Hall or dine at the Lake View restaurant. Sup Jennings real ale at the Sun Inn in Bassenthwaite; with a real fire, games room and views of Skiddaw, the seventeenth-century former farmhouse is a favourite. Across the lake, the shiny dingy walls and ceiling of the Pheasant Inn's bar are renowned for the yacht varnish cum cigarette smoke decoration. Look out for two paintings by 1920s artist Edward H Thompson; without funds for his bill he paid with art instead. Near the pub, the Dubwath Silver Meadows wetland nature reserve is a great free visit. Follow the boardwalk to Celtic and Norse-style hides made of wattle and daub and beautifully carved with creatures you can find living on the reserve.

...tired?

Thrill to the splendid isolation of Skiddaw House, a former hunting lodge where shepherds and gamekeepers resided on the high fell. Three miles from the nearest road, Skiddaw House is now an atmospheric youth hostel, the highest in Britain. Camp at Trafford's caravan park or rent the Parish Rooms in Bassenthwaite. Willow Cottage offers bed and breakfast, and the Ravenstone Hotel and Castle Inn are cosy retreats. Historic Armathwaite Hall is a magnificent country house hotel.

wind resistance as the bird flies them to the nest or favourite perch. Persecuted by gamekeepers, the osprey was made extinct in Britain as a breeding bird for 40 years. Following the return of a few birds to nest in the 1950s, the RSPB instigated Operation Osprey; 24-hour protection of the eyries.

When the chicks have fledged the birds make the immense journey to Africa. Regarded as a sign of spring, the male osprey usually returns first to Britain, flying over 3,000 miles from the west of Africa. While awaiting the return of his mate – the birds are largely monogamous – he may undertake repairs to the nest or eyrie; more sticks are added to an ever-increasing pile that grows to spectacular proportions over the years.

As if the opportunity to observe the domestic arrangements of an osprey family wasn't enough, Dodd Wood offers the further bonus of resident red squirrels.

Stroll to the gentle shore of Bassenthwaite lake across pastureland at Mirehouse, a handsome historic house and gardens with literary connections, Wordsworth and Tennyson included. St Bega's chapel, the ancient parish church of Bassenthwaite, stands at the water's edge. This tranquil sanctuary, reached on foot, is surrounded by poppies and daisies in the churchyard, while inside wildflower and bird identification books are available for general use.

CURIOUS AND CURIOUSER

Every ten years – the last time was in 2006 – the villagers of Bassenthwaite beat the bounds of the parish. This involves swimming across Bassenthwaite lake and climbing to the summit of Skiddaw, where refreshments are served.

See the extraordinary lithophone or musical stones of Skiddaw at the Keswick museum and art gallery. The tuned black stones were played at Buckingham Palace to the delight of Queen Victoria.

18

Show and Shine

Fells Romans Crag rats

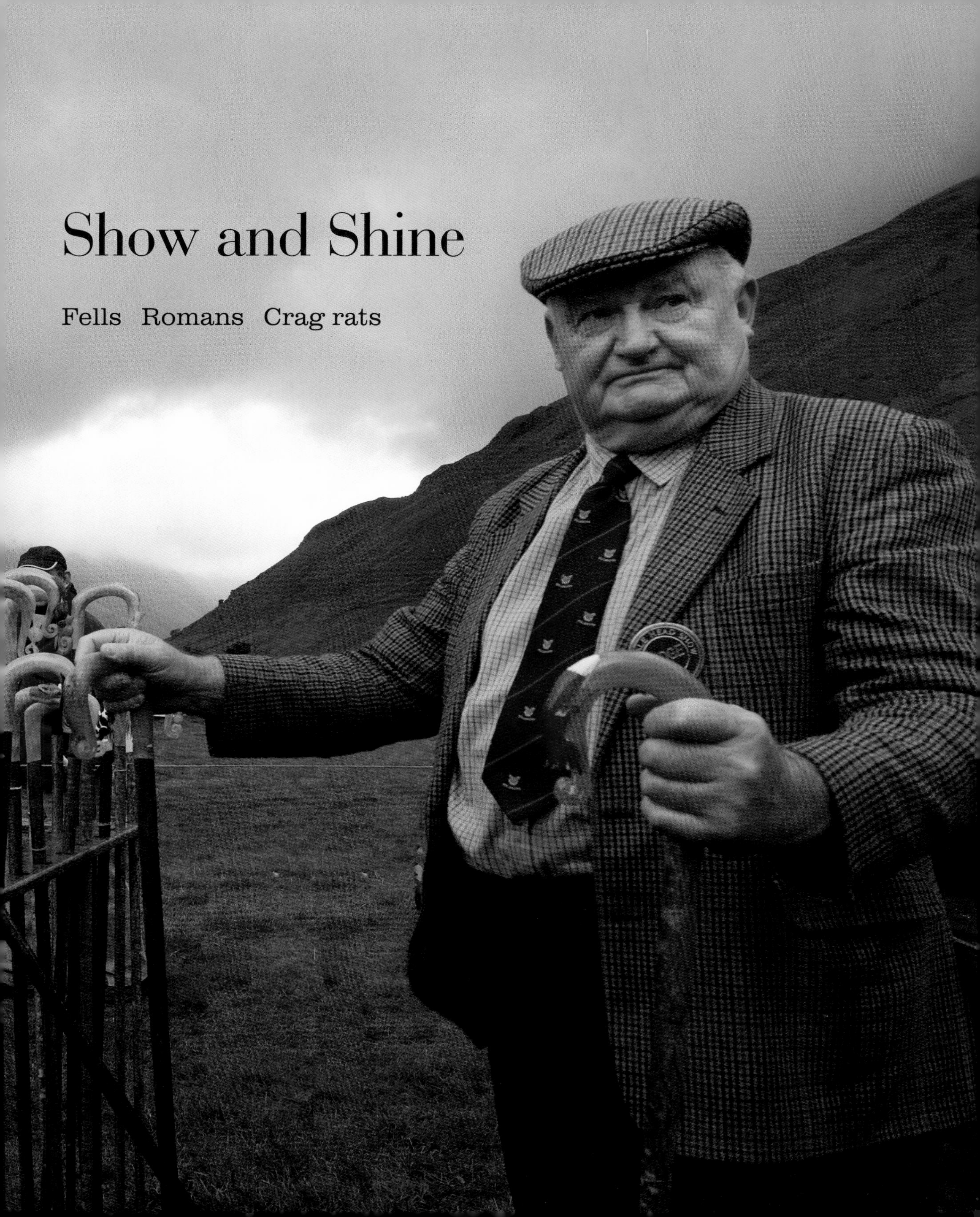

A weekend at a traditional western Lake District country show is a great escape, with the bonus of a stupendous waterfall, crazy Romans, friendly country pubs, and breathtaking walks on low and high fells. Even if your boots weren't made for walking, this is a weekend to savour.

Every second Saturday in October is a red-letter day for the Lakeland community of Wasdale. At the top of the valley country folk gather in green pastures for the Wasdale Head Shepherds' Meet and Show, where trail hounds, sheep, fell runners and vintage agricultural machines can all be found. The emerald stage is bounded by lichen-stained walls and the tawny bracken fells of England's big boys: Scafell Pike, the highest mountain in England, Great Gable, Pillar, Kirk Fell and Sca Fell. The church of St Olaf, final resting place of many a mountaineer, hides in a nest of thick yews. Beyond is a scene judged Britain's favourite view by ITV audiences in 2007; stony, heathery screes plunge into Wast Water, England's deepest lake.

The show has a competition for everyone, from the children's under-five race, run with mum or dad, in which everyone gets a prize,

to the best-looking smooth-coated dog and the best-looking rough-coated dog. And there's a highly prized trophy for the most beautifully polished shepherds' boots. Men with weathered faces collect admission fees and judges in flat caps and tweed jackets cast critical eyes over ornamental shepherds' sticks, traditionally made from hazel with a curve of four and a half inches to grasp a sheep's neck. Country stalls sell slurry boost, sheep marking fluid, bootlaces and Teflon-coated pure new wool tweed caps. Herdwick sheep are mustered in makeshift pens. Renowned for their rugged, resilient outlook, the hardy flock is gathered in from the hill for a makeover; washed, detangled and daubed with a traditional red-bloom stain based on haematite, they become allegedly more attractive to the judges. Tinted rouge, the woolly crowd appear bemused.

Herdwicks have owned the Cumbrian fells for centuries; these survivors can cope with fiercesome weather and marginal fell pasture. Their heafing instinct is strong; once acquainted with their territory, Herdwicks are reluctant to roam, unlike nearby fell runners limbering up in skimpy shorts and vests. The saying goes that the only way a Lakeland lad could woo his girl was by running up and over the peaks, hence the advent of fell running.

The first recorded races took place in 1850; many of the competitors were mountain guides accustomed to leading tourists over the hills. At the show lithe and springy athletes perform stretches against stone walls while onlookers turn their gaze to the mighty mound of Kirk Fell, shrouded in cloud. Some begin to question the sanity of the entrants. But too late, the runners are off, with the show announcer declaring, 'You know where you're going, to the top o' th'ill.' Immediately challenged by the steep incline, the rush of runners becomes a single file of worker ants pushing relentlessly upward. Binoculars are trained as they disappear into cloud, then a shout goes up when the leader comes into view, bounding down the fell, o'erleaping bracken, dodging rocks and sliding through mud in an attempt to finish within the record time of thirty-one minutes. There's jostling and overtaking as the winner hurtles towards the crowd's applause, collapsing on the finishing line, agony etched on his face. Loyal onlookers count them in safely before retiring to the beer tent.

Nether Wasdale is a well-kept village with a bright blue maypole and benches on the village green. The phone box, often adorned with floriferous plant pots, is alongside the millennium seat of Joss Naylor MBE, sheep farmer and wiry giant among fell runners. See childhood

...hungry and thirsty?

The Woolpack is special, combining country character with a superb wine list and a second-hand boot exchange for kids, who outgrow walking gear so quickly. There are fifty-two vodkas and cocktails including Woolpack Royale, made with sloe gin and champagne. Food ranges from chip butties to local lobster thermidor. On Friday the inn becomes the Hardknott Café with live comedy and music. The Wasdale Head Inn is a Mountain Rescue post, and photos on the wall reveal the early days of 'crag rats'. The King George IV in Eskdale Green boasts slate-flagged floors and a fine selection of malt whiskies; there's a lovely riverside walk from here to Doctor's Bridge. In Nether Wasdale the Strands Hotel has a microbrewery, while the Screes Inn has two beautiful pub signs (there's breakfast for non-residents with bike hire too). The Bower House has superb views from the elegant terrace, Woodlands is a good stop for afternoon tea and there's a platform café at Dalegarth Station.

...tired?

There's a luxurious yurt and bed and breakfast at Rainors Farm, basic essentials at Murt camping barn, and traditional camping at Fisherground. Shepherd's View Holidays welcome caravans and camping and offer bike hire and hot tubs. Lingmell House is close by St Olaf's Church, Low Wood Hotel offers painting courses, or stay on a working farm at Burnthwaite Cottage, Penny Hill Farm or Bowderdale Farm. Hermon's Hill is a seventeenth-century farmstead and Stanley House bed and breakfast, with impressive green credentials, is directly opposite Beckfoot Station. Creature comforts include Wi-Fi and hot-water bottles. Two favourite Lakeland youth hostels are Wast Water and Eskdale.

pictures of Joss and his hound on display in St Michael's Church, where there's a photographic exhibition of local life and magnificent felted wool seat pads on the pews. A peace shelter built in 1923 remembers people of all nations who have given their lives in the cause of patriotism and duty. Nether Wasdale was a popular stop for Victorian gentry discovering the fells thanks to the poetry of William Wordsworth and Samuel Taylor Coleridge. The latter made the first 'recorded' ascent of Scafell in 1802. In the 1880s Lake District peaks became the haunt of climbers, many from the south, known locally as 'crag rats'.

Eskdale is one of the few Lakeland valleys without a lake, yet there are still many reasons to visit; the Fell Dales Association hosts the Eskdale Show on the last Saturday of September in a field near the King George IV pub. There are classes for Herdwick sheep, hound trails, Cumberland and Westmorland wrestling, and prizes for a winning Cumberland rum butter and a knitted article in Herdwick wool. At Giggle Alley the Forestry Commission is restoring the Japanese garden of Lord Rea, a Liverpool coal and shipping millionaire. Pick up an information leaflet from the village shop and wander through an exotic woodland of maples, magnolia and bamboo. St Bega's Church, built by Lord Rea, is at the heart of the community and serves as a post office, heritage centre and bookstall.

Further up the valley, the Ravenglass and Eskdale Valley narrow-gauge railway, fondly known as La'al Ratty, terminates in the village of Boot. Opened in 1875, it carried haematite iron ore, as sported by tinted Herdwick sheep, from mines in Eskdale to the Furness railway at Ravenglass. The Lakeland journey from the fells to the sea takes 40 minutes.

From Boot you may walk to tarns, standing stones and peat scales (huts) on the moor where locals dried and stored their fuel. See the Lake District's oldest working water cornmill in the village and stroll to St Catherine's Church near Doctor's Bridge, widened by Dr Tyson so he could reach patients across the River Esk by pony and trap. Opposite the ancient church is a more daring way to cross the gin-clear water – stepping stones. Hop across to reach Stanley Ghyll Force, a thrilling torrent in a narrow gorge where rhododendrons bloom. It's a dangerous and exhilarating visit, best avoided by young children and anyone with vertigo.

The dizzy heights of Hardknott Pass at the head of Eskdale make a journey up the steep single-track road with hair-pin bends an ear-popping, heart-thumping experience. This is no place for nervous drivers,

nor is it where you'd expect to find a Roman fort. Few would send a dog to this cold and lonely outpost, let alone a legionnaire. The design of the commandant's house was inspired by Roman town houses; the soldiers lived in timber barracks. Imagine the queues for the bathhouse, still visible outside the main walls of the stronghold. Here men sought relief in hot rooms to remove sweat and cold rooms to close the pores. On a miserable day you can picture the clamour for the laconicum (sauna), which appears rather like a stone igloo. When there's no low cloud or pelting rain, the fort has commanding views down the valley and out to sea, to monitor hostile natives, but when the weather closed in on this god-forsaken garrison it must have felt like the end of the world to a lad from sunny Italy.

19

Night at the Museum

Wildflowers Sheep Vikings

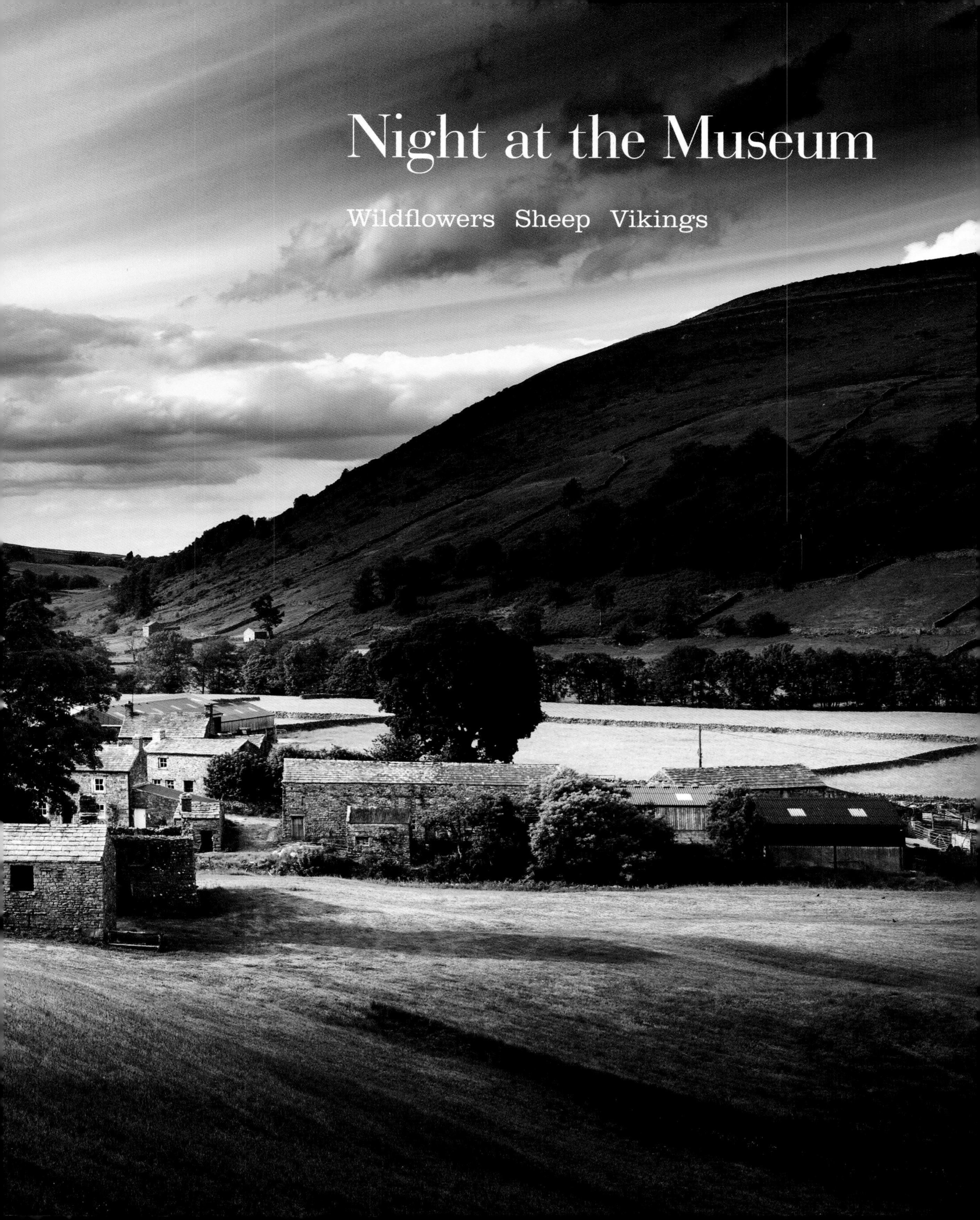

Fields of gold await in Swaledale and Arkengarthdale. Come summer Yorkshire's most northerly valleys are a perfect pastoral vision; hay meadows enclosed by dry-stone walls brim with swaying buttercups, violet-blue crane's bill, purple melancholy thistles and ground-nesting birds including lapwing and curlew.

Hills, moor and scree where hardy Swaledale sheep thrive surround ancient villages and hamlets named by Viking settlers over a thousand years ago. 'Dale' is the Norse word for valley and 'Swale' means fast. Fearsome accounts tell of the River Swale in spate rising as much as ten feet in twenty minutes.

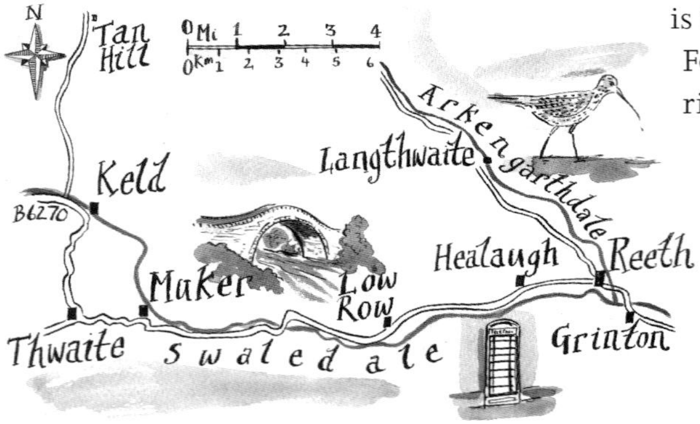

Traditional agriculture has shaped the landscape. In summer farmers lived with their sheep and cattle on high pastures, allowing hay meadows in the valley to produce winter feed. These grids of green are dotted with small neat field barns reminiscent of the teeny houses used in the board game of Monopoly. From November to May each two-storey barn stored hay above the cattle. In spring the muck was collected and spread across the meadows to nourish the next hay crop without need of artificial fertilisers. It is a process that has been re-introduced with glorious results.

To see the wildflowers of the hay meadows at their peak, visit between June and mid-July when livestock are excluded from the fields before the hay is cut. Crossing the sea of flowers is a joy. However, respect the farmers' need to protect their crop. It is not possible to reap flattened hay so follow public footpaths and take note of fingerposts that politely remind walkers: 'Meadow land, single file, please'.

Situated on the River Swale with a splendid village green, handsome architecture and fine views of the fells, the lovely village of Reeth is a great base from which to explore Swaledale and Arkengarthdale. Reeth flourished when lead and coal mining in Arkengarthdale were big business. Many miners supplemented their income with smallholdings – a couple of cows and a barn. Visit the charming Swaledale Museum in the former Methodist school room to see the tools of their trade, including a back can, made by the local tinsmith, used to carry fresh milk from cows in high summer pastures to the dairy in the valley.

Just off the village green, Reeth's community orchard is a welcoming hideaway enclosed by high stone walls. Rest on the bench seat inscribed with the first line of Siegried Sasssoon's 'Idyll': 'In the grey summer garden I shall find you'.

IDYLL

In the grey summer garden I shall find you
With day-break and the morning hills behind you.

There will be rain-wet roses; stir of wings;
And down the wood a thrush that wakes and sings.

Not from the past you'll come, but from that deep
Where beauty murmurs to the soul asleep:
And I shall know the sense of life re-born
From dreams into the mystery of morn
Where gloom and brightness meet. And standing there
Till that calm song is done, at last we'll share
The league-spread, quiring symphonies that are
Joy in the world, and peace, and dawn's one star.

SIEGFRIED SASSOON

Shapely pots and fountains and delicious local damson cheese are on sale at the Garden House Pottery in Anvil Square. From here there's a lovely twenty-minute walk to the springy bridge across the Swale, known as the 'swing bridge', although it's actually a suspension bridge. A riverside path on the opposite bank leads to the village of Grinton.

The sixteen-mile Corpse Way links the Swaledale villages of Keld and Grinton. Before the consecration of burial ground at Muker in 1586,

...hungry and thirsty?

Country pubs abound; try the Farmers Arms in Muker, the Punchbowl Inn at Low Row, hostelries on the green in Reeth, the CB Inn, Arkengarthdale, named after Charles Bathhurst's mining company, and Keld Lodge, a former youth hostel and shooting lodge in Keld. At the Tan Hill Inn, the highest pub in Britain, there's a Swaledale sheep show every May. Overton Café in Reeth is a local favourite, likewise the ice cream parlour on the green. Local cheese is available at the café and village stores in Muker.

corpses in wicker coffins were carried over Kisdon Hill and through the villages in relay to be buried at St Andrew's Church in Grinton.

Follow the river from Reeth to the village of Healaugh, which takes its name from the Norse for 'high forest clearing'. The phone box in the village is one of my favourites anywhere; on my last visit it was filled with the scent of freshly cut sweet peas in a vase. From here the road travels through magnificent walking country on the Coast to Coast Walk and close by the Pennine Way to Low Row, where the seventeenth-century Punchbowl Inn has a contemporary wooden bar commissioned from 'The Mouseman', Robert Thompson of Kilburn.

Gunnerside was formerly the centre of the local lead-mining community. Here the elegant Ivelet packhorse bridge crosses the Swale at a popular picnic spot below Oxnop Hall. Look out for the coffin stone, a slab where pallbearers on the Corpse Way rested en route to Grinton churchyard. The river and road wind into the upland meadows of Muker, which takes its name from the Norse word for meadow.

...tired?

It's a real treat to spend a night in the cottage of the Swaledale Museum in Reeth. Adjacent to the former schoolhouse, the pretty hideaway is perfect for couples. The Burgoyne Hotel is a handsome Georgian building on the village green. Enjoy tea, scones and home-made jam at nearby Springfield bed and breakfast. Swaledale lamb is on the menu at Kearton Country Hotel in Thwaite.

Hire bikes from the friendly Dales Bike Centre in Fremington and stay there too – they offer accommodation, bike wash, repair services and home-made food in a cheery café. There's camping in the wild at Hoggarth's Farm; no loos, water from a spring and eggs from free-range hens make it a big adventure. Camp by river swimming pools at Scabba Wath, Park House or near the beck at Usha Gap Campsite. For larger groups there's a bunk barn at Low Row.

A short walk from the village centre on a paved path leads through the hay meadows to Rampshome Bridge. You might come across Gordon Peacock sharpening scythes used to cut the hay in the traditional way. Gordon told me that the handle of the scythe must be as tall as the person using it.

Surrounded by magnificent landscape and extraordinary biodiversity, lovely Thwaite village is the birthplace of brothers Richard and Cherry Kearton, authors and naturalists whose studies of the local environment took them on pioneering expeditions around the world. The weird Buttertubs geological feature must have fascinated them, two miles south on the road to Hawes.

Keld hamlet is at the head of Swaledale and from nearby Kisdon Farm there is a magnificent view down the valley. A narrow steep road returns to Reeth via the fascinating industrial landscape of Arkengarthdale. Look out for the hexagonal powder house in Langthwaite, used to store explosives for the mining industry.

20

Skittish lambs race through bracken, sweet birdsong fills the air, tiny wild strawberries, fairy fruits, grow beside gushing moorland streams and an occasional tractor rumbles by.

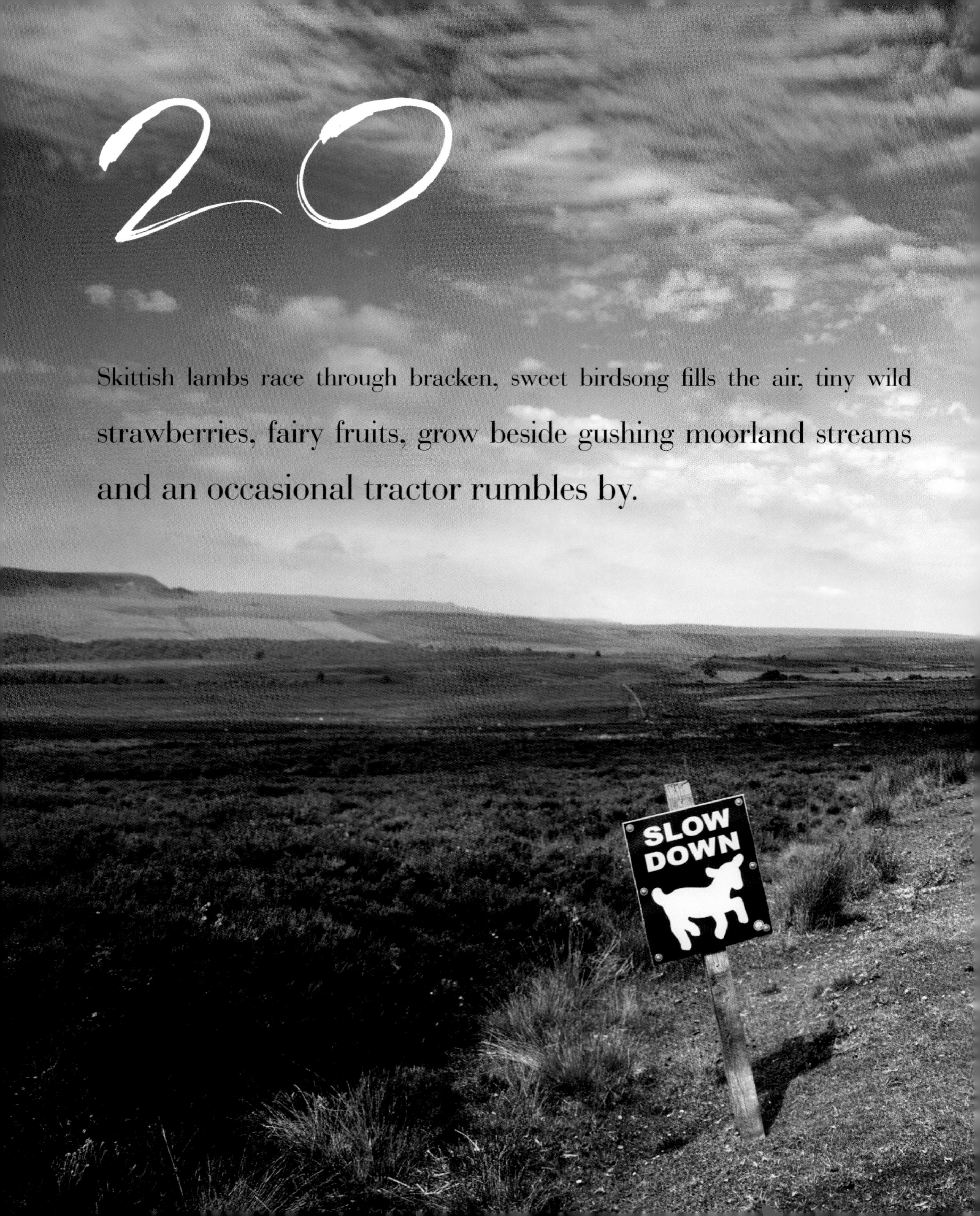

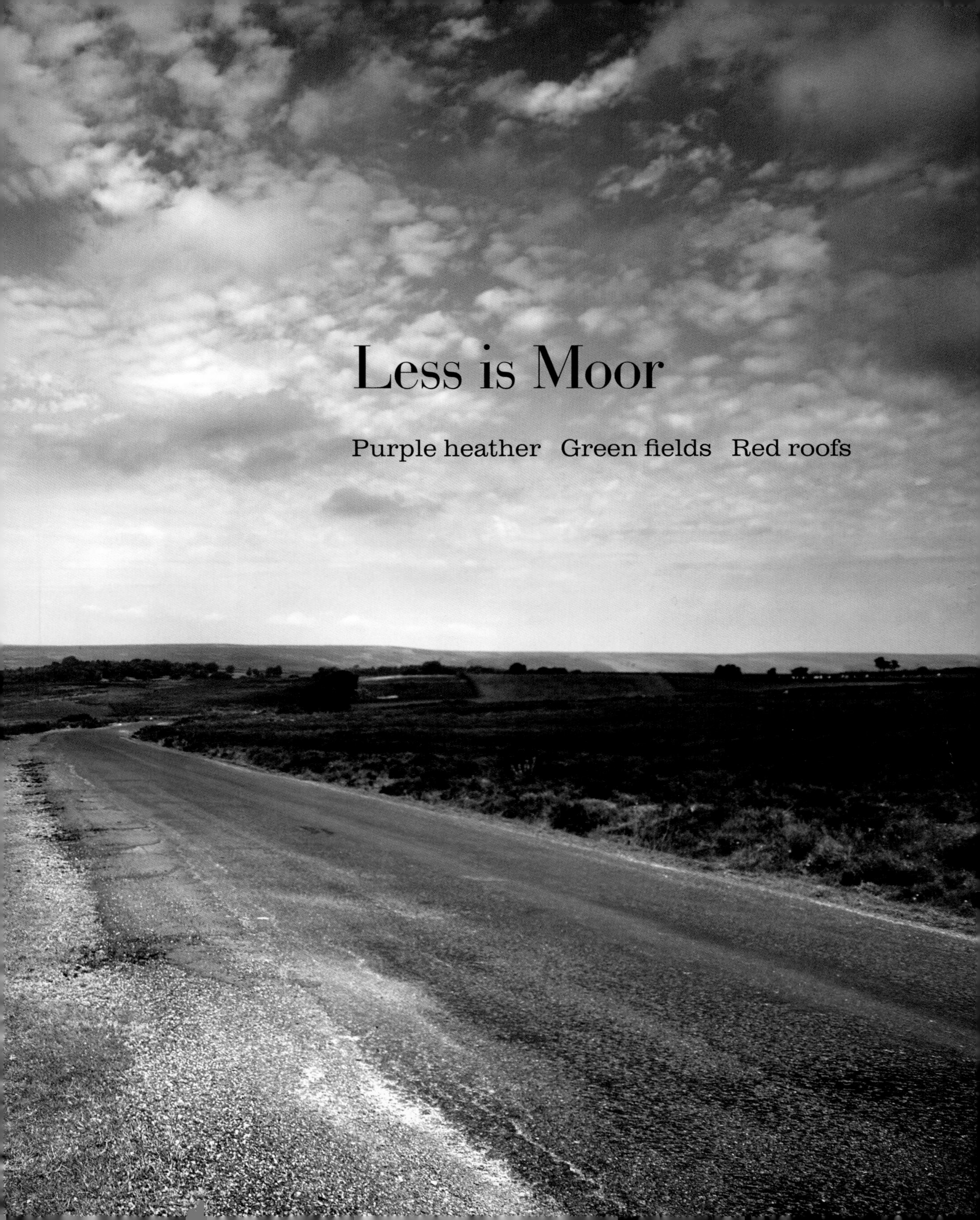

Less is Moor

Purple heather   Green fields   Red roofs

Need an escape route? Then this weekend is for you. Take to the hills of the North York Moors National Park where remote Bransdale will refresh your spirit.

The cheery country road that passes through the charming market town of Kirkbymoorside dwindles to a narrow lane beyond the hamlet of Fadmoor; leaving behind summertime hedgerows of poppies and wild roses it climbs to the patchwork of purple heather and bilberries at Bransdale. With big skies above there's a feeling of freedom and welcome separation here; the cares of the world can seem aeons away. Skittish lambs race through bracken, sweet birdsong fills the air, tiny wild strawberries, fairy fruits, grow beside gushing moorland streams and an occasional tractor rumbles by.

The North York Moors is the largest continuous tract of dry upland heath in the British Isles and the precious open landscape supports a range of wildlife including roe deer, red grouse, short-eared owls, merlin and curlew. Out of sight are lizards and adders.

Surrounded by green fields, dry-stone walls march up and down dale, criss-crossed by bridleways and footpaths. Working farmhouses stand under red clay pantile roofs, swallows swoop around barns and place names sound like a magic spell: Wind Hill, Groat Hill, Smout House, Toad Hill, Cornfield and Cow Sike. In this isolated community there are 25 families; nine of them farm the land. Previously there were 400 people including a shoemaker, blacksmith and innkeepers. Mobile telephone signals in the dale are scant. Spout House farm is a communication hub with its red phone box on the hillside and a scarlet postbox in the barn wall.

...tired?

Stay for bed and breakfast at Lidmoor Farm in the heart of Bransdale. Just beyond the dale there's also bed and breakfast at Bitchagreen Cottage and Manor Farm. Groups are welcome at Bransdale Mill independent hostel.

St Nicholas' Church is in a blissful spot on the hillside, above the beck with idyllic views down the dale. Great slabs of stone encircle the church, making a path, inviting you to explore. Headstones engraved with the white rose of York reveal the sorrow of commonplace infant deaths, yet some, like Joseph Duck aged 102, survived many seasons in the dale. Indoors the church has a barrelled roof and a stove to warm the windswept congregation. Whitewashed Bransdale School has been beautifully restored to serve as a community centre with secondary glazing and walls insulated with sheep wool. Former pupils would be astonished to find solar panels in the playground of their alma mater.

READY FOR MOOR?

Prepare for a great day on the moors and be aware of the dangers.

Weather changes quickly. Dress appropriately; take food and drink, a map and compass.

Wildfire is a huge risk. Moorland notices warn that once started fires may smoulder in dry peat for days and discarded glass can magnify the sun's energy to spark a blaze.

Dogs must be on a short lead, less than two metres, at all times. A dog worrying livestock can be legally shot.

Ticks in fern and bracken carry disease and attach themselves without your knowledge. Swift action is required to remove them with care, so check your skin thoroughly.

Adders live on moorland. Britain's only poisonous snake has distinctive black zigzag markings for perfect camouflage. Keep to the tracks.

Blanket bog can be deep and dangerous. Walk with care.

...hungry and thirsty?

There are no shops, cafés or pubs in Bransdale. Pick up supplies in Kirbymoorside. Visit Farndale, renowned for wild daffodils, on the other side of Rudland Rigg, for a friendly welcome from barman Peter at the Feversham Arms; there's accommodation too. In Gillamoor the Royal Oak is a cosy traditional pub by the village green. Take a short stroll from the pub to see the unusual village sundial and St Aidan's Church, and enjoy the 'Surprise View' over Farndale from a hilltop bench.

21

Grand Designs

Wharram Percy   Fossil Willy   Castle Howard

Discover the heart of Ryedale this weekend with a visit to Malton, a country town rich in Roman and medieval heritage and one of the top racehorse training centres in the UK. Malton and neighbouring Norton are situated on either side of the River Derwent, a strategic location favoured by the Romans who established the fort of Derventio nearby. For supplies and trading, the river gave access to the sea and, as the fort prospered, a civilian community developed on both banks of the Derwent to service the needs of the occupying army. Later, in the twelfth century, a castle and priory were built near the site of the fort and the borough of New Malton was established to the west of it. The medieval walled town was a thriving hub of wool merchants, weavers, dyers, tailors and masons. Serving rural communities, the market was famed in the sixteenth century for horses, eels, fish and corn. Traders sold agricultural tools to labourers and a multitude of pubs slaked their thirst. In the seventeenth century a spa on the River Derwent became renowned for curing liver complaints, indigestion and ulcers. Prestigious events were held at Langton Wold racecourse; the gallops on the summit of the Wold are regarded still as among the finest in the country. Vital to Malton's commercial success, river traffic on the Derwent increased hugely in the early eighteenth century before dwindling upon the arrival of the railway age.

Now remains of the Roman fort are hidden under grassy knolls at Orchard Fields, but in the small town museum there are fascinating displays of extraordinary finds unearthed by experts and locals alike. One of the most moving is an infant skeleton found buried with a tiny black bear finely worked in Whitby jet; there's also a bead and bronze bracelet and an early third-century coin, payment to Charon the

...tired?

Stay at The Old Lodge, the grand gatehouse of a Tudor mansion that was effectively destroyed by two squabbling sisters. Unable to settle a dispute as to who should inherit the family home, the Sheriff ruled that the mansion should be divided equally between them, after first being reduced to a pile of rubble. Fortunately the women put a stop to their wrangling before the same fate befell the gatehouse.

ferryman who would, the Romans believed, transport the dead child across the river Styx to the Underworld. Lightening the mood, there's the tale of Fossil Willy, a notorious faker who fooled many experts with his steady supply of Roman artefacts. Dressing-up clothes, and the opportunity to grind flour Roman-style, promise fun for children in the museum's activity centre. The upper floor of the museum explores medieval life with an evocative display of sights and sounds from a simple dwelling in Wharram Percy, the remote wolds village that was sacrificed when families working the land were cleared to make way for grazing sheep.

A gentle circular walk, available from the museum, takes in the heritage highlights of this lovely town, from the traditional wooden pens of the livestock market to a shuttered Georgian building in narrow Chancery Lane; here the offices of Smithson Solicitors inspired Ebenezer Scrooge's counting house in *A Christmas Carol* by Charles Dickens. Allow around an hour and a half for the stroll, and longer if you're likely to stop off at tempting cafés or picnic benches by the river. If you are a curious soul like me, beware the wonders of George Woodall & Sons in Market Place, established in 1884; this fascinating country store sells everything from rope and twine to ferret collars and ear tags for livestock.

Beyond Malton there's plenty more to see, including traces of medieval life in Wharram Percy, now in the care of English Heritage. Tranquil ruins in remote open countryside make this an atmospheric visit. For something quite different, visit Eden Camp, an extraordinary museum. Within the grounds of a World War Two prisoner-of-war camp, a great gathering of huts brims with military and social history from 1914 onwards. The full splendour of stately Castle Howard might demand a weekend in itself. The fabulous Baroque pile, designed by John Vanbrugh and Nicholas Hawksmoor, was constructed in the early 1700s when the third Earl of Carlisle used his power to flatten the village of Henderskelfe which stood in the way of his view. At Scampston an extraordinary vision has been achieved in a walled garden once used to grow Christmas trees. Divided into nine contrasting areas, the awe-inspiring gardens were designed in 1999 by Piet Oudolf. Wander through swaying drifts of grass, rigid topiary columns in the Silent Garden and the sensuous enclosure of the Serpentine Garden, and prepare to be inspired. The bold, beautiful design may have you rethinking your green patch at home.

...hungry and thirsty?

There are teashops, cafés and pubs galore in Malton. Kingfisher café and bookshop is a cheery place to make a pit stop on the heritage trail. Pop into the Hidden Monkey for 'proper puds, cakes and scones'. Among the locals' favourite pubs are The Spotted Cow in the Cattle Market and the seventeenth-century Blue Ball, which has an historic traditional inn yard. Malton has a weekly Saturday street market and the farmers' market takes place on the last Saturday of every month. Sumptuous Castle Howard has a farm shop, coffee shop and café. The Garden restaurant at Scampston is light and bright, with seats outdoors to savour the surroundings.

22

From the valley bottom zigzag roads, perilous in winter, zip around windswept hills before romping across bleak moors; it's a dramatic environment that has spawned much creativity.

Well Versed

Poets Packhorses Playtime

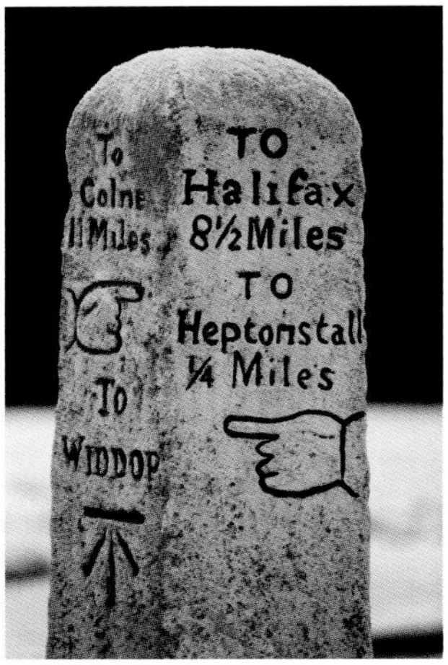

Welcome to the good life in West Yorkshire. Discover a vibrant community, with breathtaking countryside, colourful independent shops, and a dynamic arts scene; all part of a bohemian weekend in the Pennines.

The mill town of Hebden Bridge crams into a deep valley where achingly steep pavements squeeze between sucked-in houses, holding their breath. Few places are flat; space is at a premium. Double-decker homes, built for textile workers, pile one family upon another, weaving a close-knit community. From the valley bottom zigzag roads, perilous in winter, zip around windswept hills before romping across bleak moors; it's a dramatic environment that has spawned much creativity.

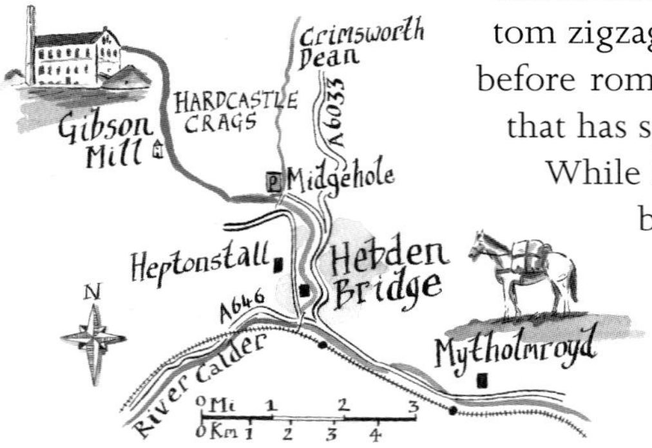

While Hebden Bridge has grown much larger than its neighbour Heptonstall, the market town remains, historically at least, the junior partner. Heptonstall was an important settlement on the Long Causeway, an ancient trading route between Burnley and Halifax, and on the packhorse track from Widdop to Colne.

Stone setts scale the hillside to Weavers Square, near the cloth hall where home workers sold hand-loomed kersey cloth to merchants. Look out for cottages with weavers' lights, windows designed to shed light on the loom.

Heptonstall's dead lie beneath a vast pavement of headstones in the historic graveyard, farmers alongside weavers in the stony ranks between two churches; one a ruin, dedicated to St Thomas à Beckett,

...tired?

The annual Ted Hughes Festival takes place in October; you can stay at Ted's House, the childhood home of the former Poet Laureate in Mytholmroyd. In Hebden Bridge elegant Holme House bed and breakfast is centrally situated by the canal, station and shops. Angeldale has views over the town's cobbled streets and Croft Mill offers self-catering apartments in a historic building. Rambles bed and breakfast is on the Mary Towneley Loop of the Pennine Bridleway and Coiners' Barn enjoys panoramic moorland views.

On a budget? Then try the independent Hebden Hostel or Mankinholes Youth Hostel. Sporty campers may be inclined to pitch up and hire bikes at Hebden Bridge Camping Company before attempting Cragg Vale, England's longest continuous ascent.

other a replacement for its storm-struck neighbour, dedicated to St Thomas the Apostle.

Across the lane is the grave of American poet and writer Sylvia Plath, first wife of former Poet Laureate Ted Hughes. Ted Hughes grew up in nearby Mytholmroyd, and seven boyhood years there deeply influenced his work. With older brother Gerard he escaped to explore hidden valleys and camp on the wild moors; Crimsworth Dean was a favourite place. Hughes met and married Plath, a Cambridge University Fulbright scholar, in 1956. The potent creative team had a daughter and son; Hughes also had a mistress, Assia Wevill. Plath and Hughes separated before Plath tragically took her own life in 1963. Suicide shadowed Hughes; in 1969 Wevill took her life and that of her four-year-old daughter and in 2009, after his father's death in 1998, Ted and Sylvia's son Nicholas killed himself too. His mother's headstone bears an inscription chosen by his father from Chinese literature: '…even amidst fierce flames the golden lotus can be planted'.

See Heptonstall's Octagonal Methodist Chapel, founded around 1742 and the oldest still in use in the world. Tradition is important here; the Pace Egg play has been performed by locals on hundreds of Good Fridays, with much mirth generated around a dastardly character called Toss Pot. Visit the snug museum in the former boys' grammar school, complete with original desks and stone-flagged floors, for reports of Civil War battles and the notorious coiners who made new dosh from clipped fragments of coins in circulation.

The steep valleys of Hebden were perfect for water-powered mills

WIND

This house has been far out at sea all night,
The woods crashing through darkness, the booming hills,
Winds stampeding the fields under the window
Floundering black astride and blinding wet

Till day rose; then under an orange sky
The hills had new places, and wind wielded
Blade-light, luminous black and emerald,
Flexing like the lens of a mad eye.

At noon I scaled along the house-side as far as
The coal-house door. Once I looked up –
Through the brunt wind that dented the balls of my eyes
The tent of the hills drummed and strained its guyrope,

The fields quivering, the skyline a grimace,
At any second to bang and vanish with a flap;
The wind flung a magpie away and a black–
Back gull bent like an iron bar slowly. The house

Rang like some fine green goblet in the note
That any second would shatter it. Now deep
In chairs, in front of the great fire, we grip
Our hearts and cannot entertain book, thought,

Or each other. We watch the fire blazing,
And feel the roots of the house move, but sit on,
Seeing the window tremble to come in,
Hearing the stones cry out under the horizons.

TED HUGHES

...hungry and thirsty?

After scaling the Buttress walkway from Hebden to Heptonstall, Towngate Tea Room in Heptonstall is a godsend. Poets Ted and Sylvia drank at Stubbing Wharf canalside pub renowned for real ale, cider and perry. The Packhorse Inn at Widdop has refueled travellers for centuries; on the Mary Towneley Loop, they offer bed and breakfast and stables too. In Hebden Bridge, Innovation café is a local favourite. Green's is a popular vegetarian and vegan restaurant and Organic House café bar does Sunday brunch. For picnics buy quality bread and cakes from Saker co-operative bakery and prepare a feast from Pennine Provisions. There are friendly cafés at Hebden Bridge Station and Gibson Mill.

and the market town's proximity to Halifax gave access to wool markets. With the arrival of the canal, roads and water-powered mills, Hebden Bridge flourished while the industry of Heptownstall dwindled.

Vibrant Hebden Bridge buzzes with independent local shops; if it's retail therapy with character you seek, then this is Nirvana. Find Polish pottery at Polka Dot Lane, rainbow colours at Jules tableware, kitchen essentials at the Pot Shop, haberdashery heaven at Ribbon Circus, ethically sourced homeware at Spirals and fashion stores offering anything from Vivienne Westwood to the latest in hemp. There are quirky lamps at Radiance and great reads at The Hebden Bridge Bookshop. For cinema and performances there's the Picture House, and the Trades Club is a traditional cultural hub; both venues are worth checking out before your visit. For a town trail leaflet, call at the visitor centre on the wharf. Here you'll also discover information about the town's canal history, with boat trips too.

Gibson Mill at Hardcastle Crags is a favourite three-mile circular walk; from Midgehole car park follow the rocky Mill Walk beside Hebden Water, with the bonus of stepping stones for sploshy fun. Now in the care of the National Trust, the mill, powered by a 22-foot waterwheel, was built in 1803 by Abraham Gibson. See the workshop where 22 workers, including children, laboured at spinning jennies to produce cotton until 1890. When cotton was no longer king, the mill became a romantic dancehall in the woods. Bright young things trekked for miles across the moors to attend.

Today the mill is a glowing example of sustainable development; off grid, it boasts photovoltaic panels, solar hot-water panels, a hydro-electric turbine, a wood-burning ceramic stove using local timber, walls insulated with Thermafleece and roof insulation from a recycled news-

paper product. There's minimal water wastage and visitors are even invited to fill drinking bottles at the spring-fed tap in the Nature Room. Don't miss Barry Clark's inspired recycled glasswork in the stairwells.

GO FOR GREEN

The Calderdale community is passionate about green transport, so aim to play your part too. Hebden Bridge rail and bus stations are close by the town centre and canal. From here there are three great walks – easy, moderate and challenging – posted on information panels. Alternatively discover the area on bicycle; check out the Calder Cycle Way and Calderdale Festival of Cycling. For horse riders, mountain bikers and walkers there's superb scenery along ancient packhorse routes on the Pennine Bridleway, inspired by Mary Towneley. The challenging Mary Towneley Loop is perfect for a long weekend. Heptonstall post office sells leaflets of walks around the village.

MORNING SONG

Love set you going like a fat gold watch.
The midwife slapped your footsoles, and your bald cry
Took its place among the elements.

Our voices echo, magnifying your arrival. New statue.
In a drafty museum, your nakedness
Shadows our safety. We stand round blankly as walls.

I'm no more your mother
Than the cloud that distills a mirror to reflect its own slow
Effacement at the wind's hand.

All night your moth-breath
Flickers among the flat pink roses. I wake to listen:
A far sea moves in my ear.

One cry, and I stumble from bed, cow-heavy and floral
In my Victorian nightgown.
Your mouth opens clean as a cat's. The window square

Whitens and swallows its dull stars. And now you try
Your handful of notes;
The clear vowels rise like balloons.

SYLVIA PLATH

23

Tunnel Vision

Longest Highest Deepest

Deep down below boatmen on wooden barges lay flat on their back on planks laid across the bow to walk the walls, legging their way along the route in a journey of four hours' darkness.

This weekend celebrates stupendous achievements in the moorland heart of the Pennines; seize the opportunity to explore the Huddersfield Narrow Canal and experience a wonder of the waterways network; the longest canal tunnel, the highest canal summit and the deepest canal tunnel in the UK.

Magnificent Marsden Moor is dramatically situated on the fringes of northern towns that flourished when the textile industry was at its peak. While the industry has dwindled and mills have been converted, the unenclosed moor, in the care of the National Trust, remains spectacular. Far-reaching views are uplifting and walks across open country on ancient packhorse routes are a perfect way to blow away the cobwebs and savour the sense of freedom.

A visit to Buckstones Edge car park and picnic site sets the scene; from this panoramic vantage point much of Marsden Moor Estate is visible. Helter-skelter roads wind around windswept hills, deep cloughs (narrow upland valleys) are interlocked, reservoirs provide water for the Huddersfield Narrow Canal and moorland birds including twite, golden plover, red grouse, skylark and curlew thrive. Far below the River Colne passes through compact neighbourhoods.

This is splendid walking and cycling country; a car is not necessary. Take the train to Marsden Station where a small National Trust visitor centre is located in the former stable of the railway goods yard; an exhibition traces the history of wildlife and people living on the moor and the historic importance of transport routes across it. The Roman military road from Chester to York is still visible on the south slopes of Pule

...hungry and thirsty?

After the chill of the tunnel, the café at Tunnel End offers welcome warmth. Watch boats go by from picnic benches outside the Standedge Visitor Centre, feast on hand-made bread, tasty cheese, olives and more from the friendly Radish deli in the village. Mozzarella's food and wine bar is a favourite local haunt, while the Riverhead Brewery Tap has outdoor seats near the weir, the ducks and Mick Kirby Geddes' sculpture of the canal and village. A favourite Marsden treat is a thick vanilla ice-cream shake at A Month of Sundaes, where sublime ice cream is made in small batches; tangy rhubarb is a big hit with locals. Marsden meets the Med at The Olive Branch, a popular restaurant with rooms, The Railway is a friendly local beside the lock and the station, and rooms at the New Inn, owned by the same team as Marsden's Hey Green hotel, are named after famous local folk, including Lancashire dialect poet Samuel Laycock. In the village centre, The Shakespeare is a popular venue during the Marsden Jazz Festival in October.

Hill. Coal, peat, lime, lead, charcoal, finished cloth, salt and corn were transported by packhorses over raised causeways, likewise ladies from London en route to the North, who were also classed as parcels!

From the National Trust visitor centre at Marsden Station, it's an easy walk of fifteen minutes along the towpath of the Huddersfield Narrow Canal to the stupendous Standedge Tunnel. Alternatively, hop on the Marsden Shuttle, a seasonal water taxi between the station and visitor centre. At 3.2 miles long and 643 feet above sea level the Standedge Tunnel is the longest, highest and deepest tunnel in the UK. Commissioned by Act of Parliament in 1794, the project to link the Ashton-under-Lyne and Huddersfield Canals took seventeen back-breaking years to complete; thousands of navvies armed with shovels and pick-axes were encamped across the moors with their families. Working by hand and by candlelight, progress was slow; floods caused death and delays, compounded by the awful realisation that diggers at either end of the tunnel, at Marsden and Diggle, were not destined to meet in the middle. At vast expense Thomas Telford was drafted in to get the project back on course.

When the tunnel opened in 1811 barges carried bulky cargo too large for the heavily taxed turnpike routes. Boats were laden with wool from Yorkshire, cotton from Lancashire, stone and coal, and manure to fertilise poor Pennine soil. Finished cloth from local mills was sent to Liverpool from where it was exported worldwide. While canal-boat horses trekked over the top of Pule Hill, deep down below boatmen on wooden barges lay flat on their back on planks laid across the bow to walk the walls, legging their way along the route in a journey of four hours' darkness. It was twenty-two years before a team of professional leggers was employed to relieve congestion and take boats through the tunnel for a fee. Empty boats were often punted through the dark. Despite the tedious journey, demand for the waterway was high; at its peak, the canal was open day and night when possible, although drought and ice often caused closures in summer and winter.

The expansion of the railways sounded the death knell; in 1845 the first of three Standedge railway tunnels was built. The route followed the line of the canal tunnel and thirty transverse passages allowed spoil to be removed by boat and heaped at Tunnel End. As railways gathered momentum, so canals declined, and by 1944 the Huddersfield Narrow Canal was abandoned by Act of Parliament. In 2001 the waterway was restored to full navigation thanks to the drive and ambition of local people. The fascinating story of the canal's conception, construction, demise and revival is told at the Standedge visitor centre, a former canal warehouse. A trip aboard a glass-roofed narrowboat to discover the tunnel with informed and enthusiastic guides is a must; the experience is awe-inspiring. Take a thirty-minute journey or travel the full length of the tunnel in two hours and walk back over the moors, following the route of the canal-boat horses.

Wrapped around the canal and River Colne, lovely Marsden village is rich in industrial heritage, from the Mechanics Hall, built in 1861, where hundreds of labourers attended evening classes, to the 1929 temperance drinking fountain in the park. Funded by the British Women's Temperance Association, the fountain served to quench thirsty workers who might otherwise head for the pub. For a bracing stroll and great views over the village, join locals on a favourite walk up Old Mount Road or seek out footpaths onto the moors from the ancient packhorse bridge at Eastergate, off Blake Lea Lane. Notice the low parapet allowing strings of horses burdened with wide loads to make the crossing safely.

...tired?

For bed and breakfast, stay at Weirside in Marsden or a little further away at The Shippon in Delph. In a converted textile mill, Titanic Spa is a luxurious retreat and the UK's first eco spa.

24

Bewitched

Moors Fells Food

The Ribble Valley promises enchantment in outstanding scenery; discover characterful Clitheroe, charming villages in the Forest of Bowland, and Pendle Hill, renowned for the witch trials of 1612 when ten men and women from the Forest of Pendle were hanged for the murder by witchcraft of seventeen people.

Pendle Hill dominates the Lancashire landscape of heather moors, farms, woodlands and textile mills that inspired JRR Tolkien, author of *The Lord of the Rings*, 'matchstick' artist LS Lowry and George Fox, founder of the Quaker Movement. Fox wrote that from the top of Pendle Hill in 1652, 'the Lord let me see in what places he had a great people to be gathered'.

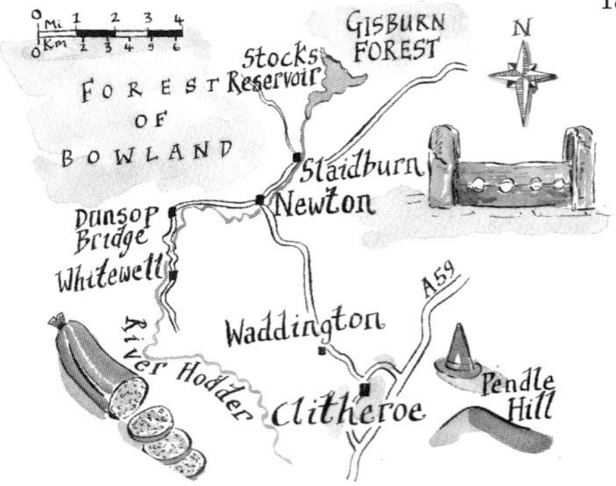

Clitheroe's damp climate offered ideal conditions for the spinning and weaving of textiles in the eighteenth century. Cotton was king and the town grew quickly to accommodate a spinning mill, weaving mills, bobbin works, bleach works and textile printing works. Today just one manufacturer remains; at Holmes Mill, Thornber Home and Leisure Ltd weaves over 100,000 metres of fabric a week.

Contemporary Clitheroe, food capital of Lancashire, is a thriving market town of great character. Sophisticated independent stores and markets on Tuesdays, Thursdays and Saturdays are popular. The Norman castle is a favourite place with a thrilling skate park, a fascinating museum, 16 acres of formal gardens and the only labyrinth in the county. Between Clitheroe and Waddington discover sika deer and otters on the Ribble Valley Sculpture Trail, a 45-minute stroll around works of art inspired by the landscape.

Ducks dabble in the splashy beck that gurgles through lovely Waddington village. Colourful communal gardens commemorate the Coronation of 1953 and ancient village stocks outside St Helen's Church bear witness to rural crime and punishment. From here the road rises to Waddington Fell in the former royal hunting ground of the Forest of Bowland. There are few trees in a landscape that offers some of the most remote walking in Lancashire; it's an important and protected breeding ground for nationally threatened birds including ring ouzels, merlins, red grouse, peregrines and hen harriers, the symbol of the Forest.

The road continues up and over Bradford Fell to the historic riverside village of Slaidburn. On land behind the new village hall, Slaidburn's hatters dried pelts at Skin Croft. Nearby Stocks Reservoir on the Bowland Estate is the most important for wildfowl of United Utilities'

...tired?

Snuggle down at the historic Inn at Whitewell; fourteen cosy rooms have open fires. The Waddington Arms country inn has a walled suntrap garden. Clark House Farm at Chipping offers bed and breakfast for horses and riders and a camping barn too. In Slaidburn, a seventeenth-century coaching inn is now a popular youth hostel. The historic Red Pump Inn at Bashall Eaves has exclusive fishing rights on the River Hodder for residential guests. The Parkers Arms in Newton-in-Bowland offers gourmet weekends and cookery courses.

...hungry and thirsty?

Food glorious food! There's plenty of it this weekend. My Clitheroe favourites include Cheesie Tchaikovsky, with a cheese-maturing room and olive oil on tap. For fine wine and malt whisky visit the cellars of D. Byrne & Co, wine merchants since the 1870s. The smell of beans being roasted at Exchange Coffee House is intoxicating – they stock thirty different varieties. Find delicious home-baked cakes at Mansell's Coffee Shop, exotic delights at Taste deli, award-winning meats at Cowmans Sausage Shop, black puddings and sheepskin rugs at Harrison & Kerr Butchers, and cocktails with stylish homewares at the Emporium, a five-storey converted Methodist chapel.

160 reservoirs; up to thirty species can be seen in winter. Adjacent to the reservoir, Gisburn Forest, the largest in Lancashire, has mountain bike trails for all abilities. Cycle Adventures, Off the Rails and Pedal Hire all offer bike hire and delivery. Walking routes around the reservoir and village are available from the village store and tearoom.

Surrounded by stone-walled fields, Newton-in-Bowland overlooks the River Hodder, an important corridor for rare migratory wild North Atlantic salmon and sea trout. Curlews nest and feed in meadows and the walled Friends Burial Ground offers quiet contemplation in a semi-wild place. In spring the small village green puts on a grand show of tulips.

It seems a shame to me that a telephone kiosk denoting the position of Dunsop Bridge as the geographic centre of the kingdom – taking into account mainland and offshore islands – is a standard-issue box without pomp or design to celebrate the village's unique position. The small and sumptuous chapel of St Hubert, designed by Edward Pugin for the Towneley family, is breathtaking. It is believed that the chapel was funded by race winnings; in 1861 Colonel Towneley's horse Kettledrum won the Derby. Spy four small carvings of a horse's head on the pillars of the altar and look out for a painting of Kettledrum near the Towneley family coat of arms.

The historic Inn at Whitewell sits cheek by jowl with St Michael's Church on the banks of the River Hodder. From the car park it's a short walk to stepping stones across the river. Soak up the scenery from the inn's riverside terrace, which has views down the valley to the Forest of Bowland. Further delights include four rods on the River Hodder with access to seven miles of trout, sea trout and salmon fishing for residents, and independent vintners within the inn itself.

For more good food and views visit Bashall Barn Food Visitor Centre between Bashall Eaves and Waddington. Look out for Hen Harrier beer from Bowland Brewery, a 'pale and refreshing bitter with soft peach and citrus flavours'. Further afield, treat your tastebuds to Lancashire's traditional creamy cheese, hand-made at Leagram Organic Dairy in the cobbled village of Chipping.

There's a romance about this post-industrial landscape, birdsong resounds, clean white water rushes over weirs and cascades, wildlife thrives, footpaths meander along the riverside and industrial remains appear scenic.

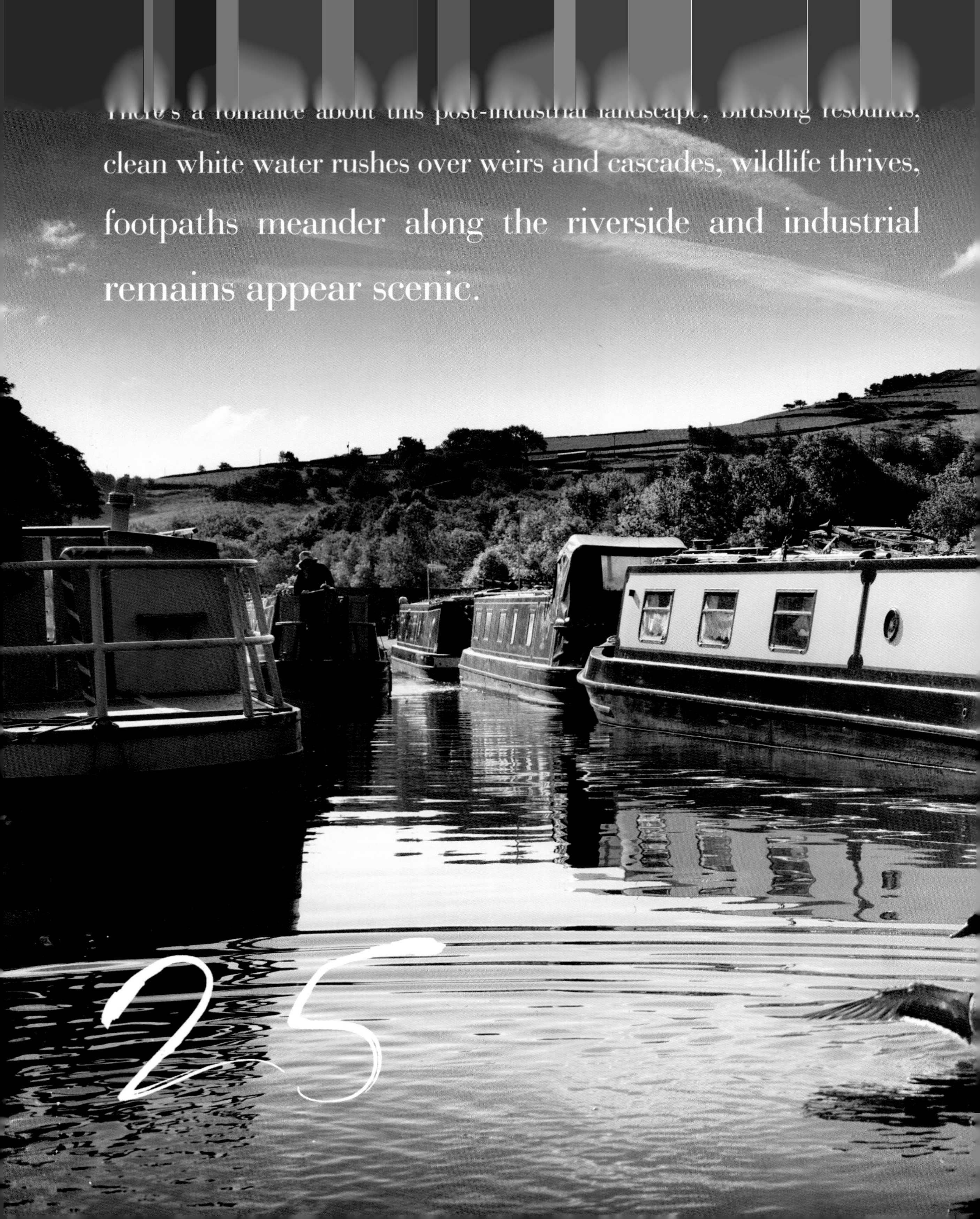

25

Watersmeet

Mills Archie Trespass

Before the arrival of mechanised mills, Britain's textile centres were rural communities. This weekend in the beautiful Goyt and Sett valleys reveals how the geology and geography of a country landscape contributed to Britain's industrial triumph.

Flowing from the Derbyshire Peak District into Cheshire, the River Goyt weaves through a deep sandstone gorge known as the Torrs beneath the town of New Mills. Cut by glacial melt water, the gorge was a prime site for eighteenth-century inventions to harness water-power; the confluence of the rivers Goyt and Sett sparked an industrial revolution in a pastoral landscape.

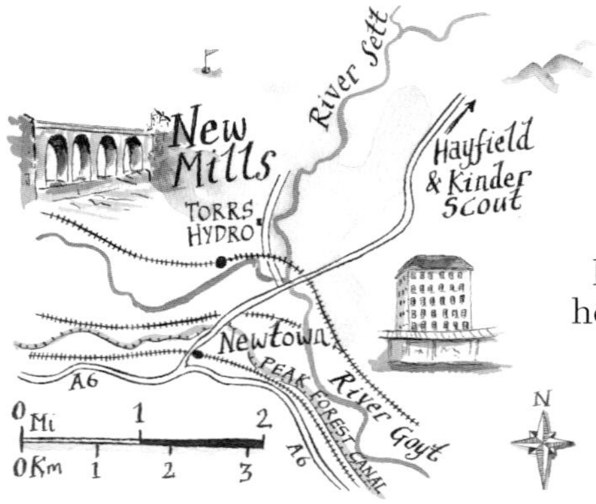

Wide sandstone terraces provided room for five mighty mills served by soft water from the rivers. To overcome the deep and inaccessible site, raw cotton, and later coal to provide steam-power, was delivered down slopes in carts with horses acting as brakes; finished cloth was loaded and hauled back uphill. As industry boomed, farmland above the gorge gave way to homes, schools, parks and pubs, and a hamlet that had originally taken its name, New Mill, from a medieval corn mill, became known as the town of New Mills.

As the textile industry declined, most of the mills were abandoned and from the 1930s clearance orders forced the demolition of the workers' cottages. The scarred gorge lay quietly under the town, closed to the public. But in 1974 campaigners succeeded in reopening the Torrs as a riverside park complete with industrial remains: weirs, leats (watercourses), aqueducts, chimneys and extraordinary bridges, high and low. In December 1999 the character of the gorge changed

again with the installation of the spectacular Torrs Millennium Walkway. Partly attached to a huge retaining railway wall and partly on immense pillars in the river, the magnificent aerial walkway sweeps 525 feet around the gorge above the River Goyt. Opposite stands Torr Vale Mill, where textile manufacturing ended in 2000 after 210 years, making it the longest continuously worked cotton mill in the country.

There's a romance about this post-industrial landscape; birdsong resounds, clean white water rushes over weirs and cascades, wildlife thrives, footpaths meander along the riverside and industrial remains appear scenic. To imagine the eighteenth-century sounds and smells that spewed forth, visit the heritage and information centre where an intriguing scale model portrays a time when the mills were in motion.

A stroll around the gorge and town is fascinating; pick up the heritage trail leaflet from the information centre. Street names like Rock Mill Lane and Dye House Lane, where notorious drunkard Thomas Handford was a regular in the local gaol, evoke times past. Seeing his drinking partner drop dead in the pub, Thomas reformed his ways and became teetotal; he even bought the prison and made it a comfortable dwelling. Proud of his achievements, he recounted them on a sandstone plaque built into the wall of his home in 1854.

In the gorge look out for 'Archie', now harnessing water-power, just as the mills did; the green reverse Archimedes screw turbine produces a quarter of a million units of green electricity for the UK's first community-owned and funded hydropower scheme. Most of the power is sold to the local Co-operative Food Superstore, with the surplus resold and added to the national grid. The Torrs Hydro New Mills Ltd was

...tired?

Twiggys bed and breakfast at Hague Bar, New Mills, is well situated for exploring the Torrs and The Waltzing Weasel Inn at Birch Vale is a great favourite with walkers in the Sett Valley. Hayfield Campsite at Bowden Bridge is near the spot where the mass trespass ramblers rallied en route to Kinder Scout.

incorporated as an Industrial and Provident Society in 2007 with 230 shareholders; mainly local individuals and businesses wishing to support renewable energy schemes. Future profits will fund a community grants programme.

A superb web of interconnected footpaths extends from New Mills; routes available from the information centre include the E2 walk, which runs from Stranraer in Scotland via Dover to Nice in France. A much shorter local favourite is the Sett Valley Trail, a 2½-mile traffic-free route for walkers, cyclists and horse riders along the former New Mills to Hayfield railway line.

At the foot of Kinder Scout, the highest point in the Peak District, Hayfield is a charming village. Follow the Calico Trail, a thirty-minute walk through the village, to discover how an abundant water supply made Hayfield ideal for finishing and printing on calico. Momentous events took place just outside the village in 1932. Benny Rothman rallied fellow ramblers at Bowden Bridge for a mass trespass on Kinder Scout, owned by the Duke of Devonshire. Frustrated at not being allowed to roam the peak, the trespassers made their way up it until they encountered the Duke's gamekeepers. A scuffle ensued and six ramblers were arrested. Held overnight in New Mills police station, they were charged with unlawful assembly and breach of the peace. Five of the six were found guilty and jailed for between two and six months. The Kinder Scout mass trespass prompted a nationwide campaign for access, which culminated with the implementation of the Countryside and Rights of Way Act in 2005. In 1951 the Peak District became the first National Park and in 2002 Andrew, the 11th Duke of Devonshire, publicly apologised at the seventieth-anniversary celebrations of the trespass for his grandfather's 'great wrong' in 1932.

WALK THIS WAY

There's great walking, cycling and horse-riding this weekend, from strolls around the industrial archaeology of New Mills, to the Sett Valley Trail's traffic-free former railway route, and towpath walks on the Peak Forest Canal. For more challenging terrain, there's the Pennine Bridleway, Kinder Scout and beyond. Routes, including the Trespass Trail, are available from information centres at New Mills and Hayfield. For golfers, New Mills Golf Club is a extraordinary experience; one thousand feet up, the hilltop course has fabulous panoramic views of the Cheshire Plain, Kinder Scout and Welsh mountains.

...hungry and thirsty?

There's no shortage of pubs with great character in New Mills and Hayfield, too many to mention! A short hop from New Mills centre there's the Beehive pub by the canal, where the upstairs Art Lounge opens at weekends for relaxed chat and jazz surrounded by changing exhibitions. Potts Bakers is a New Mills institution, call in for leek and potato cakes. Llamedos Café (read it backwards!) is a local favourite and there's good coffee at the New Mills Heritage Centre. Find picnic benches in the Torrs and at Hague Bar picnic site. In Hayfield there are secret seats in the hideaway Memorial Gardens by the weir, and benches in the community garden by the village hall. Rosie's Tea and Coffee Room serves Elvis sandwiches with peanut butter and banana, and has benches outside for weary ramblers.

26

A River Runs Through It

Limestone   Wildflowers   Well dressing

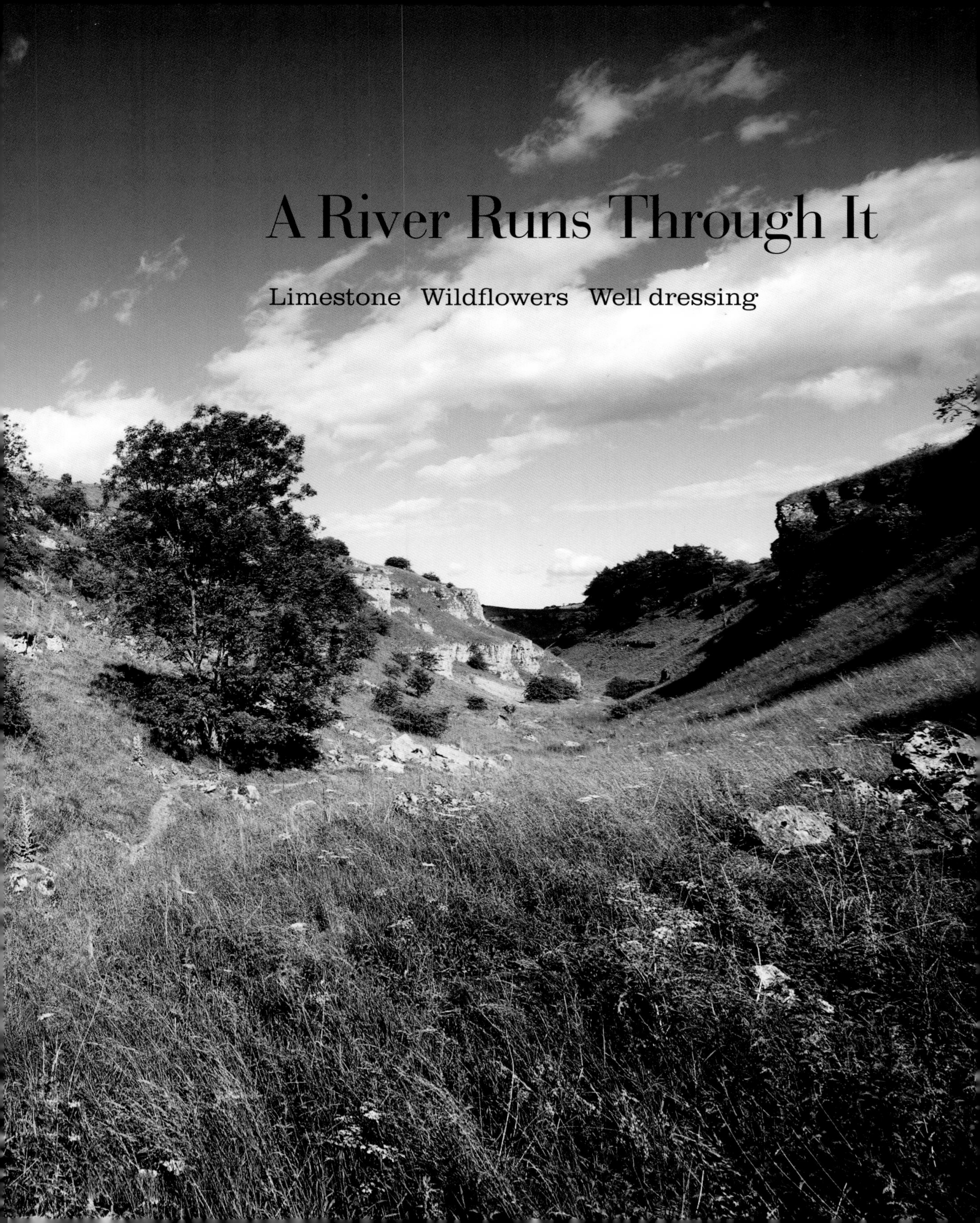

This walking weekend follows a circular route of 11 miles around Lathkill Dale, a most beautiful yet little-known limestone valley. Lovely Lathkill is one of five dales that make up the Derbyshire Dales National Nature Reserve and this memorable ramble on good paths follows the crystal-clear river through uplifting scenery.

To walk into Lathkill Dale from Monyash on a calm summer's day is magical; from the small car park the flat path soon narrows to weave its way through the bottleneck entrance of the steep-sided valley. Around 350 million years ago this area of the White Peak was part of a tropical lagoon and the limestone of the dale has fossils to prove it. Now the summer scene is awash with a haze of wildflowers, purple orchids, pink wild thyme and stately yellow verbascum. The rare wild blue Jacob's Ladder thrives here and is fenced off to afford protection from grazing sheep. Ramble on to Lathkill Head Cave, from where the source of the river gushes in winter only to withdraw in arid summer and rise instead at springs in Psalm Pool near Over Haddon. Lead mining in the area has lowered the water table; as the river leaks into mineshafts along its course the flow becomes a trickle.

On reaching the junction with Cales Dale look out for the medieval sheep-wash used to soften the fleece before shearing. The river flows on beneath the dappled canopy of ancient Low Wood where busy woodpeckers hammer in search of food. At waterfalls bobbing dippers flit across rocks to dive and swim for freshwater shrimps and insect larvae. Hear the splosh of water voles at the site of Carter's corn mill and look

...hungry and thirsty?

Refuel at The Lathkil Hotel in Over Haddon; the pub has a reputation for well-kept beer and superb views across the dale. The Cock and Pullet is a friendly pub in Sheldon, where the landlord has a collection of chiming clocks. The Bull's Head, near the Old Smithy tearoom and bistro in Monyash, has a spacious beer garden and there's a further Bull's Head in Youlgrave, along with the Farmyard Inn, where resident guests can tuck into Youlgrave sausages for breakfast. Join weekenders stockpiling sweet and savoury pies from Hollands Butchers shop (established 1865). Minced lamb and leek is a local favourite. There are lovely views at Edge Close Farm tearoom in Flagg and Youlgrave's seasonal charity fundraising garden café Dying for a Drink. In Over Haddon Uncle Geoff's Diner is a quirky backyard café much appreciated by touring cyclists and weekend riders enjoying the countryside astride the magnificent Hanoverian horses from Over Haddon stables.

out for remnants of Lathkill's lead-mining industry among the trees of Palmerston Wood (closed to visitors on Wednesdays in the shooting season). In one of many bids to boost drainage of the lead-mining area, Mandale Mining Company constructed an immense sough, or underground channel. Take a short diversion from the outlet of the sough to see the remains of Mandale Mine Engine House. Medieval Conksbury Bridge carries the road to Youlgrave across the river, while the low arch of Coalpit Bridge was the route for packhorses laden with fuel from Chesterfield.

At Alport the rivers Lathkill and Bradford are united, and from here the walk follows Bradford Dale into the terraced village of Youlgrave. Maps and signs reveal that the village is also spelled Youlegrave and Youlgreave, although strangely locals have yet another name for it – 'Pommie'. Choose to divert from the riverside to visit Pommie or return to Monyash via Middleton and save Youlgrave for the following day. There is much to see in the village: dinky stone cottages with colourful coun-

...tired?

Local villages offer accommodation from hotels to yurts; here are just a few. Lathkill Dale Campsite is perfectly situated for the start of the weekend walk with many more campsites on local farms along the way; look out for walkers on the long-distance Limestone Way with tightly packed tents on their backs. Knotlow Farm offers camping, bed and breakfast, glamping in cosy yurts, plus stabling for horses. The Reckoning House at Mandale Farm campsite is a camping barn. For a stylish vegetarian bed and breakfast weekend, choose Sheldon's Luxury Retreat. In Youlgrave, Meadow Cottage bed and breakfast is close by the clapper bridge in Bradford Dale and there's a friendly youth hostel in the former Co-operative stores opposite the fountain. Castle Farm in Middleton offers bed and breakfast, a camping barn and a small site for Caravan Club members. Haddon Grove farm has a campsite and cottages for long and short breaks.

try gardens, an elegant church, the tranquil tangle of Bankside wildlife garden and an attractive tank, known as the fountain, on Church Street to which river water was piped for the villagers' use. I especially like the allotments; dry limestone walls corral a colourful patchwork of fruit and veg.

Before the arrival of the fountain in 1829, locals drew water from the river or five wells around the village. Every June the precious water supply is celebrated by dressing the wells with huge images made from natural materials, a tradition that may stem from the pagan ritual of placing flowers around a spring to placate the spirits residing within. The ritual involves the whole community; children gather moss, leaves and flowers and the fiddly work of layering petals is carried out by those with patience and expertise. To ensure the final images remain fresh, the boards are first soaked in the river for ten days, smothered with clay and the design outline pricked into the surface. Ace teams work intensively over just a few days and images soon begin to bloom. Materials least likely to fade are placed first; mosses and lichens followed by delicate, vibrant petals. Sited at wells throughout the village the tableaux are outstanding. On the Saturday nearest John the Baptist's Day, the silver band leads a procession to each of the artworks and the community celebrates a thanksgiving service at Holy Well.

EXPLORE MORE

Close by Lathkill Dale is the immense stone henge of Arbor Low. Approached from a farmyard, the henge is not visible until the last moment. During the Neolithic period and early Bronze Age this was a place of ritual; when I last visited two pagans were enjoying a picnic in the sanctuary area of the stone cove, a circle within the outer circle, found only at major sacred sites.

27

A framed document marked 'Most Secret' contains the operational orders issued to 617 Squadron Leader Guy Gibson for the attacks on

Rest and Repose

Spa Dambusters Kinema

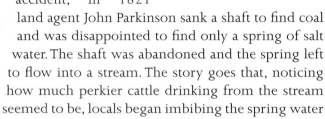

Fashionable Edwardians were attracted to the genteel inland resort of Woodhall Spa in Lincolnshire by the promise of rest and repose. With a unique cinema, an outdoor swimming pool, the National Golf Centre and Dambuster connections, the refined retreat in the pinewoods still offers a spiffing weekend.

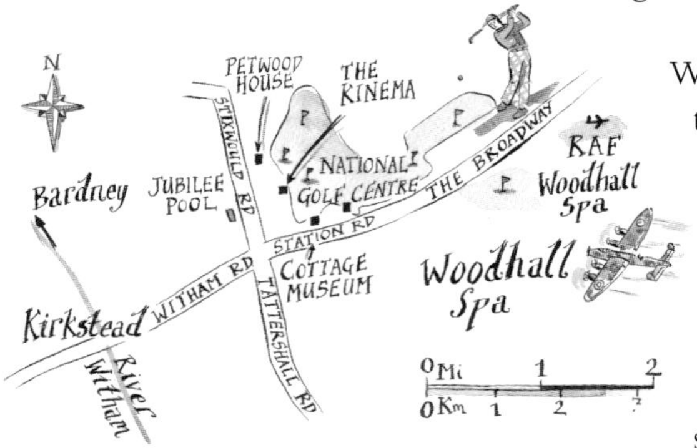

The development of Woodhall spa baths was the result of a happy accident; in 1821 land agent John Parkinson sank a shaft to find coal and was disappointed to find only a spring of salt water. The shaft was abandoned and the spring left to flow into a stream. The story goes that, noticing how much perkier cattle drinking from the stream seemed to be, locals began imbibing the spring water themselves. The squire decided to build a bathhouse and an infant resort opened for business.

By 1839 such was the demand among sufferers of gout and rheumatism for the bromine and iodine-rich mineral water that the Victoria hotel opened, with gentle woodland walks in the grounds for sickly guests. In 1848 the Great Northern Railway Company built a station at nearby Kirkstead on the River Witham and tourists were able to travel from much further afield. Visitor numbers increased again when Woodhall Spa Station on the Horncastle branch line opened in 1855. Sensing a business opportunity, a syndicate of investors appointed London architect Richard Adolphus Came to create a stylish planned resort three miles from Old Woodhall. Attractive residential homes and boarding houses would recreate the ambience of a German spa town, indeed many of the houses were given German names. Everything would be top notch, right down to broad tree-lined avenues. To emphasise gentility, there would be no 'streets', a decree that still applies.

On Station Road the Royal Hydropathic Hotel and Winter Gardens welcomed the smart set and in 1905 the

18-hole Hotchkin Golf Course opened. Named after a local landowner, the course, built on sand with notoriously pesky bunkers, is now within the National Golf Centre, the home of amateur golf in England.

Nearby, Grace Maple, daughter of the furniture company magnate, Sir Blundell Maple, had a spectacular country house built in what she regarded as her pet wood. In 1933 it became the Petwood Hotel and

> 'There is nothing rough or trained to shock the eyes or assault the nostrils in the heart of outlying quarters of this spa.'
>
> *THE MELLOW OBSERVER*, 1890

was requisitioned for use as the officers' mess soon after the opening of RAF Woodhall Spa in 1942. A visit is fascinating; the hotel flies the RAF ensign and there are the remains of a bouncing bomb in the car park. In the entrance a plaque states this was the officers' mess for 97 Squadron 1942–3, 617 Squadron 1943–4 and 671 Squadron 1944–5. They all flew from RAF Woodhall Spa. In May 1943 617 Squadron took part in Operation Chastise and would be immortalised thereafter as The Dambusters.

Don't miss the squadron bar; it is a humbling experience. Dedicated to the heroism of the RAF, there are photographs, newspaper cuttings,

...hungry and thirsty?

Visit Janet's tearoom, opposite the Dambusters' memorial, to be surrounded by RAF memorabilia; there are Lancaster bombers and Spitfires on the placemats, flags, photographs and aspidistras all around. For good books, coffee and milkshakes, stop at Bookfayre. The Bardney Station tearoom is a welcome pitstop on the Water Rail Way. At weekends fish and chips are served from the Bardney Fryer, a 1957 brake-ballast van on the platform. Find picnic treats at Woodhall Spa's bakery and deli and enjoy your lunch among the ruins of Tupholme Abbey or Bardney Abbey, or beside the River Witham at Stixwould platform, a peaceful spot with picnic benches.

and even the bough of a tree above the bar. In 1944, the timber cut through the nose and into the cockpit of a Lancaster bomber captained by Nicky Knilans en route to bomb a German battleship, the Tirpitz. Forced to refuel in a field, the bough pierced the bomber as it brushed against trees on take-off. Serving to remind all of a lucky escape, it was hung over the bar on the crew's safe return to Petwood.

A framed document marked 'Most Secret' contains the operational orders issued to 617 Squadron Leader Guy Gibson for the attacks on the Ruhr Valley. The newly formed, hand-picked squadron had trained to fly specially modified Lancaster bombers dangerously low at night, and three key dams were to be destroyed by bouncing bombs designed by Barnes Wallis. The essence of the operation was surprise; precision bombing would result in bridges and power plants being swept away, crippling the enemy. The success of the extraordinary raid was a huge boost to British morale. The *Daily Telegraph* of 18 May 1943 reported that 'with one single blow the RAF has precipitated what may prove to be the greatest industrial disaster yet inflicted on Germany in this war'. The squadron adopted the motto 'Après moi le deluge' (After me the flood). Their memorial, in the form of a burst dam, stands on the site of the former Royal Hydro Hotel.

RAF Woodhall Spa closed in December 1945 and Petwood returned to its owners. Much changed after the war, the resort's spa baths closed in 1946, although Grace, by now Lady Weigall, gifted to the village her gardens and private outdoor swimming pool. The pleasure grounds became known as Jubilee Park. Enjoy a swim at the outdoor pool where the water is heated to around twenty-nine degrees. Should one of the lifeguards have to enter the pool, an air-raid siren sounds!

Another Woodhall Spa leisure attraction is England's only rear-projection cinema, the Kinema, known fondly by RAF personnel as the 'flicks in the sticks'. Films have been screened continuously since 1922; the quaint building evolved from a barn, screened silent movies and the best seats in the house were front-row deckchairs. The atmosphere is great, with pot plants, velvet curtains and hooks along the wall to hang your overcoat while enjoying the latest big picture.

A Victorian corrugated-iron prefabricated bungalow is another treasure; the Cottage Museum is a quirky delight managed by volunteers. The most prized artefact is a unique donkey-drawn bath chair. Outside, a monument remembers the men of the 1st Airlanding Brigade who left Woodhall Spa to fight at Arnhem.

In 1922, to further promote the resort, Kirkstead Station was renamed Woodhall Junction, rather overshadowing the community on the banks of the River Witham. Tourism was booming and two dozen railway staff were required to service business. The stationmaster's house is splendid, built with accommodation for the family's fourteen children. Now a private residence on a disused platform, look out for a neatly clipped steam-train topiary in the garden. Holidaying workers from the city of Sheffield have a special relationship with the area; hundreds would board the Fisherman's Train to take part in All England fishing matches on the Witham. Now the line is part of the Water Rail Way, a mainly traffic-free route between Boston and Lincoln for walkers, horse riders and cyclists. You can hire bicycles from Bardney Station Heritage Centre. The path runs alongside the river, which carried packet boats and barges, linking towns, villages and farms, a vital trade route for the export of wool from the seaport at Boston.

...tired?

There's gracious living at Petwood Hotel and a seasonal campsite in Jubilee Park. Beyond the village, Rose Cottage bed and breakfast is a pretty 400-year-old 'mud and stud' thatched building, and rail enthusiasts will be delighted by the opportunity to sleep in a converted brake van on Platform One at Bardney Station.

Hooked!

Horseshoes Gallows Gardens

28

ORVIS

Multum in Parvo, or 'Much in Little', is the boast of England's smallest county, Rutland, and it is not wrong; great weekend pursuits on and around the reservoir-cum-playground of Rutland Water include miles of traffic-free cycling and the finest still-water fly fishing in Europe.

If you're a stranger to Rutland, there is something you should know. Be aware that locals are fiercely proud of their status as an independent rural county; the idea that Leicestershire should absorb their patch is anathema.

The first challenge to independence came under the 1945 Local Government Act. Despite skirmishes the county survived a second challenge under the Local Government Act of 1958. But in 1974 the battle was lost and Leicestershire swallowed up Rutland. Determined campaigning culminated in the restoration of Rutland County in 1997. For local people it was a momentous victory; near the offices of Rutland County Council at Catmose House in Oakham, a plaque on the car park wall marks the location of the Rutland Independence Time Capsule of 1997.

From Anglian Water's huge reservoir 270 million litres of water per day are pumped continuously. After treatment the water is distributed to to 500,000 people in five counties. Learn more at Normanton Church visitor centre and museum, formerly the church of St Matthew; the landmark building was deconsecrated and almost demolished when the reservoir was built in the 1970s.

At the heart of Rutland, the water is a magnet for leisure activities. Top-quality rainbow and brown trout attract anglers from all over the UK; stock fish grow well on natural food, building up superb muscle tone, and make a much-prized catch. Anglian Water host fishing courses for trout and pike and a range of fishing permits, including

...hungry and thirsty?

Enjoy tapas on the terrace of the Olive Branch in Clipsham, which has accommodation and a Michelin star. Uppingham's Lake Isle is a stylish hotel and restaurant, and there's good food at the Blue Ball in Braunston, the oldest inn in the county. Look out for the pagan sheela-na-gig in the churchyard opposite. The landlord of the King's Arms in Wing cures his own meat and smokes his own trout, while The Crown Inn in Uppingham serves traditional home-made pies with real ale, and the terrace of the Finch's Arms, overlooking Rutland Water, is a special place for lunch on a warm day. The Castle Cottage café in Oakham is a wonderful colourful hideaway and the Veranda café–bar at Wing Hall is a great place for breakfast and home-made cakes.

special deals for short breaks, is available from the tackle shop near the Fishing Lodge at Normanton. Rutland Water Fly Fishers Club organises a series of bank and boat competitions to international and reservoir rules. Rob Waddington is one of several local experts teaching novices and improvers fly-fishing skills over a full or half-day. 'A bad day's fishing beats a good day's working' reads the sign on the wall of his fishing cabin on the lakeshore. In this den of rods and flies, with an angler's map of Rutland Water on the wall, Rob's lively lessons inspire even the most reluctant landlubber to embrace fly fishing from a boat.

Further leisure pursuits on the lake include sailing and windsurfing. Hire equipment and enrol for lessons at the Rutland Watersports Centre in Whitwell. Cruise the lake on the *Rutland Belle*, which plies from Whitwell on the north shore, calling at Normanton on the south shore. Sailings operate between April and October with special sunrise and evening cruises to observe Rutland's ospreys hunting for fish. Lyndon Visitor Centre and nature reserve is the best place to see these magnificent birds. Live images from osprey and kestrel nests are beamed to visitor centre screens, while bird hides on the shore make it possible to observe from a safe distance.

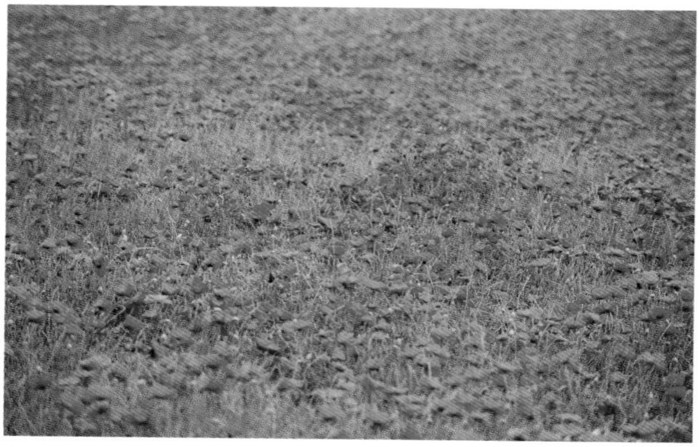

The Anglian Water bird-watching centre in Egleton overlooks a variety of habitats; a shallow lagoon attracts tufted duck, coot and goosander, waders use muddy banks and channels to feed and breed and a deeper lagoon attracts diving ducks and hosts a colony of reed warblers. There's also a purpose-built badger hide and family activities around the reserve throughout the year, and popular guided walks including Birdwatching for Beginners.

One of the best ways to see Rutland Water is by bike; there's a superb traffic-free circuit of seventeen miles, or twenty-three miles including the Hambleton Peninsula. From electric bikes to tandems and trailers, bike hire and sales are available from Rutland Cycling near the shore at Normanton and Whitwell. Events include exciting night rides where you can try a range of bikes from top cycling brands.

Attractive Oakham, the county town of Rutland, is perfect for a spot of retail therapy combined with fascinating heritage. Don't miss the Rutland County Museum of farming and rural life in the former riding school of the Rutland Fencibles, a volunteer cavalry regiment raised in 1794. The small museum has some outstanding exhibits, including gruesome portable black gallows first used in 1813 and the only surviving 'new drop' gallows in the United Kingdom. A design flaw meant that the drop was too short to break a neck cleanly. On a happier note, look out for the small mobile plumber's workshop, which served as a changing room for Oakham Rugby Club. The museum also serves as the town's cinema; exhibits make way for the big screen.

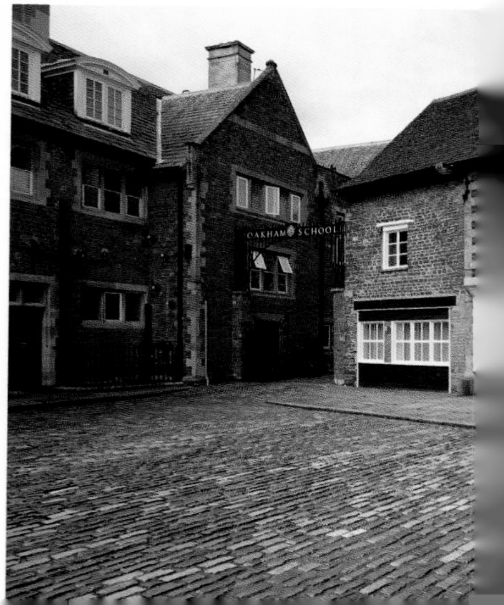

..tired?

There are trout carved into the stone fireplace of Rob Waddington's Lakeside bed and breakfast overlooking Rutland Water, where sunsets are dreamy and fishing lessons are fun. Number 17 Northgate offers bed and breakfast in a 300-year-old thatched cottage, while rural Broccoli Bottom has a drying room for waders and wetsuits. For a good look at the ospreys, stay at Lyndon Top campsite; for local food, including bread from Hambleton bakery, real ale and Rockingham cider, pitch up at Wing Hall farm shop, deli and campsite. Rutland caravanning and camping park is an affiliated Caravan Club site. Hambleton Hall is a luxurious country house hotel with elegant gardens; Barnsdale Lodge welcomes good-mannered dogs and provides stylish dog beds too. Barnsdale Hall offers golf breaks in association with Rutland County Golf Course and Normanton Park hotel is close by Rutland's landmark, Normanton Church.

Oakham Castle is the great hall of a fortified manor house stuffed with hundreds of oversized horseshoes. An old custom decrees that every peer setting foot in the town must present a horseshoe to be hung inside the castle. The extraordinary notion may have come from French barons who were lords of the manor, hence the upside-down position of the horseshoes, which is the way the French display them for good luck.

For antiques, galleries and books visit the bijou market town of Uppingham. Gardeners will enjoy the six-acre sculpture garden, Art de Jardin, at Wing where there's also a rare turf medieval maze, one of only eight remaining in England. The design of the maze (or labyrinth to be precise), is similar to that on the floor of Chartres Cathedral. There's another great visit at Barnsdale, associated with television gardener Geoff Hamilton. Allow plenty of time to enjoy Britain's largest collection of individually designed gardens; there are thirty-eight in total.

SHROPSHIRE UNION
RAILWAYS AND CANAL COMPANY,
GENERAL CARRIERS
TO
CHESTER, LIVERPOOL,
MANCHESTER,
NORTH, AND SOUTH, STAFFORDSHIRE,
AND
NORTH WA

29

Along for the Ride

Lakeland Crusaders Races

Enjoy a watery weekend in the Shropshire lakelands; discover beautiful meres, tranquil canals and the magnificent River Dee in the borderland of England and Wales. Historic pubs ooze charm and character, inspirational gardens offer colour and you can have a flutter at country races in Bangor-on-Dee.

The historic market town of Ellesmere grew up around the huge kettle-hole mere created by glaciers. The calm pool, 60-feet deep, is one of several meres in the area fed not by rivers or streams but by water draining from the surrounding land. Fringed by woods and fields with an elegant promenade and boathouse, Ellesmere is the perfect place to relax at the water's edge. Take a stroll, feed ducks and swans, join the fishermen or simply watch the world go by from a bench among lavender flowerbeds beneath an avenue of lime trees. There's an exciting children's playground and BMX dirt track in Cremorne Gardens, where Victorian gardeners planted specimen trees; in season, a pretty steam launch, *Lady Katherine*, takes visitors around the Mere's man-made islands. If you're feeling energetic, explore the Mere under your own steam and hire a rowing boat.

Imposing Ellesmere House, built by the canal duke, the Duke of Bridgewater, overlooks the Mere. From the town wharf the Ellesmere Canal was intended to link the River Mersey at Netherpool, now known as Ellesmere Port, to the River Dee at Chester and the River Severn at Shrewsbury. Engineering problems prevented the grand scheme and the plan was revised, although engineers Thomas Telford and William Jessop achieved spectacular success with breathtaking aqueducts at Chirk and Pontcysyllte.

The church of the Blessed Virgin Mary also overlooks the Mere, and here lies the tomb of Sir Francis Kynaston, Cupbearer to Elizabeth I. High in the wall nearby is the rather cute tomb effigy figure of a fourteenth-century scrivener, complete with his inkhorn, pencase and small dog. A pavement of richly patterned tiles lends a Gothic touch. Each pattern is significant: the fleur-de-lys represents the Virgin Mary and the winged ox is the symbol of St Luke. Don't miss a curious collection of crusaders' relics sent back from the Holy Land by local knights. Treasures include earthenware pots and the sorry remains of a crusader's sandal.

From the mereside promenade there's a gentle waymarked circular walk of about an hour around the town and along the banks of the canal. Explore the town first and you can return through the wooded nature reserve to the Mere Visitor Centre and boathouse restaurant. Historic buildings in town include coaching inns, which served travellers on the London to Holyhead route. Find boats bedecked with flowers at the canal wharf and walk along the towpath where boat-builders, coach-builders, timber merchants and wheelwrights plied their trade. The circular walk returns to the Mere through Plantation Wood, which is especially lovely on a spring morning when bluebells and primroses are in flower and church bells ring out across the country landscape.

Before leaving Ellesmere do walk up St Johns Hill and the Mount, where medieval houses mingle with fashionable eighteenth-century homes like Sheraton House. Lodgings in these streets catered for cattle drovers and later pupils from all over the country attending the town's small boarding schools. A visit to the dizzy heights of the bowling club

...tired?

In Ellesmere, Mereside Farm is close by the shore. The Grange offers bed and breakfast and residential weekends and Teal Cottage is self-catering. Enjoy wood sculptures in the garden of Yew Tree House bed and breakfast. The Garden House offers luxurious accommodation and the Stableyard at Bangor-on-Dee is well placed for the races.

atop the former castle mound is rewarded with panoramic views of the Mere and seven distant counties. Take the greatest of care not to tread on the precious greens of the historic bowling club, among the oldest in the country and still active.

At Erbistock a hand-operated chain ferry across the River Dee brought travellers to the historic Boat Inn on the grassy banks of the winding river. From here it is a short walk to the grounds of Garden House where you'll find the National Collection of Hydrangeas. For more views of the Dee, visit the Cross Foxes pub where stage coaches stopped between Chester and Shrewsbury; outdoor tables in terraced gardens have a great view of salmon fishermen in the river. Nearby Overton-on-Dee just across the England–Wales border is a small town dominated by the ancient yews of St Mary's Church. The trees, up to 2,000 years old, are among the Seven Wonders of Wales cited in traditional verse:

Pistyll Rhaeadr and Wrexham steeple,
Snowdon's mountain without its people,
Overton yew trees, St Winefride wells,
Llangollen bridge, and Gresford bells.

Bangor-on-Dee, or Bangor-is-y-Coed, has a famous boast too; it is the only racecourse in the country that does not have a grandstand. Who needs one, when the gentle slope of the hillside creates a perfect arena

...hungry and thirsty?

Ellesmere Boathouse café has been a landmark since the 1930s. Find maps and local history at the visitor centre where you can also buy day fishing tickets and bags of grain to feed wildfowl. In town, the Corner House Café and Talgarth Tearooms are local favourites, the White Hart is Shropshire's oldest pub, and La Belle Vie restaurant in the former town hall is a friendly place to loaf around on a Sunday morning. Check out the brick-built Cavern below. On frosty mornings a mega mug of hot chocolate from Coco Coffee goes down well with bargees from the canal, while booking is always advisable at the Black Lion Hotel, renowned for good food. Vermeulen's traditional bakery and continental delicatessen sells good food for picnics.

Erbistock has two great pubs serving good food, the Cross Foxes and The Boat. In Overton the White Horse Inn serves beef and ale pie. Woodlands delicatessen sells farmhouse ice cream, vegetables grown in the village and local cheese, meat and bread.

for spectators and competitors alike with glorious countryside views to boot. The left-handed jumps racecourse offers a great day out, whether you plan to picnic on the grass or dine in the Paddock restaurant overlooking the parade ring. Novice and champion racegoers are all most welcome.

CURIOUS

Ellesmere has connections with thirteenth-century and more recent crusaders; Eglantyne Jebb, co-founder of Save the Children, now one of the biggest international charities, was born in the town. With her sister Dorothy she began the charity in 1919 out of a subcommittee of the Fight the Famine Council. Their first project was to raise funds for starving children in the Balkans. Later Eglantyne drew up the Declaration of the Rights of the Child, which she persuaded the League of Nations to adopt. See her memorial in Cross Street.

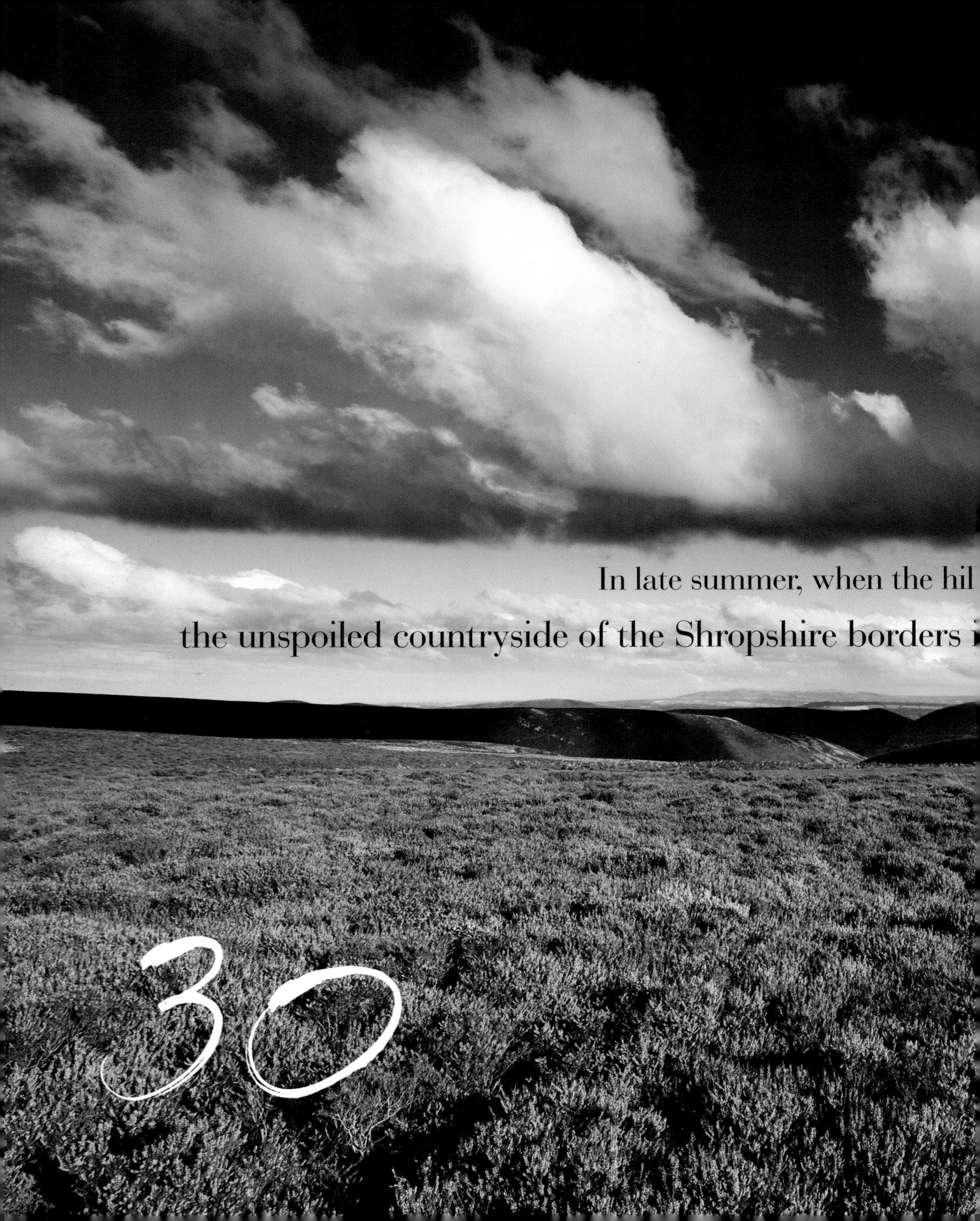

In late summer, when the hil

the unspoiled countryside of the Shropshire borders i

30

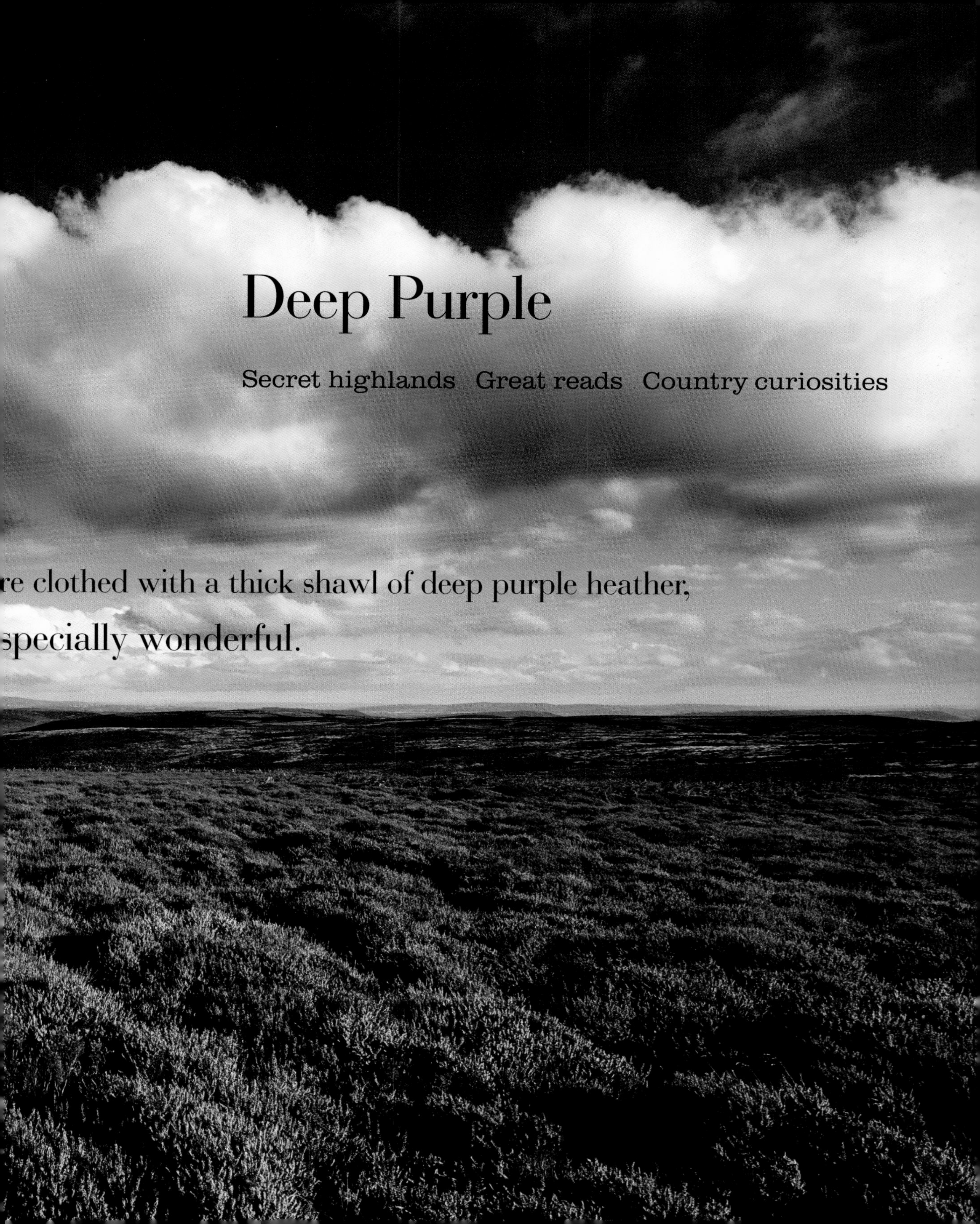

Deep Purple

Secret highlands   Great reads   Country curiosities

re clothed with a thick shawl of deep purple heather,
specially wonderful.

Make base camp near the market town of Church Stretton to discover the heights of the Long Mynd and Stiperstones, dramatic highland landscape that inspired thrilling tales by writers Malcolm Saville and Mary Webb.

In the *Open Air Scrap-book* Malcolm Saville described Shropshire as an unspoiled 'secret sort of county'. The highlands in the east, close to the border with Wales, contain 'enchanting country – forests, mountains and wild moorland – richer in folklore and legend, perhaps, than any other part of England'. Saville was intimately acquainted with this territory; his wife and children were evacuated here during the Second World War and he was a frequent visitor. At the end of the war the family returned regularly for holidays. His first novel, *Mystery at Witchend*, is set on Long Mynd and his Lone Pine series recounts the adventures of Lone Pine club members Mary, Dickie, David and Peter (aka Petronella), exploring the Shropshire hills on foot and bicycle, solving mysteries as they go.

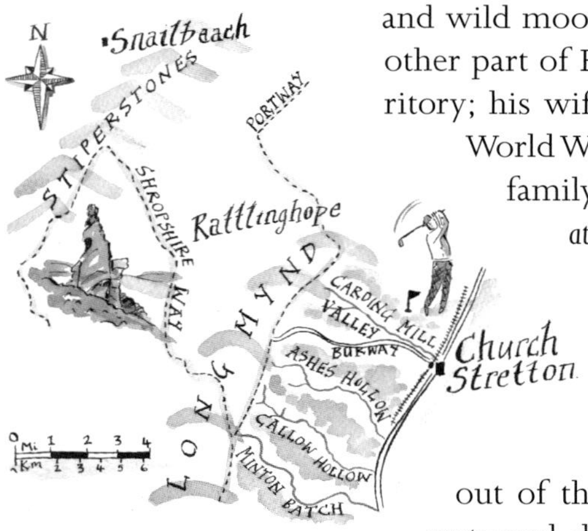

Mary Webb's novels tell of extraordinary characters born out of the Shropshire hills; in *Gone to Earth*, Hazel Woodus is the untamed daughter of a beekeeper cum coffin maker and a Welsh gypsy. Her ways 'were graceful and covert as a wild creature's'. Treasuring an orphan fox, Hazel fears Squire Jack Reddin of Undern Hall, 'a man who rode down small creatures'. The intense sexual attraction that brings them together disturbs her: 'She was afraid of him, yet days without him were like saltless food.' In *Precious Bane*, wild child Pru Sarn is the victim of a country curse; a hare crossed her mother's path during preg-

'Shropshire is a county where the dignity and beauty of ancient things lingers long.'

MARY WEBB

nancy to inflict the baby with a 'hare shotten lip', her precious bane.

Four valleys split Long Mynd, or the Mynd as it is known, each with a stream running from bogs at the top. 'Mynd' is from the Welsh for hill. The valleys, or gutters, around Long Mynd are Minton Batch, Ashes Hollow, Callow Hollow and Carding Mill Valley. Some say Callow Hollow is the most attractive while Carding Mill is the least wild. The Portway, a high route used by Neolithic traders, runs along the Mynd, skirting ancient burial mounds. Packhorse routes trek through knee-deep heather and bilberries, collected in the past by locals to dye fabrics brown, purple and blue. Here they are called whin berries.

...hungry and thirsty?

Find food, drink and accommodation at the Bucks Head in Church Stretton, the Stiperstones Inn and the Crown Inn at Wentnor, where there's a lovely painting of the hills on a farm wall. The riverside Bridges country pub is the 'Hope Anchor' in Saville's *The Neglected Mountain*. The thatched church at Little Stretton is close by the Ragleth Inn and Green Dragon. In Church Stretton don't miss the Studio Restaurant in a former artists' studio, Van Doesburg's deli, Berry's Coffee House, Acorn wholefood café and Mr Bun the Baker. Entertaining Elephants is a den of inspiration and the Secret Garden stocks pretty homewares. Stop for tea at Stretton antiques market and the Bog Visitor Centre seasonal café. The Chalet Pavilion tearoom in Cardingmill Valley is the genuine article, relocated from Switzerland.

...tired?

For Saville fans there's Stable Cottage within the grounds of the house where he stayed at Cwm Head. Mary Webb followers may camp at Brow Farm close by Ratlinghope churchyard and the sin-eater monument. Small Batch campsite is family run and wonderfully situated, while Long Mynd Hotel is a much-loved Shropshire Hills institution with great views and a sculpture trail. For bed and breakfast there's The Belvedere and Highlands. Jinlye is a walkers' landmark, Mynd House has rooms named after the hills and Victoria House is inspired by the life of Victoria and Albert. You may take your horse to lovely Lawley House, where grazing is available. All Stretton Youth Hostel is perfect for an early start on the hills and Bridges Long Mynd Youth Hostel offers camping in the small garden.

From Church Stretton the snaking single-track Burway ascends the hill. The steep incline is nerve-racking however you do it, but the rewards at the top are many; when the wind whips up your hair and clouds race overhead, there's a tingling sensation of freedom in wild open space. Happy ramblers with rucksacks on their backs swing their arms as they follow tracks threading through mounds of honey-scented heather. Trees are few and buildings fewer still – this is the domain of red grouse, merlin, snipe, whinchat, stonechat and silent soaring gliders. Wherever you turn, distant views are stupendous.

In contrast to the Mynd's smooth contours, Stiperstones is a jagged ridge upon which it is said the devil sits in a rocky chair of quartzite tor, dominating the skyline. The challenging Stiperstones Stomp is a popular six-mile ridge walk over rough terrain with outstanding views across green pastures stitched together by hedges. When low cloud creeps in, locals retreat; the devil is reclaiming his chair and it's time to leave the hill. The friendly Bog Visitor Centre reveals industrial heritage, geology and local folklore of Bog village, demolished in 1972. Nearby Snailbeach was one of the most productive mines in Britain; visit old workings to see the ghost of a thriving community that died when it could no longer compete with iron ore mined more cheaply overseas.

There are many curiosities in the area; among my favourites is the poignant monument to Richard Munslow, sin-eater, in St Margaret's churchyard, Ratlinghope. Richard revived the local tradition after the tragic deaths of four of his children, three of them in one week. The sin-eater was paid to attend the funeral of a person unable to recant their sins before death, the sin-eater taking on the unspoken sins, declaring over the corpse, 'I give easement and rest now to thee, dear man. Come not down the lanes or in our meadows. And for thy peace I pawn my own soul. Amen.' Richard Munslow died in 1906 and the community erected his monument. Mary Webb writes about the practice of sin-eating in *Precious Bane*.

In Church Stretton, St Laurence's Church is beautiful with bold contemporary artworks within. Over a door outside there's a rare sheela-na-gig, or female fertility symbol with open legs. See the curious gravestone of Ann, wife of Thomas Cook, which reads:

On a Thursday she was born
On a Thursday made a bride
On a Thursday her leg was broke
and on a Thursday she died.

Maybe Ann ran her errands on a Thursday, market day in Church Stretton. At the heart of the Shropshire hills, Church Stretton has a walking festival and an arts festival in summer. Traditionally the town hosted a sheep fair in September and a mop fair in May; country girls with mops at the ready gathered in town to find employment as servants. Explore tranquil Rectory Wood, a Georgian landscaped garden, from where there's access to the Hundred Steps, a gruelling short-cut to the top of the Mynd. From the town there are walks into Cardingmill Valley, which is in the care of the National Trust. Follow paths to Light Spout waterfall and the Shooting Box on a moorland Bronze Age bell barrow. Golfers with a head for heights will enjoy a round at Church Stretton, Britain's third highest golf club; springy well-drained turf makes for year-round play with heavenly views.

UPS AND DOWNS

Getting around the Shropshire highlands is easy; Church Stretton railway station is in the centre of town, with an especially pretty garden. See the plaque advising that the town is 613 feet above sea level and real noon is eleven minutes and twelve seconds later than Greenwich.

There are bridleways over Long Mynd for use of those on foot, bicycle or horseback. The Jack Mytton Way, named after eccentric Mad Jack Mytton, is a favourite. Perhaps this hunting, shooting squire inspired Mary Webb's Jack Reddin.

Mountain bikers will find routes, maps and good advice at Plush Hill Cycles in Church Stretton, where there's electric bike hire too. For walkers there's the Shropshire Way. Find more routes and maps at the Bog Visitor Centre and Church Stretton information centre.

Between April and September abandon the car and head for the hills with the Shropshire Hills Shuttle bus service. And for something completely different, soar over the Mynd with the Midland Gliding Club, where pioneer aviator Amy Johnson was a member. The club is renowned for its use of the rare bungee launching technique when the wind is westerly and above 20 knots. High-flyers are welcome to use the club's overnight bunkhouse accommodation and residential holiday courses are available.

31

After Apple Picking

Architecture Battle Orchards

Raise a glass to traditional cider and perry this weekend and discover the historic castles and churches of Mortimer Country. Here medieval villages of distinctive black and white timber-framed houses nestle in rolling green hills surrounded by the apple and pear orchards of Herefordshire.

Two great routes explore this undulating landscape; for walkers the Mortimer Trail is a waymarked long-distance path of 30 miles through Shropshire and Herefordshire from Ludlow to Kington. The Black and White Trail is a 40-mile circular exploration passing through distinctive medieval villages. Follow the trail by road or take the cycle route version, a tour of either nine or 15 easy miles.

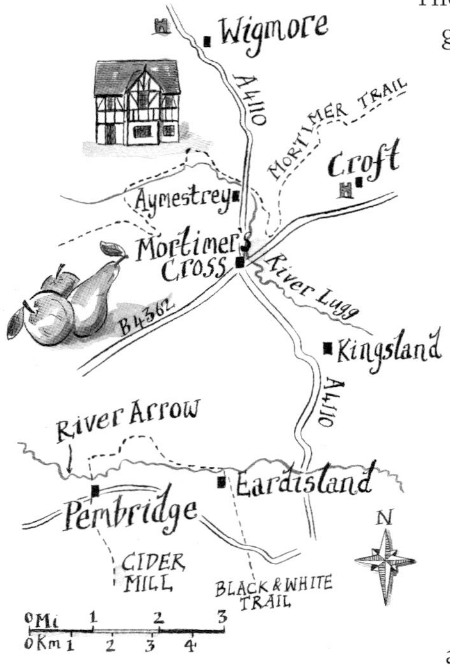

The iconic traditional timber-framed houses were built with green, unseasoned oak grown nearby. Skilled carpenters, trained for many years, constructed skeletal oak frames, which were infilled with lath and plaster, and occasionally brick. Look out for distinctive cruck frames of Celtic heritage, huge curved blades that remind me of whalebone arches. While the strong structures have survived since medieval times, the vogue for black and white paintwork was introduced by Victorians keen to emphasise the skilful timber construction.

Medieval Pembridge was a bustling commercial centre, where prosperous families could afford handsome homes. The town is an architectural delight with over ninety listed buildings, including the rare sixteenth-century market hall, an important focal point where traders and villagers gathered on Mondays to buy, sell and gossip under a hipped roof supported by eight immense oak pillars. Annual festivals included the Cowslip Fair in May and the Woodcock Fair in November. Cheek by jowl with the marketplace is the characterful New Inn; sit at benches on the cobbled yard or indoors by the vast open fire. The grand size of St Mary's Church is further evidence of Pembridge's medieval wealth. Look out for the fine oak north door with a sanctuary knocker. The detached octagonal bell tower is an extraordinary structure that offered a safe haven when the town was under siege; see the arrow-slit windows and musket holes in the oak doors.

Eardisland is a dreamy black and white village. The languid River Arrow flows under a handsome stone bridge, colourful country gardens spill onto the water's edge and a magnificent Georgian dovecote serves

.....hungry and thirsty?

The Riverside Inn at Aymestrey offers fly fishing, walking routes and maps to resident guests. Enjoy lunch at picnic tables by the River Lugg. Visit the follies of Westonbury Mill Water Gardens and take tea at Sally's Pantry. Locals gather at the Garden Tea Room and Deli in Kingsland and Eardisland Tea Rooms, tucked behind the village church. The doors of the Monument Inn at Kingsbridge commemorate the Battle of Mortimer's Cross, likewise the 1799 monument nearby. The Kings House restaurant in Pembridge is in a magnificent black and white hall built by wealthy merchant Robert King. Buy local cider and foodie treats from two vibrant village shops, the Eardisland Community Stores and Mortimer Country Stores in Wigmore. Picnic with views in the ruins of Wigmore Castle; the open space and playground of the Millennium Meadows at Pembridge are perfect for young children.

as the lively village store and heritage centre. Don't miss the splendidly restored 1920s AA box, believed to be the oldest in England. Formerly located at Legions Cross, it was saved from demolition by local AA man Harry Gittoes. The black and yellow cabin stands in a lovingly tended flowerbed by the black and white Cross Inn. Historic AA artefacts are on display at the dovecote opposite.

Surrounded by ancient forests, the romantic ruins of Wigmore Castle are situated on high ground, dominating the Welsh Marches. William the Conqueror presented the fortress to Ralph de Mortimer and from this time the Mortimers began their campaign to become one of the most powerful families in England. As Marcher Lords they policed the Marches (border areas) and were able to raise armies without the sovereign's consent. Victorious in the fierce winter battle of Mortimer's Cross in 1461, during the War of the Roses, Edward, Earl of March, saw off the Lancastrian army and was later crowned Edward IV. Before the battle he took heart from the occurrence of a meteorological phenomenon, a parhelion, giving the appearance of three rising suns. Edward later adopted the 'Sunne in Splendour' as his symbol. Near the castle, St James' Church is in an elevated position. Visit this peaceful place to see Saxon herringbone brickwork dated around 1050.

There are further curiosities at Mortimer's Cross; a rare one-man-operated 1750 watermill, open to the public in season, and a small museum adjacent recording the events of the Battle of Mortimer's Cross. Mortimers Mill Coracle Club offers the opportunity to paddle a basket boat on the River Lugg at weekends. Nearby is the handsome historic pile of Croft Castle in the care of the National Trust. For panoramic views of Herefordshire and the Welsh borders, walk from the castle car park to Croft Ambrey Iron Age hill fort and Fishpool Valley.

The apple and pear orchards of the area make superb real cider and perry. Try fruity golden alcohol made by small producers and enthusi-

asts like Peter Keam of Brook Farm Cider. John Tedstone planted fruit trees as a young man around his father's farm. 'Boy, you're making yourself some work,' his dad told him. The harvest from John's orchards is bought by Dunkertons to make organic cider with a traditional press. There's no charge to visit the mill at Pemberton, where you can learn more about the meticulous production process and savour the fruits of their labours.

...tired?

The Old Rectory in Pembridge is a handsome, brick-built Gothic retreat on the banks of the River Arrow. Nearby Lowe Farm offers cycles for guests' use, fresh eggs from rescue chickens and deep relaxation in a candlelit hot tub. At Croft Castle the National Trust lets Garden Cottage, a charming house built into the walls of the garden. Campers and caravanners are welcome at Townsend Touring Park and wooden pods are available for hire; there's also coarse fishing, a farm shop and butchery. Pear Tree Farm in Wigmore offers stylish evening meals, while food at the Old House in Kingsland is cooked expertly on an Aga.

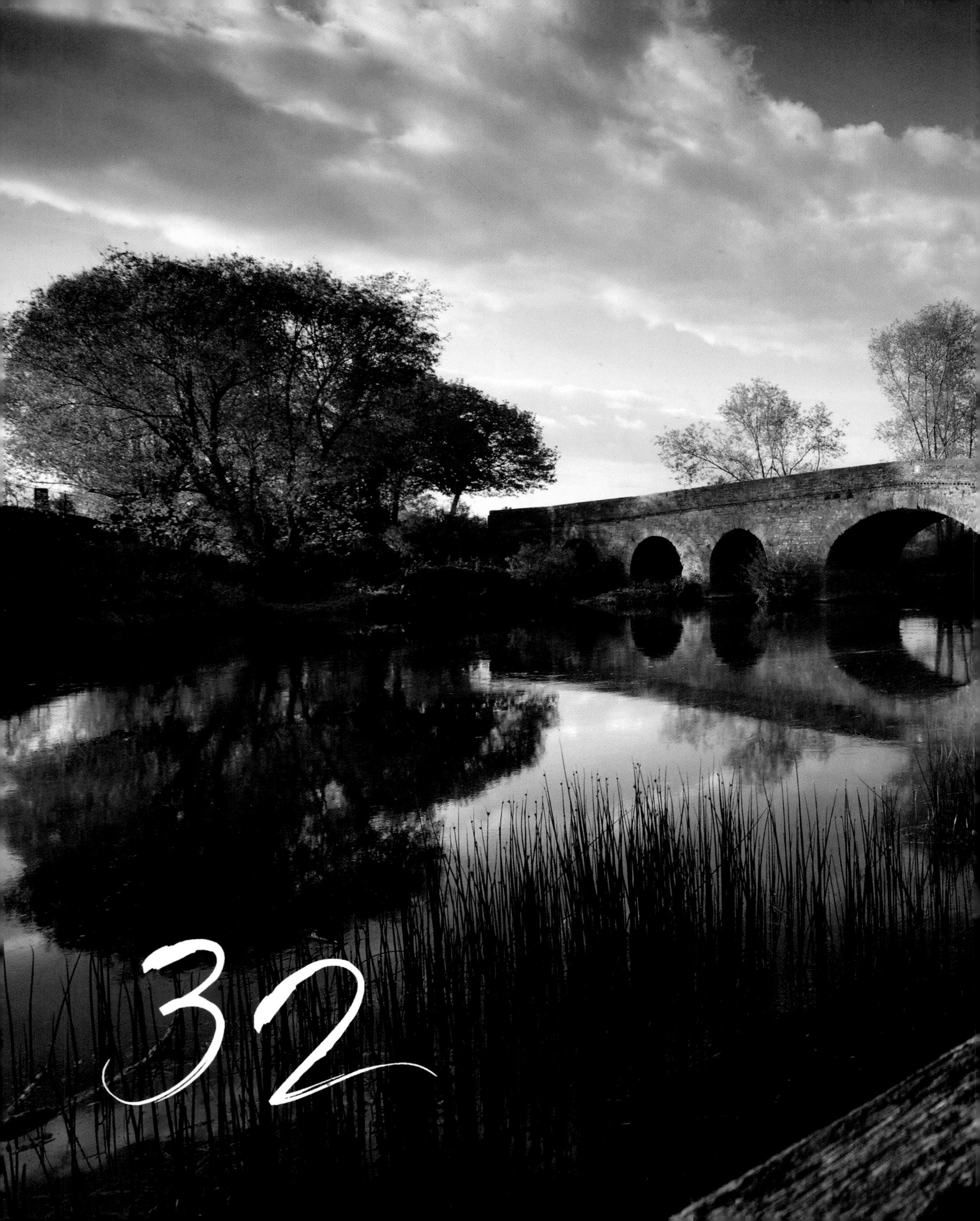
32

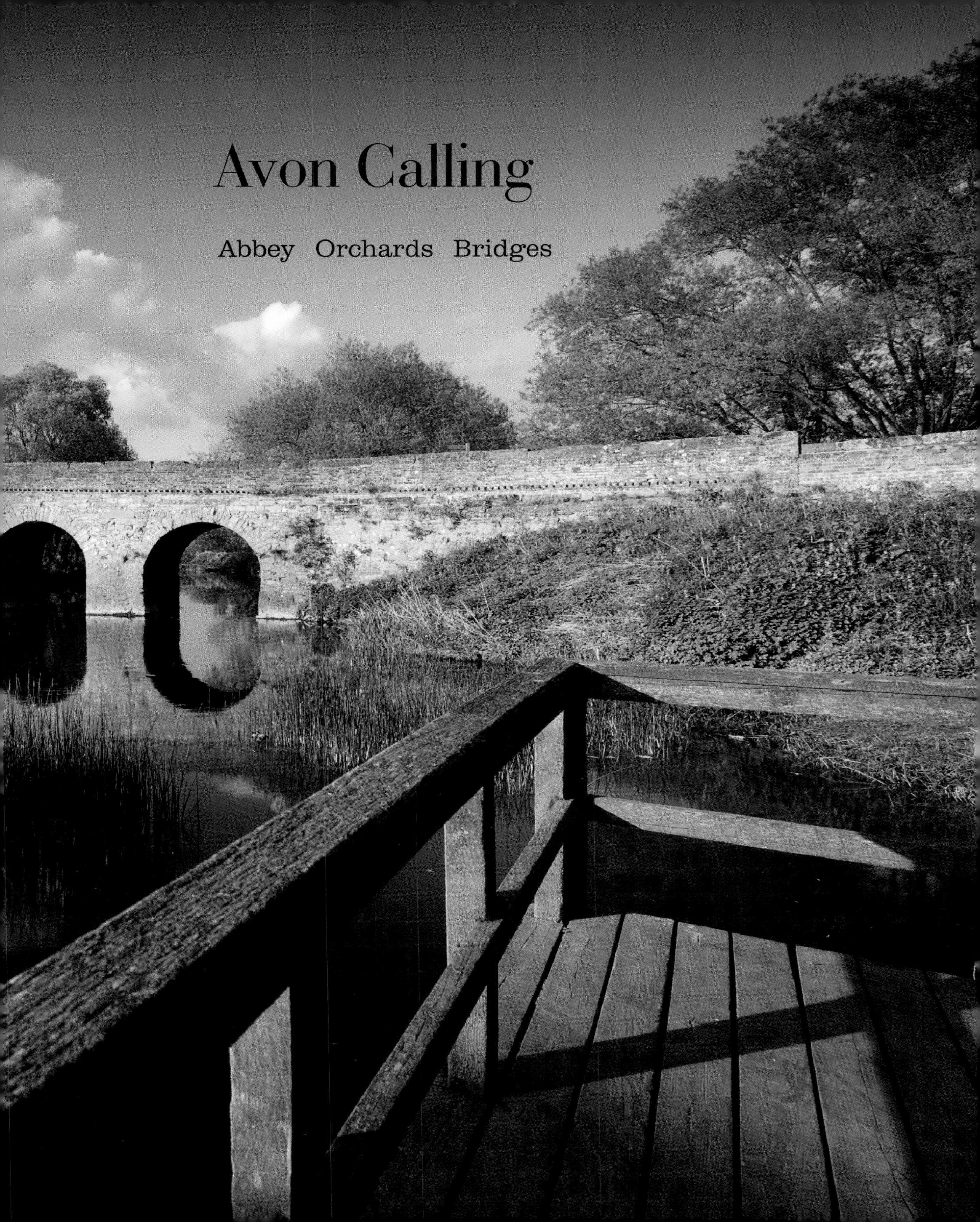

Avon Calling
Abbey Orchards Bridges

Easily reached by rail and road, the elegant Georgian market town of Pershore on the River Avon is cosseted by rolling hills, ancient woodlands and fruit orchards bearing plums, apples and pears. Follow riverside walks and country cycling routes to pretty villages and characterful inns for a great weekend in Worcestershire.

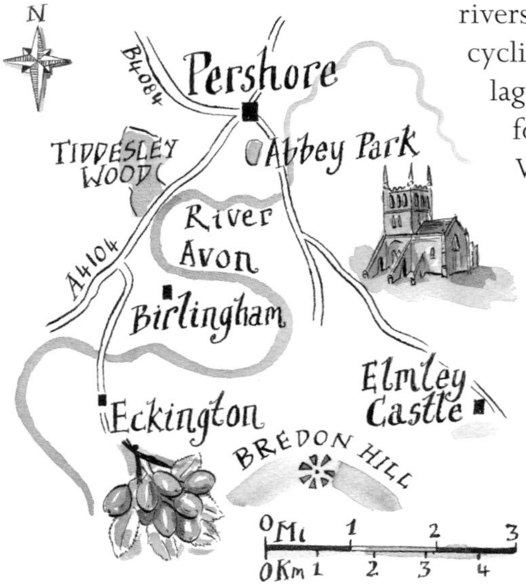

Pershore's handsome Bridge Street boasts fine Georgian architecture with elegant wrought-iron balconies; many of the colourful buildings are listed. Close by is Abbey Park, an inspirational open space where you'll find a medieval abbey sitting happily alongside a skatepark and an immense beech-trunk sculpture. Add to this a community orchard and a small wetland area where newts and insects thrive, plus a bowling green and safe water-play area and you understand why this much-loved park is truly at the heart of the community.

...hungry and thirsty?

Pershore Bridge picnic place on the River Avon is well loved by locals who sit in quiet contemplation at the water's edge or enjoy takeway fish and chip suppers at picnic benches. Stop at Quintessence Deli and Belle House Traiteur on Bridge Street for picnic treats. Local, seasonal food is served in stylish surroundings at Belle House restaurant.

The Swan Inn is a thatched vision in Birlingham. With rambling roses around the door, the black and white village pub is a lovely hideaway with a small restaurant, sunny south-facing beer garden and sales of local honey. Surrounded by snowdrops, crocus and cyclamen, the nearby church of St James is a heavenly sight in January and February. The Old Stable Tea Rooms at Revills Farm Shop is popular with cyclists. In season local asparagus, know locally as 'gras', is served with bread, butter and hollandaise sauce. Feast on juicy fruit at the annual Pershore Plum Fayre on August Bank Holiday Monday and buy a plum tree from Pershore College Plant Centre to grow your own.

The handsome Georgian buildings of Pershore have turned their backs on the lovely River Avon, so wander through the archways of historic inns to find beer gardens and moorings at the water's edge with views of the weir and lock. What fun it must have been when these hostelries hired punts for trips along the river.

Locals have a tradition of caring for the abbey and grounds; in 1540 the Benedictine Abbey was largely demolished under the Dissolution of the Monasteries. Raising four hundred pounds, the community stepped in to preserve the Monk's Quire and Tower. This curious remnant of the fine Norman building became the abbey church of the Holy Cross. Amid flying buttresses, immense stone pillars and an extraordinary bell-ringing cage suspended under the central tower, you'll find a warm welcome. In the tradition of the Benedictines, visitors are invited to help themselves to tea and coffee.

The Pershore Bridges five-mile circular walk is a splendid weekend ramble. The circuit may be joined at any point, though many walkers set out from Pershore Old Bridge just outside the town. Information panels along the way recount the history of important crossing places. The Ancient Monument of Pershore Old Bridge features in English Civil War history; in 1644 King Charles I ordered that the bridge be demolished to prevent Parliamentarians pursuing his troops. During the deconstruction of the central arch, forty Royalists fell into the river and were drowned. Later repairs to reinstate the bridge are clearly visible.

...tired?

From sixteenth-century Rye Cottage in Elmley Castle there are bracing walks up Bredon Hill. Pensham Fields bed and breakfast offers views of the hill with yoga therapy and reiki treatments to follow. Lovely Eckington Wharf is a great place to launch a canoe on the Avon; nearby bed and breakfasts include Harrowfields, a seventeenth-century cottage, and Myrtle Cottage for home-baked bread and views of the Malvern Hills. Luxurious Eckington Manor offers romantic retreats and Aga cookery courses. Pensham Hill House is within walking distance of Pershore with views over the River Avon. There's a small campsite at the Defford Arms from where you can take the bus to Pershore.

The walk passes through Tiddesley Wood Nature Reserve, almost 200 acres of ancient and rare trees. This landscape has been forested since the last Ice Age and through the centuries the woods have provided locals with timber and a place to turn out pigs for pannage (the swine feeding on acorns). A two-mile trail wanders through the reserve. In May the sight and scent of the sea of bluebells is magnificent.

Acquired by The People's Trust for Endangered Species, Rough Hill is a traditionally managed orchard on the banks of the Avon. Newly planted saplings stand alongside dead and dying trees clothed in mistletoe; these provide important habitats for rare invertebrates, which attract hungry bats at dusk. Birdsong rings out across the steep terraced hillside. Listen out for the woodpeckers while enjoying open views of historic riverside grazing pasture towards Pershore Abbey and Bredon Hill. A public footpath on the high bank of the lovely orchard cum wildlife sanctuary leads to Upper End and the Swan Inn at Birlingham.

CURIOUS

At the foot of Bredon Hill, the village of Elmley Castle is named after a long-gone fortress which stood on a hill to the south of the village. There are curious finds in St Mary's Church, including a controversial 1960s abstract painting of the Pregnant Madonna by Donald Pass, a medieval carving of a happy hare in the porch and an extraordinary carved alabaster memorial to the Savage family. Eight figures are featured: Sir William Savage and his son Giles lie beside his wife Catherine, who clasps her infant daughter; at their feet kneel the couple's four sons. Opposite is an outlandish memorial to the first Earl of Coventry, erected by his second wife. A lengthy inscription eulogises about the earl but since it's all in Latin few will ever know just how magnificent he was. The monument was intended for nearby Croome but it was refused admission and was squeezed into St Mary's instead, blocking out a window in the process.

Listen for the splosh of water vole among the lily pad
and the hum of insects goin

Fentastic!

Dragonflies   Ditches   Devil's Dyke

33

he call of cuckoos proclaiming their territories
about their business.

The drama of big skies over a flat watery landscape is the essence of this weekend. Discover the historic village of Burwell and the unique National Nature Reserve of Wicken Fen in East Anglia.

Situated at the fen edge, where chalk upland meets the marsh, the Burwell Museum is something of a surreal experience. To find this hidden gem, look out for the white wooden sails of a historic windmill above the rooftops of the modern housing estate that surrounds it. Among curiosities on display is a shepherd's hut, complete with lambs, and a selection of ice skates known as Fenland Runners, which locals used to sprint from one village to the next when the waterways froze in winter. Fiercely fought competitions attracted speedy skaters with the promise of a fine pork pie for the winner.

Fenland is defined as low-lying ground that historically floods in winter. For centuries humans have influenced the Cambridgeshire landscape by digging ditches, for peat blocks used for fuel and insulation, and with waterways, used for transport. Isolated communities eked out a living by harvesting reed and sedge for thatch, animal fodder and bedding. Their staple fenland diet consisted of wildfowl, eels and other fish. In medieval times vessels on the fenland lodes (waterways) carried sedge, fuel and a chalky local stone known as clunch to Ely and Cambridge. Centuries later, barges on Burwell Lode carried fertiliser and bricks made from local clay. Despite the nineteenth-century decline of this traffic, many of Cambridgeshire's lovely lodes are still navigable.

The National Trust Visitor Centre at Wicken Fen describes the precious habitats of the nature reserve as 'a window on a lost world'. When the fenland economy declined in the 1890s the species-rich landscape was under threat; wetlands around Wicken were drained for agriculture. But with the support of naturalists and locals, the National Trust intervened to buy Wicken Fen in 1899. Today the reserve is home to around 8,000 species including an array of dragonflies, hen and marsh harriers, reed and sedge warblers, secretive bitterns and otters. Launched in 1999, the Trust's ambitious Wicken Fen Vision is a 100-year project to turn intensively farmed land into 20 square miles of nature reserve and green lung extending from Wicken Fen to Cambridge.

One of my favourite times to visit the fen is after sunrise on a calm summer morning when the rustle of gently swaying reeds invites you to follow boardwalks at the water's edge to bird hides and the working wind pump with white wooden shutters. Listen for the splosh of water vole among the lily pads, the call of cuckoos proclaiming their territories and the hum of insects going about their business. As the day warms up, you'll be glad of sun hats and sun cream – there's little shade on the fen – and mosquito repellent may be useful too.

Managing the landscape involves cutting Sedge Fen in rotation on a three-year basis; waterways are dredged and spoil thrown to the side. Grazing animals play a part too; placid Konik ponies, originally from Poland, and a herd of Highland cattle from the Isle of Mull clear the

...tired?

For an early morning fenland start stay at Dragonfly Cottage bed and breakfast at Wicken Fen or nearby Meadow View campsite. For bed and breakfast a little further afield, there's The Old Vicarage in Isleham and The Meadow House and Chestnut House in Burwell.

scrub, encouraging wildflowers and insects. The Dragonfly Centre in Lode celebrates the twenty-one species of beautiful darting dragonfly and damselfly that thrive at Wicken Fen, making it one of the best places in the country to see them; call in to learn about their fascinating lifecycle. Don't miss a visit to Fen Cottage along the lane, where you will stoop at the door to enter a charming home straight out of a Beatrix Potter book. The last inhabitants were Reggie Butcher and his mother Alice who lived there until 1972. Reggie's unusual middle name, Octavius, came from a visiting naturalist who paid the pregnant Alice to name her baby after him.

LODES MORE

To discover more of this fascinating landscape follow the Fen Rivers Way long-distance path between Cambridge and Kings Lynn. Walk from north to south for dramatic views of Ely Cathedral. The Lodes Way is a nine-mile cycle ride from Wicken Fen passing Anglesey Abbey to Bottisham. Seasonal bike hire is available from the National Trust at Wicken Fen. To glide along the lodes try inland stand-up paddle-boarding with the Fen Paddle Company.

Close by Burwell is the extraordinary Devil's Dyke, a defensive Anglo-Saxon earthwork designed to keep marauding neighbours and more distant British tribes at bay. The mighty embankment rises above arable fields and travels in a straight line for almost eight miles between Reach and Woodditton.

...hungry and thirsty?

Take breakfast, lunch and high tea in style at By Jove! in the Old Schoolhouse at Burwell. Teapots are clad in hand-knitted cosies, seasonal crumbles bathe in piping-hot custard and Empire scones are accompanied by rich clotted cream. Work off the feast with a gentle meander around St Mary's Church and the ruins of Burwell Castle opposite. Enjoy soup and freshly baked cakes at the National Trust's Wicken Fen café, next to the visitor centre, from where you can buy flour from Wicken Mill, which opens occasionally to the public.

In Burwell the Five Bells pub has red-brick patterned chimneystacks, while The Fox offers the unusual combination of a historic inn and modern Mexican restaurant. Enjoy an evening stroll past boats moored at the Five Miles From Anywhere No Hurry Inn at Upware. The pretty garden of Dyke's End pub in Reach overlooks the magnificent chestnut tree on Fair Green, a short walk from Reach Lode where the Romans had a vital port. Locally sourced food and open fires make the Maid's Head at Wicken a popular watering hole.

34

Broadly Speaking

Waterways Wherries Wildlife

The watery delights of the Norfolk and Suffolk Broads, Britain's largest nationally protected wetland, promise a fascinating weekend whether you are afloat or not. Extraordinary habitats and abundant wildlife make the slow-moving tidal waterways a pleasure to explore.

The shallow lakes of the Broads are the remains of medieval peat diggings flooded when sea levels rose around 500 years ago. Along a vital trade route between coastal and inland ports, most Broadland towns and villages had small quays or staithes and dykes connecting them to rivers.

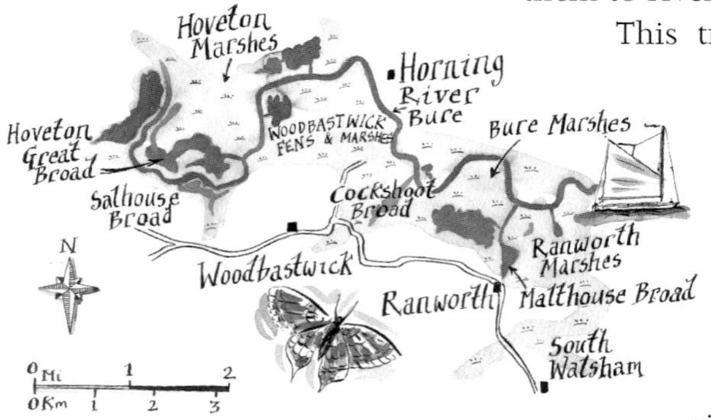

This transport network made Norwich the second largest city in England after London in the sixteenth century. As river traffic evolved, the Norfolk wherries of the 1800s replaced Norfolk keels to become the most distinctive vessels on the Broads. Both boats were designed for shallow rivers but the advantage of a wherry was that it could be sailed by just one man. With their iconic black gaff-rigged sails the trading boats sailed close to the wind. The forward-placed mast created more space for crew and cargo and the white-painted nose made the black hull more visible after dusk. The graceful barges were soon a common sight on the waterways between Great Yarmouth and Lowestoft. But hundreds of wherries could not compete with the growth of the Victorian railways. Without cargo contracts, enterprising wherry owners converted their barges to carry tourists and the tradition of the Broads as a scenic holiday destination was established.

Discover the special features of the Broads at Norfolk Wildlife Trust's floating visitor centre on Ranworth Broad. Situated in the middle reaches of the River Bure Marshes National Nature Reserve, Ranworth Broad is not accessible by boat or vehicle and is best reached on foot or by ferry from the staithe at Malthouse Broad. I'd suggest walking there and taking the ferry back. From Malthouse staithe an intriguing boardwalk winds to the visitor centre through a variety of habitats that reveal what happens when nature reclaims the waterways. Free from human

interference, open water becomes open fen followed by fen scrub, carr woodland and then oak woodland. As you journey to the broad through evolving swampy surroundings, look out for alders sinking into the marsh under their own weight, listen for the plop of water voles going for a swim and be prepared for the stench of methane gas produced by the bog. In summer you'll see precious milk parsley, the food plant of endangered swallowtail butterflies, rare ferns, yellow flag iris and wild roses.

Ranworth Broad is a magnificent wildlife haven. Depending on the season, visitors are often rewarded with sightings of otters, migrating ospreys, marsh harriers, great-crested grebes and common terns circling in the air. It is on Ranworth Broad that Dick and Dorothea of Arthur Ransome's *Coot Club* learned to sail. Because the broad is closed to public boat traffic, early morning visitors often have this magical place to themselves.

And so, rejoicing in their freedom, the outlaw and his friends sailed on their way, through a country as flat as Holland, past huge old windmills, their sails creaking round,
pumping the water from the low-lying meadows on which the cows were grazing actually below the level of the river. Far away over the meadows, other sails were moving on Ant and Thurne, white sails of yachts and big black sails of trading wherries.

FROM *COOT CLUB*
BY ARTHUR RANSOME

Binoculars and telescopes are available at the visitor centre; climb to the first floor for the best views over the water, and friendly volunteers will advise on where to train your lens. Children may borrow wildlife detective bumbags. Displays illustrate the active management of the marshes and a sightings board records wildlife highlights. For exclusive seasonal access to Ranworth Broad and Cockshoot Broad by water, book a 45-minute trip on the electrically powered *Damselfly* boat, or take the ten-minute foot ferry to Malthouse.

For more great views, climb eighty-nine rather scary uneven steps and two ladders in the tower of St Helen's Church at Ranworth, known as the cathedral of the broads. The altar cloth and kneelers are stitched with scenes of Broadland wildlife including dragonflies, kingfishers and butterflies. A colourful parade of saints on the extraordinary rood screen is unmissable. Look out for the rare Medieval Latin service book, known as an antiphoner, in a protective cabinet. Atop the tower a wonderful weather vane features Brother Pacificus and his dog. Entrusted with the restoration of the rood screen in the sixteenth century, Pacificus paddled his coracle daily from St Benet's Abbey to the church accompanied by his four-legged friend.

Salhouse Broad is unusual; sand and gravel extraction rather than peat digging created this lovely expanse of water. It is the only broad with a beach and the small sandy shore is a popular destination in high summer. A circular walk, canoe hire and sunset cruises also make Salhouse special. There's mooring for sixty-five boats, with the fees fund-

...tired?

For bed and breakfast or camping stay at the thatched Old Hall Farm in South Walsham. In the same village Oak Farm offers bed and breakfast and packed lunches. Leeward bed and breakfast is a ten-minute walk from South Walsham Broad.

ing further conservation work. Deposit your recycling at the depot in the car park and the money raised goes to help the local youth club. Take a ferry from here to the protected wilderness of Hoveton Great Broad, cut off from road, rail and footpath. Wear stout shoes to discover bird hides along the short nature trail through carr woodland (note, dogs are not allowed in the reserve).

Curiously, the medieval churches of St Mary and St Lawrence in South Walsham share the same churchyard. Look out for carved poppy-heads on the nave benches in St Mary's. The restored church of St Lawrence now hosts exhibitions, concerts and workshops and a small, tranquil Sacristan's Garden is planted with medicinal herbs. Nearby Fairhaven woodland and water gardens are beautifully situated on a private broad, but beware the allure of flora and boats. In *The Handbook to the Rivers and Broads of Norfolk and Suffolk*, (1882), G Christopher Davies has strict advice for female holidaymakers: 'Ladies, please don't gather armfuls of flowers, berries and grasses which, when faded, you leave on the boat or yacht for some unfortunate skipper to clear up. Don't play the piano in season and out of season (the reedbird's song is sweeter on the broads).'

NO WHERRIES

Once a common sight on the Broads, just a handful of iconic Norfolk wherries remain. Several were sunk in Ranworth Broad to prevent enemy seaplanes landing in World War Two. If you're lucky, you may see the black sail and hull of the trading wherry *Albion* or the white hull and black sail of purpose-built pleasure wherries like *Hathor*, built for the daughters of the mustard-selling Colman family and named after the Egyptian goddess of love. The interior features hieroglyphics inspired by artefacts in the British Museum. The luxurious *White Moth* has the definitive white hull and white sail of a wherry yacht. Less glamorous, the more modern mud wherries of the Broads Authority carry dredged sediment to disposal sites.

If taking your own boat to the Broads, there are public slipways and slipways at boatyards you can use for a small charge. Remember that all boats must have a licence; contact the Broads Authority, which can also advise on entering the Broads from the sea.

...hungry and thirsty?

Friendly cafés at Fairhaven Garden and St Helen's Church are popular with locals. The Granary at Ranworth serves ploughman's lunches and there's good food at The Ship in South Walsham, twenty minutes walk from South Walsham Broad and thirty minutes from Ranworth.
The Salhouse Bell enterprisingly offers boaters a free lift to and from Salhouse Broad, while the Kings Arms in South Walsham combines a bar with a Chinese and Thai restaurant. The Maltsters pub at Ranworth is close by the water's edge and the Fur and Feather at Woodbastwick offers real ale from the cask; Woodforde's Brewery is next door. Try a glass of Wherry, a zesty champion bitter with crisp floral flavours.

35

Feeling like a time traveller is easy in Lavenham – with over 300 listed buildings it is one of the best-preserved medieval villages in England.

Dyed in the Wool

Friars Peasants Merchants

Amid farmers' fields thick with poppies, the medieval market towns of East Anglia promise a dreamy weekend escape. Wander through historic lanes, stroll by the River Stour, explore secret gardens, take afternoon tea by a village green and prepare to be wowed by the loveliness of it all.

Historic and lively, the small country town of Clare in Suffolk is best enjoyed on foot. The town trail starts in the car park of the riverside country park complete with ruins of a Norman castle. The town's railway line was built on the castle grounds and the former station house now houses the country park rangers.

Clare Priory, the mother house of the Augustinian order in England, is nearby; a telling sign at the gate reads: 'Founded 1248, Suppressed 1538, Restored 1953'.

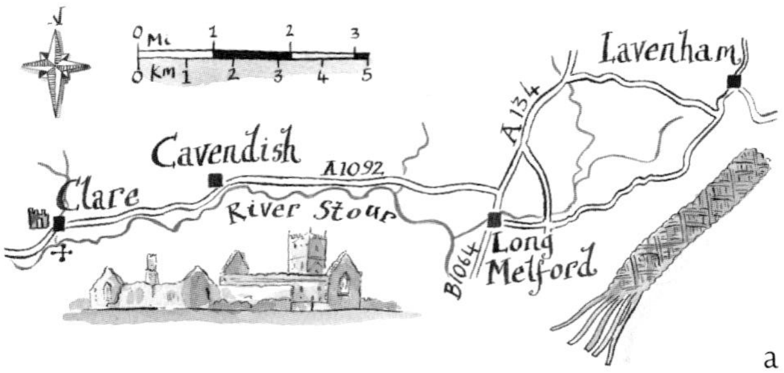

Founded by Richard de Clare, the priory was suppressed by Henry VIII and was in private hands until 1953 when the Augustinian Friars were invited to buy back their home for a fraction of its value. Having restored it, they converted a large medieval barn into the Catholic parish church of Our Lady of Good Counsel and in 1998, to commemorate the 750th anniversary of the Augustinians in Clare, the beautifully simple Shrine of The Mother of Good Counsel was established. Today the home of a mixed Augustinian community is also a retreat centre. The parish church and ruins within the peaceful grounds are open to all visitors.

In the Middle Ages the region revelled in wealth created by the cloth industry and the spacious former Catholic church of St Peter and St Paul

...hungry and thirsty?

Pick up tasty treats at Number One deli in Clare and picnic in the lovely country park. Seasonal food is home-made and delicious at Café Clare in the medieval Moot Hall courthouse. Beside the village pond or waiver, Cavendish Tearoom serves elegant lunches in airy modern surroundings. The George on the green offers fine food and cosy rooms. Once the home of poet Stephen Spender, the Great House in Lavenham is a chic French restaurant with rooms. There are just a handful of tables at characterful Sweetmeats tearoom in a 500-year-old weaver's cottage; their home-made ice cream and old-fashioned sweets are irresistible. Lavenham Farmers' Market takes place in the modern village hall on the fourth Sunday of the month; the friendly café serves home-made soup and cakes. Get on your bike at The Greyhound pub, which offers a range of cycles for hire, complete with kit including helmets and backpacks.

in Clare is testament to immense local prosperity. Clare market was renowned for wool and woollens; merchants based in Ipswich, Colchester and London exported local broadcloth throughout Europe. Accruing vast fortunes, clothiers funded fine half-timbered buildings, works to grand churches, new market crosses and repair of old roads, but when the industry declined there was no cash left to update the towns, hence the survival of so many extraordinary medieval buildings.

One of the most exquisite buildings in Clare is the Ancient House, opposite the church. Formerly a priest's residence, it is now the town museum, housing curios including tools to test the ripeness of wheat and barley. Look out for the double-handled mug with the traditional 'Farmer's Arms' poem and fine examples of eighteenth-century straw plaiting for which the town was famed; families of poorly paid agricultural labourers were eager to learn a skill that brought them extra income. But perhaps the most attractive part of the house is the creamy exterior lavishly covered in raised plaster flowers. This decorative process and local craft, known as pargetting, was applied in the seventeenth century to block out draughts caused by

The Farmer's Arms

Let the Wealthy & Great
Roll in Splendour & State
I envy them not. I declare it.
I eat my own Lamb,
My Chickens and Ham.
I shear my own Fleece & I wear it.
I have Lawns. I have Bow'rs.
I have Fruits. I have Flow'rs.
The Lark is my morning alarmer.
So Jolly Boys now,
Here's God speed the Plough,
Long Life, & success, to
The Farmer.

...tired?

The Ancient House at Clare was almost shipped off to the USA before a local farmer stepped in to save it and it is now the town museum. The Landmark Trust has a delightful guest apartment in this medieval masterpiece. The Ship Stores bed and breakfast in Clare has an external staircase, which led to drinking rooms for sheep farmers, and Cobbles bed and breakfast has a detached garden hideaway for two. The luxurious Grain House on the banks of the River Stour is perfect for coarse fishing. Get close to nature at School Barn Farm in a yurt with log burner, compost loo and barbecue.

The maze of medieval beams in Lavenham's Swan Hotel is a sight to behold. Curiously, this elegant retreat houses part of the dismantled Wool Hall, relocated within the building to prevent it too being shipped across the Atlantic. Home to Benedictine monks in the thirteenth century, lovely Lavenham Priory is a refined bed and breakfast cosseted by three acres of grounds in the centre of the village.

shrinking timbers. In the church of St Peter and St Paul opposite there are more country flowers, and you will discover carved poppy-heads on the choir stalls and sanctuary chairs.

The neat village of Cavendish is another medieval delight. Thatched pink almshouses cosy up to an immaculate village green, still an important gathering place for the community. The village sign recalls scenes from 1381 when the son of landowner Sir John Cavendish was tasked with suppressing the Peasants' Revolt. During negotiations at Smithfield he delivered a fatal blow to the peasants' leader Wat Tyler. As the culprit's father, Sir John was pursued to Cavendish Church where he clung in vain to the sanctuary knocker that remains today. Under medieval law individuals were afforded the right of asylum if they could reach a sanctuary knocker, although Parliament overruled this in 1623. Desperate Sir John was taken to Bury St Edmunds where he was beheaded by a mob.

Feeling like a time traveller is easy in Lavenham – with over 300 listed buildings it is one of the best-preserved medieval villages in England. In the fourteenth century this was the wealthiest town in England, famous for the production of coarse woad-dyed broadcloth in three shades of blue: azure, plunket and brown-blue. Oak-framed half-timbered buildings lean at jaunty angles across narrow lanes; it's a wonder so many survive. Among my favourites is Corpus Christi Guildhall in the care of the National Trust, where plants used in the medieval dye works are grown in a secret garden. The root of yellow flag iris coloured wool black, while the flowers made it yellow, and lily of the valley produced soft apple green.

There's another lovely garden within the grounds of Little Hall House, built in the 1390s for a family of wealthy clothiers; a visit offers the opportunity to see the domestic arrangements of a fine medieval home. Follow your nose around Lavenham or hire a walking audio tour from Lavenham Pharmacy for a ninety-minute treat. Tearooms and galleries are plenty; a favourite is the Wildlife Art Gallery, with three rampant tortoises – Tilly, Toby and Tommy – in the garden. Here you'll find the work of artist owner Andrew Haslen. His illustrated book, *The Winter Hare*, is a beautiful record of the two years he spent in the company of orphan hares.

36

'Not on one strand

are all life's jewels strung…'

Villiam Morris Old Father Thames Chimney Meadows

Take it easy this weekend. Discover the youthful River Thames and meander by boat, on foot or by road from the medieval market town of Lechlade to a nationally important nature reserve on floodplain meadows near the hamlet of Chimney. Enjoy traditional country pubs, a wild swimming pool and the inspirational country retreat of Arts and Crafts guru William Morris, who believed that 'not on one strand are all life's jewels strung'.

For hundreds of years, three ancient trackways brought drovers, livestock, goods and travellers to Lechlade on Thames: the Salt Way, the Welsh Way and Lambourne Lane. From Lechlade's wharfs, cheese, malt and corn were loaded onto barges bound for London. Barges from the capital delivered cargoes of gunpowder and timber destined for Bristol and Liverpool; at Inglesham, just outside Lechlade, the Thames and Severn Canal links with the River Thames to serve a national network of water transport routes.

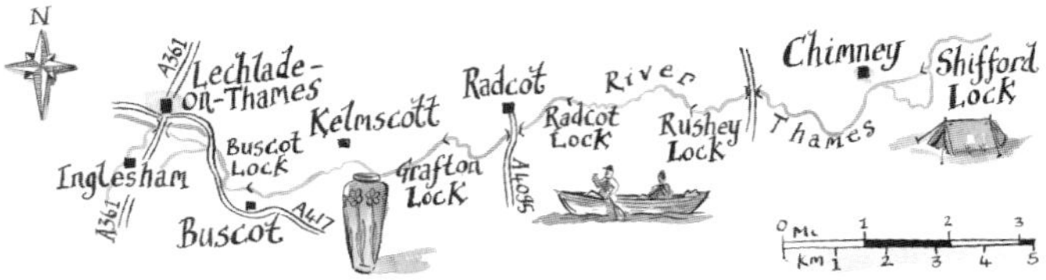

The former tollhouse on Ha'Penny Bridge reveals the importance of the river crossing, which permitted speedier boarding and unloading from Lechlade Wharf than the small ferry. From 1839 resentful locals refused to pay the fee and pedestrian tolls were abandoned.

Take a weekend trip down the narrow river by cruiser or canoe, or hire electric boats, rowing boats and day boats by the hour. Boat hire is available near St John's Lock, the first of forty-four on the river. Here a statue of Old Father Thames, commissioned for the Crystal Palace's new grounds of 1854, reclines at the water's edge.

Lechlade high street is good for supplies, including practical essentials from Tight Lines fishing and camping store, and there are treasures to be found in cavernous antique and junk shops. On a sweet summer evening in 1815, Percy Bysshe Shelley felt moved to write poetry

...hungry and thirsty?

Watch boats from the Riverside Inn at Lechlade where Colleys café and restaurant has a reputation for stylish eccentricity. Enjoy live jazz on summer Sunday nights at the Trout Inn. There's no food but great beer at the Crown Inn and Halfpenny microbrewery, where Thames Tickler is the local favourite. Cheery Buscot tearoom has a pretty garden. At Kelmscott Manor, the Stables restaurant serves morning coffee, lunch and afternoon tea. The Swan Hotel at Radcot offers real ale and fishing permits. The Trout at Tadpole Bridge has log fires, cask ales, stylish rooms and lovely moorings too. Riverside inns are popular with boaters and walkers on the Thames Path; it is wise to reserve your table and your moorings.

about the graveyard of St Lawrence church adjoining the marketplace. Look out for a tablet in the creamy stone wall inscribed with lines of verse from 'A Summer Evening Churchyard, Lechlade'. Shelley's Walk passes along an avenue of yew trees surrounded by headstones. See the statue of St Agatha of Sicily in the church; a sword pierces her chest, recalling that as punishment for refusing to marry Quintianus her breasts were cut off. St Agatha, now patron saint for breast cancer, celebrates her feast day on 5 February.

Cheese Wharf, downriver towards Buscot, is now a favourite place to swim and launch canoes, yet in the late eighteenth to mid-nineteenth centuries the quayside was busy with barges loading cargoes of cheese, some in the shape of pineapples and hares, bound for London. Beside Buscot weir and lock, the former lock-keeper's cottage conceals a deep pond beneath the floor; this held fish in water channelled from the river for Buscot Park estate owner Edward Loveden, nicknamed 'Old Father Thames'. Under his ownership tolls at Buscot Lock were among the highest on the river. Robert Tertius Campbell bought the estate in 1859 with funds acquired from Australian goldfields. The tycoon set about major water works, creating weirs and digging irrigation channels to create an industrialised farm. Brandy Island was among his most extraordinary projects; here expert foreign workers used sugar beet from local farms to distil spirit alcohol, which was then shipped via London to France.

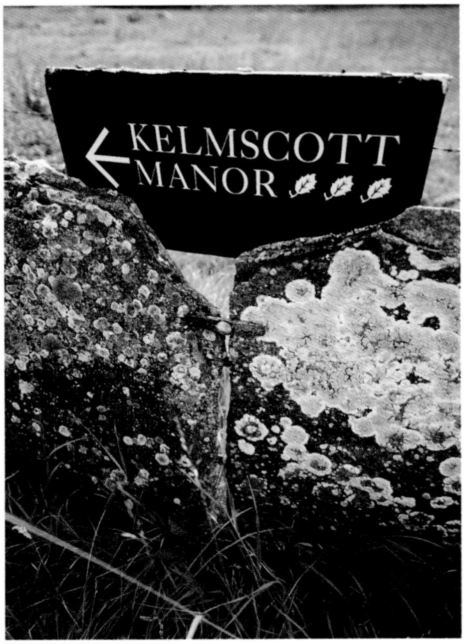

Buscot Park Estate is now in the care of the National Trust, and Buscot weir pool, in the shade of weeping willows, is a blissful place to swim (wear goggles for safety). After your exertions, doze on the grassy banks before strolling half a mile into the village for refreshment at the village tea shop.

Further downstream it is possible to moor temporarily near Eaton footbridge, from where a path leads 200 yards to Kelmscott Manor, described by William Morris as 'the loveliest haunt of ancient peace'. He shared the rent with painter and poet Dante Gabriel Rossetti,

founder of the Pre-Raphaelite Brotherhood. A visit to the Tudor farmhouse offers the opportunity to see outstanding examples of furniture, pictures and metalwork designed by Morris and used by his family.

The hamlet of Kelmscott is an idyllic collection of farm buildings and cottages in honey stone. Look out for the plaque featuring Morris on Memorial Cottages. The designer, his wife Jane and their children Jenny and May are buried at St George's Church nearby. There are further examples of Morris's work in the west window of St Michael and All Angels' Church at Eaton Hastings on the opposite bank of the river.

Meadows around Grafton Lock are renowned for the delicate snake's head fritillaries that bloom in spring. From here the river flows to the oldest bridge on the Thames at Radcot, a former commercial centre where stone was loaded onto barges for construction use in Oxford and London. Now leisure boats moor nose to tail around the snaking bend in the river. Passing under Old Man's Bridge, the Thames, or Isis as it is at this point, twists and turns to Rushey Lock and on to Tadpole Bridge.

Shifford is the most isolated lock on the Thames. According to lock-keeper Tom, 'What makes this a special place is the effort required to get here.' There's a small orchard on the tiny island opposite his cottage, an Eden of plums, walnuts, cherries, pears and apples. Walk from the towpath to Chimney Meadows, a low-lying nature reserve surrounded by watercourses. The range of habitats makes this a nationally important and sensitive site; wet grassland, ex-arable land under reversion to flower meadows, hay meadows, crop fields, woodland, seasonal and permanent ponds and scrub. On a still summer's afternoon the air is full of birdsong and the long grass alive with the electric buzz of insects; it is a deeply peaceful place.

...tired?

For bed and breakfast there's Buscot Manor, an elegant Queen Anne House. Horses and dogs are welcome and there's storage for canoes and kayaks. Accommodation at Manor Farm is a five-minute walk from William Morris's country retreat. There's rustic camping on the river at Shifford Lock although vehicle access is not possible. Access is strictly from the water, or on foot from the towpath or Chimney Meadows. The lock-keeper's house at Buscot is a National Trust holiday cottage. Several inns along the route offer camping by the Thames, including the Trout Inn at Lechlade and The Swan Hotel at Radcot. The inviting Plough inn at Kelmscott also serves seasonal, locally sourced food.

Between Holmscote and Hurstcote
The river-reaches wind,
The whispering trees accept the breeze,
The ripple's cool and kind;
With love low-whispered 'twixt the shores,
With rippling laughters gay,
With white arms bared to ply the oars,
On last year's first of May.

FROM 'DOWN STREAM'
BY DANTE GABRIEL ROSSETTI

37

Standing on Ceremony

Sacred sites Millionaire's mission White horses

[redacted]

This weekend explores ancient monuments and sacred sites around Avebury in Wiltshire. Here chalk white horses canter across the hills, Europe's largest man-made prehistoric mound rises defiantly above farmland and the world's largest stone circle encompasses a pretty English village.

My best advice when planning to visit the immense Neolithic stone circle at Avebury is to get your timing right. Arrive at high noon on a summer's day and you'll join the trudge of coachloads doing the rounds, but prepare well and the Unesco World Heritage Site will be quite a different experience at dawn or dusk. Late afternoon on a bright autumn day is special; the stones cast lovely long shadows.

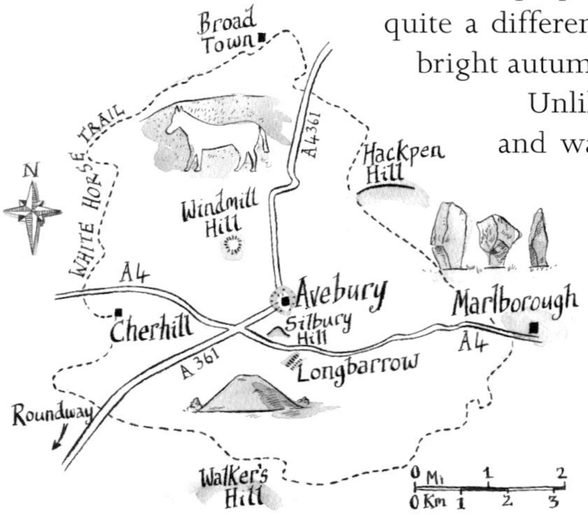

Unlike Stonehenge, you may touch the Avebury stones and walk between them. The privilege of this close contact is sensational. Constructed around 5,000 years ago, the henge covers an area of around 28 acres, making it 14 times the size of Stonehenge and 500 years older. To walk slowly on the high chalk bank above the ditch that contains the circle of ancient stones is an extraordinary feeling; what were the builders thinking of as they toiled with antler picks and shovels made from ox shoulder blades? What rituals took place in the surrounding landscape where sheep and cattle graze and tourists stare in awe?

Avebury's stones have rugged natural shapes and names, and there are many theories about their placement, in relation to the sun, moon and stars. Each stone weighs between 10 and 60 tons. The tall rectangular-shaped stones are thought to represent the male, while the diamond-shaped stones suggest the female. Selected for these forms, stones were dragged to the site on sledges and sunk into pre-dug holes. Originally the outer bank and ditch surrounded one circle with two smaller circles within it. While there are gaps where stones have disappeared – some buried, others recycled for use in construction of the village – the overall impact of this ancient monument is immense.

The henge is part of a wider sacred complex, all within walking distance, although a full day and plenty of stamina are required. Around a hundred pairs of upright stones form West Kennet Avenue, a processional route to the Sanctuary, which was a complex arrangement of stones and is now, sadly, a concrete replica of much smaller proportions beside thundering traffic on the A4 carriageway. Rising out of agricul-

tural landscape, Silbury Hill is the tallest artificial prehistoric earthen mound in the world. At just over 100 feet it has survived erosion due to sophisticated building techniques. The exact purpose of the monument remains unclear. The domes of West Kennet and East Kennet barrows were burial places and sites of ritual; at the time of their construction human remains, archaeologists believe, may have been used in rituals. At Windmill Hill, Neolithic tribes gathered, reared animals and grew crops.

English Heritage holds guardianship of the Avebury stone circle, which is owned and managed by the National Trust. To discover more about the site, visit the Trust's exhibitions and Alexander Keiller Museum. In the 1920s archaeologist (and heir to a marmalade fortune) Keiller funded scientific research and the re-erection of Avebury's stones to restore their prehistoric appearance. Despite his flamboyant lifestyle, four wives, many mistresses and millions in the bank, Keiller appears to have been a loner whose true love was the henge. He even bought Avebury Manor so he could reside as close as possible to it.

On hillsides around Avebury, a series of huge horses has been carved out of the turf to expose the white chalk. Linking eight of the existing

...tired?

Wake to outstanding views of the stone circle from The Lodge vegetarian bed and breakfast in Avebury, and if you plan to stay a while, the National Trust has holiday accommodation in the village: Isobel's Cottage and Fishlock's Cottage. Guests are welcome to picnic on the River Kennet running through the field of The Old Forge bed and breakfast at East Kennet.

horses, the Wiltshire White Horse Trail is a long-distance path of 90 miles. For weekend visitors the horses at Cherhill, Hackpen Hill, Broad Town, Alton Barnes and Preshute are all within easy reach by car, as is the horse created to mark the Millennium on Roundway Hill, north of Devizes, the only Wiltshire white horse to face right. The horses vary in age and appearance; I have two favourites. I like the Cherhill horse, carved in 1780 at the command of an eccentric local doctor who shouted design instructions with a speaking trumpet to workers above him on the hill; a layby on the westbound A4 carriageway permits a good view of their achievement. But best of all is the happy gait of the 1863 Broad Town horse, restored by the local community and adopted as the symbol of the local school from where it may be viewed.

...hungry and thirsty?

The Circle is the National Trust's only vegetarian restaurant. Food is fresh, tasty and seasonal; eat indoors or al fresco by the stones. Indulge in cream tea and work it off with a stroll around the garden of Avebury Manor. After a trot to the Cherhill white horse and nearby Lansdown monument, refuel with home-cooked food, quality coffee and freshly baked cakes at Divine Café on the A4. The friendly village shop in Broad Hinton is a good pit stop, serving takeaway tea and coffee.

One of the oldest pubs in Wiltshire, the lovely Goddard Arms in Clyffe Pypard, is a traditional free house serving real ale and home-cooked food with the benefit of YHA bunkhouse accommodation too. The beer garden of the New Inn at Winterbourne Monkton looks over fields towards Avebury, and the pub also offers bed and breakfast.

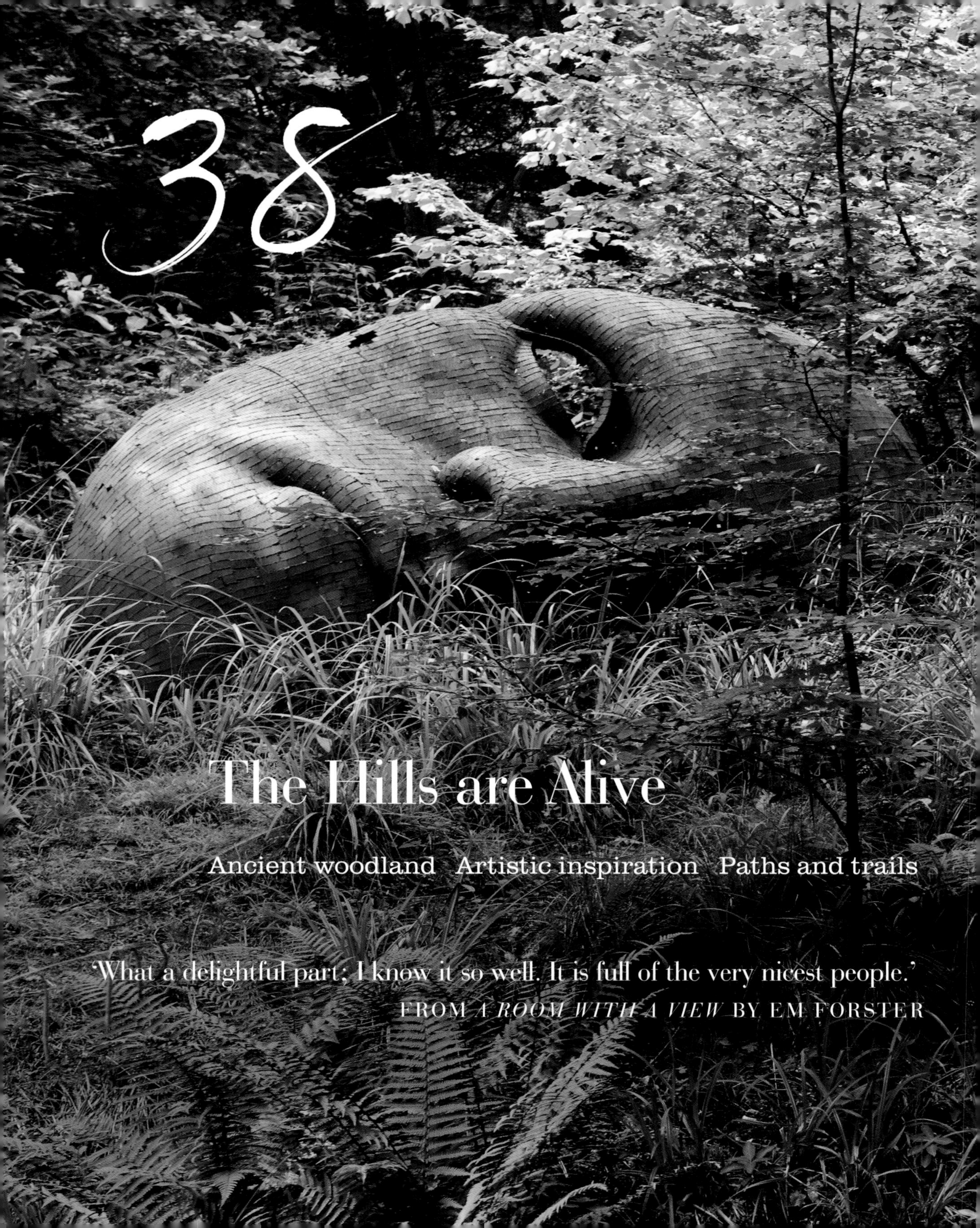
38
The Hills are Alive
Ancient woodland Artistic inspiration Paths and trails
'What a delightful part; I know it so well. It is full of the very nicest people.'
FROM A ROOM WITH A VIEW BY EM FORSTER

There's something quintessentially English about the Surrey Hills, just 30 miles from London. EM Forster referred to it in his Edwardian comedy of manners *A Room with a View*. While holidaying in Florence, Miss Lavish and Miss Honeychurch are keen to impress their English social status upon each other; that both have smart connections in the Surrey Hills delights them and seals their friendship. EM Forster lived in Surrey for over forty years and was passionate about the landscape of wooded hills, open heath land, chalk downs and valleys. This weekend is an invitation to explore unexpected tranquillity and outstanding art in countryside close to the capital city.

Leith Hill is the highest point in southeast England. The mighty mound is topped with a prospect tower, reminiscent of a single candle on a birthday cake. The monument was built in 1765 by Richard Hull of Leith Hill Place. Hull so loved it that he arranged to be buried beneath it. Now in the care of the National Trust, it is possible to climb the tower and peer through a telescope at the distant English Channel or St Paul's Cathedral. There's a steep ascent to the hill from Landslip car park, or a more gentle approach from Starveall Corner.

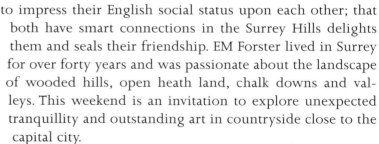

Leith Hill Place has connections with two men whose work is quintessentially English – dinner-service tycoon Josiah Wedgwood III, who bought the property in 1874, and composer of 'The Lark Ascending', Ralph Vaughan Williams, who inherited it in 1944. Wedgwood's wife Caroline was the sister of yet another English icon, Charles Darwin. On the Surrey hillside she created Rhodendron Wood, a collection of spectacular specimen plants including Wellingtonia, Japanese Cedar and rhododendrons from China, India and Tibet. Follow winding paths through the plantation, which reaches peak fragrance and flower power in April, May and June.

In *A Room with a View*, EM Forster writes of fictional Summer Street village, inspired by Holmbury St Mary. The idyllic real village ticks all the boxes: duck pond, well, village green, cricket club, choral society, fine church, post office and pubs. There are musical master classes and open-air galas at Woodhouse, a private concert hall and arts venue; it's well worth checking their performance programme before your visit. Hidden in a woodland glade is a purpose-built youth hostel, from where there are walks to Holmbury Hill Iron Age fort, trails through the leafy Hurtwood and a bike ride of just under five miles to the foot of Leith Hill. Holmbury Hill has further musical connections: watching warm spring sunshine illuminate the Surrey landscape, George

...tired?

Holmbury St Mary Youth Hostel is perfectly situated for a mucky weekend in the woods. Groups are invited to stay at the National Trust's Henman Basecamp in the Tillingbourne valley of Leith Hill. Tumblers bed and breakfast at Forest Green is good for Leith Hill walks and matches at Hurtwood Park Polo Club. Ockley's Gatton Manor is a hotel and golf club and there's accommodation at the Inn on the Green. In Peaslake there's the Garden Room bed and breakfast and The Hurtwood Inn.

Harrison wrote 'Here Comes the Sun' in Eric Clapton's hillside garden.

The lanes of Peaslake village are a sight to behold at the weekend. Muddy mountain bikes and road cycles are propped up against garden walls in the delightfully named main street, Walking Bottom. There's a buzz of wholesome fun with long queues of cyclists outside the village stores and the Pedal and Spoke shop, where bikes can be hired, serviced or bought after trying them out over challenging terrain. Parents associated with Peaslake Village School organise popular Mountain Bike Orienteering events around the area and new riders are invited to join them. If the thought of such exertion makes you feel faint, consider instead culinary fun under the tutelage of master chef Kevin Hooper at the Taste of Surrey Cookery School in the village.

One of my favourite Surrey Hills places to visit is Hannah Peschar's magical sculpture garden. Step away from the hills and follow deep, narrow lanes where exposed and mangled roots of trees perched on high banks grip the earth firmly. Descend into a secret dell littered with inspirational art and be prepared for sensory overload; the sound of the breeze in the trees, splashing water over the weir and the rustle of secretive deer observing you. Mysterious music combines with art works in a setting you will never forget. The sculpture garden is the work of Dutch owner-curator Hannah Peschar and her husband Anthony Paul. Innovative planting by landscape designer Anthony is every bit as beautiful as the artworks within, much of it inspired by the rainforests of his native New Zealand. Hannah and Anthony live in a fairytale house at the heart of the garden.

...hungry and thirsty?

The Surrey Cycle Way passes by the door of the sixteenth-century Scarlett Arms at Walliswood. The pub is great – authentic Malaysian food, bike racks and emergency parts, jet-washing facilities, a sculpture garden and a lawn to park your horse. There's even a cyclist-friendly menu to keep you expertly fuelled. Walk from the pub into lovely Wallis Wood. The Kings Head and Royal Oak in Holmbury St Mary are traditional village pubs. For fine food and excellent picnic fayre visit Butchers Hall and Country Store at Forest Green. The shelves of the small cheese room are packed with tasty treats and the home-made white tractor bread is delicious. The neighbouring Parrot pub and restaurant overlooks the village green and cricket pitch. Peaslake village shop and deli is to be congratulated for serving tea and coffee in proper mugs. Cyclists and walkers take them into the lanes, sup up and return them. The cheese straws, banana milkshakes and pork and leek plaits are popular too. The Servery in the tower at Leith Hill serves delicious home-made cake.

39

Blooming Marvellous

Medieval romance   Railway obsession   Garden party

To Kent and East Sussex this weekend; discover an elegant country town, a moated medieval castle and explosive colour in an extraordinary garden. Throw in a ride on England's finest light railway and some gentle boating on a reedy river to make this a glorious escape to remember.

Tasteful Tenterden is one of those impeccable historic towns where the supermarket is concealed carefully behind the handsome high street. Browsing attractive independent stores is excellent retail therapy. To discover greens where markets were held in the nineteenth century and clever mathematical tiles masquerading as bricks, pick up a copy of the heritage walking trail from the Tenterden Gateway. Explore medieval lanes leading to St Mildred's Church where, for 28 years, Horatia Nelson, the adored love child of Lord Nelson and Emma Hamilton, was the vicar's wife. She had ten children with her husband Reverend Philip Ward.

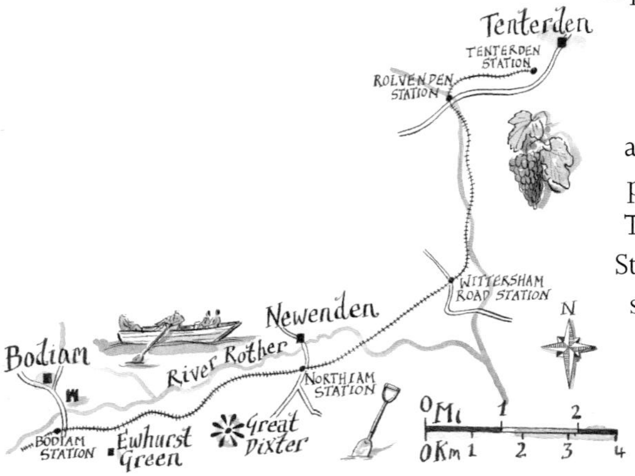

In 1449 the town on the River Rother was incorporated into the confederation of Cinque Ports as a limb of the port of Rye. The Cinque Ports provided men and ships against the threat of French invasion, and in return they were largely self-governing and exempt from national taxation. The town's coat of arms features a three-masted vessel. Using timber from Wealdon Forest, ships built in the town helped the port of Rye to meet its quota. By the end of the eighteenth century, the silting of the River Rother had caused Tenterden to lose all access to the sea, yet songs of the ocean wave are still heard in the town; the annual folk festival held over the first weekend of October welcomes singers, dancers and musicians from throughout Britain and Europe.

...tired?

The friendly White Dog Inn at Ewhurst Green has rooms with a view of Bodiam Castle. Spring Farm bed and breakfast is a traditional East Sussex white weatherboarded building and Wellington House bed and breakfast is close by Great Dixter. In Tenterden, the stylish Tower House offers bed and breakfast in a romantic Georgian building with a walled garden.

Don't miss an entertaining visit to the Colonel Stephens Railway Museum at Tenterden Town Station. Allow about an hour to do it justice. Somewhat obsessed by light railways, Holman Fred Stephens built or was associated with sixteen of them. There is much railway ephemera on display alongside the smallest standard-gauge locomotive in Britain, the Shropshire and Montgomeryshire locomotive 'Gazelle'. The tearoom is in Britain's first bus station, a building relocated from Maidstone. Imbued with light-railway knowledge, take a train from Tenterden Station on the rural Kent and East Sussex light railway, to Bodiam Station ten miles up the Rother Valley. From here it is just a six-minute walk to one of my favourite British castles.

Romantic Bodiam is one of a handful of fortresses that I might choose to live in. I'm very choosy, yet the style, size and location of this dreamy stronghold are perfectly inviting. It is easy to imagine midsummer parties by flaming torchlight, musicians on the causeway and rowing races around the moat. The castle presides over the water meadows of the River Rother and the backdrop of an organic vineyard on south-facing slopes is especially beautiful. Sir Edward Dalyngrigge began construction of the castle and landscaped estate in 1385 with the intention of impressing his pals and striking fear into the hearts of his enemies. The Rother waterway has silted up so dramatically that it's hard to imagine what was then the very real threat of French invasion from the wharf where the National Trust tearoom serves cream scones and cake.

The castle walls are intact although the interior was destroyed in 1645 on the orders of Oliver Cromwell. Since then there have been no further residents (I am biding my time). In 1828 eccentric local squire Mad Jack Fuller bought Bodiam and welcomed artistic types inspired by the setting. JMW Turner painted it, Edith Wharton wrote a poem about it. Her companion Henry James pronounced his famous summer after-

noon quotation while admiring it on a day trip from Rye: 'Summer afternoon – summer afternoon; to me those have always been the two most beautiful words in the English language.'

Lord Curzon bought the castle in 1917 and bequeathed it to the National Trust on his death in 1925.

The colour explosion of Great Dixter makes it one of my favourite gardens; here it is always fiesta. Even on misty October mornings blazing red and glowing amber dahlias can't wait to get the party started. Bold colour quickens the heart. Blooms leap out, tendrils entwine; resistance is futile. Lose yourself in a leafy jungle of banana and canna, swoon at tall tasselled grasses exploding like fireworks. Catch your breath on a bench in the sombre shade of a rustic barn before heading back to the shindig where plants will still be romping long after you are in bed. Velvety roses flirt with cactus dahlias and topiary peacocks taunt the vegetable patch. The audacious designs of Christopher Lloyd and Fergus Garrett make this one of Britain's greatest gardens, set against the backdrop of a historic house restored and extended by Edwin Lutyens.

ROW YOUR BOAT

If the romance of a rowing boat appeals then, weather permitting, hire one by the day or by the hour from the Bodiam Ferry Company at Newenden. Meander along the reedy Rother to Bodiam Castle in the company of kingfishers and herons. Alternatively cruise from Newenden Wharf on Bodiam Ferry, the *Dannie Lee*, a 24-seater open boat. There's also a tea garden and camping paddock at the wharf and day-fishing tickets too. If you fancy the idea of being king or queen of the road, there's short-break motorhome hire with bicycles, tents and barbecues from Motorhomes Hire Kent.

...hungry and thirsty?

Make time for delicious local, seasonal food at the award-winning Curlew restaurant, a former coaching inn near Bodiam Station. Visit three local vineyards to discover fine English wines: Biddenden is Kent's oldest commercial vineyard, Sedlescombe is a family-run organic vineyard and the talented team at Chapel Down vinery also brew beer. In Tenterden the historic Vine Inn has a sheltered walled garden. Nutmeg Delicatessen in Sayers Lane is great for picnic treats and takeaway coffee, which can be enjoyed in the lavender sanctuary of the town's millennium garden behind Pebbles, the house where Horatia and her husband lived while the rectory was being done up. The National Trust tearoom at Bodiam provides welcome relief for weary rowers.

40

Friends and Lovers

Bloomsbury Set   Firle Beacon   Cider and perry

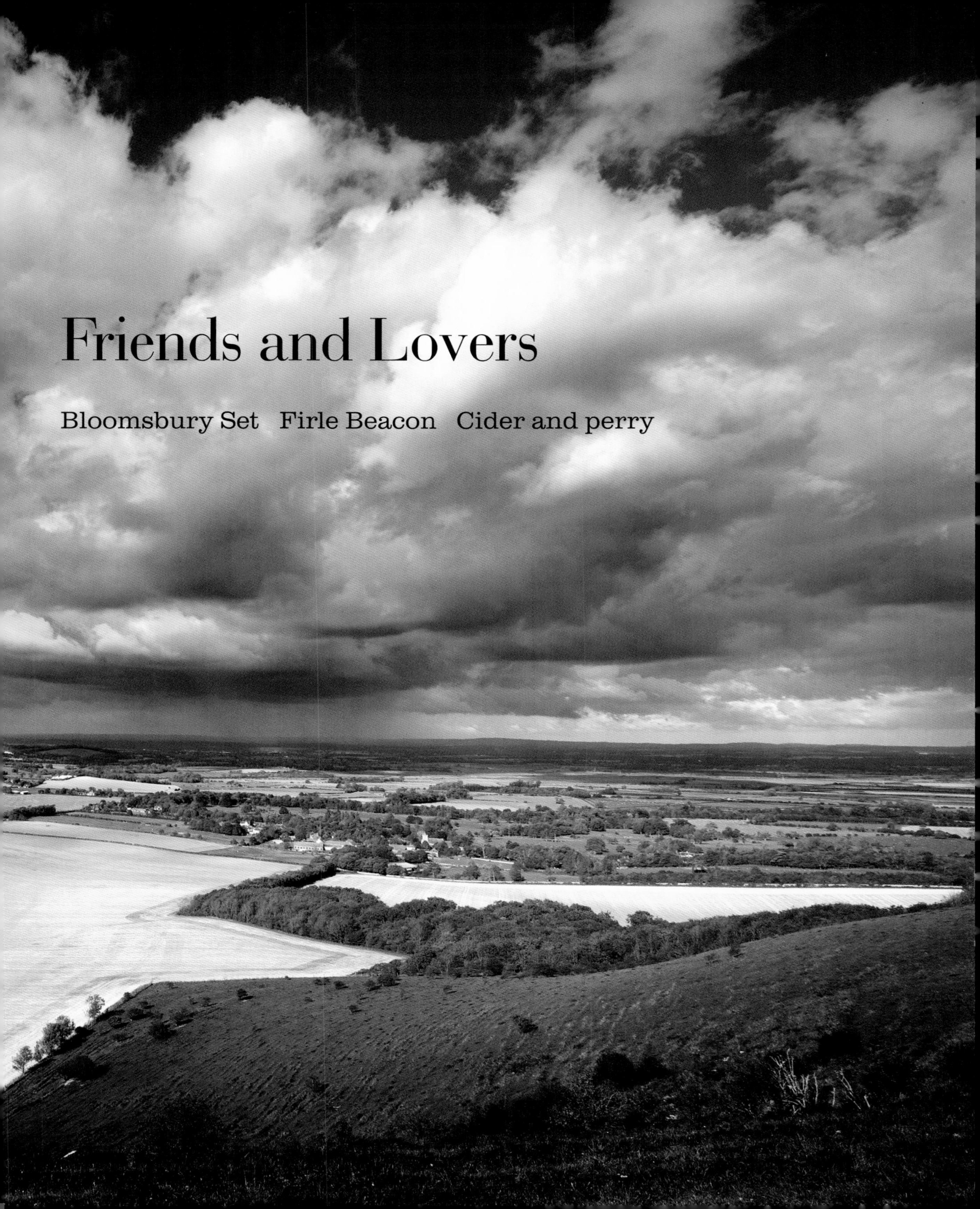

Remember when your parents forbade you from drawing on the walls of the family home? Well, this inspirational weekend in Sussex shows what happens when grown-ups allow their painterly imaginations to fly all over the walls, furniture and garden. One visit to Charleston farmhouse, the country retreat of Bloomsbury Group artists Vanessa Bell and Duncan Grant, and you may be inclined to get your paintbox out.

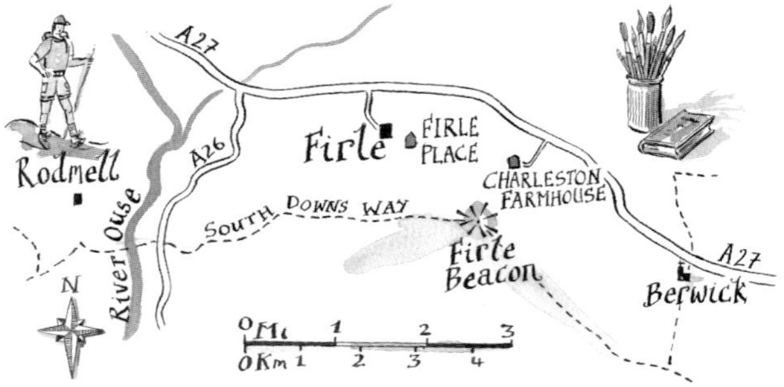

It was Virginia Woolf, Vanessa Bell's sister, who discovered Charleston while walking on the hillside of the Firle Beacon, the highest point of the South Downs National Park. From 1916 it became the Bohemian home of Vanessa Bell, Duncan Grant, their family, friends and lovers.

The bedroom arrangements of the curious household were intriguing. Vanessa Bell ultimately chose a ground-floor room next to the communal artists' studio which was formerly a chicken coop; Duncan Grant (her lover), Clive Bell (her husband) and other male guests slept upstairs.

With zest the house was transformed into a vibrant work of art. Vanessa and Duncan painted on the walls, doors, fireplaces and more, they made mosaics, designed textiles and remodelled the walled garden. Duncan painted Vanessa's bed with a dog at the foot to protect her through the night and a cockerel at the head to wake her. His mother Ethel sewed cushions to Vanessa's design.

Traditionally, rural Downland churches were decorated with murals and when, in 1941, Bishop Bell (no relation) of Chichester was inspired to revive the tradition at St Michael and All Angels in Berwick, Duncan Grant, much influenced by Italian frescoes, seemed the ideal candidate. With Vanesa Bell he set about depicting rural English scenes in an Italian way. The seasons of life are depicted in harmony with the farmer's seasons. The pulpit is swathed in fruit and flowers. Artist Edward le Bas posed tied to an easel for the picture of Christ on the cross and Angelica, daughter of Bell and Grant, was the model for Mary at the annunciation.

...tired?

Accommodation at Firle's historic Ram Inn is stylish and luxurious, and the Bloomsbury Room has views across the village to the Downs. You can walk to Firle Beacon and the South Downs Way from Dairy Farm bed and breakfast, or enjoy lovely gardens at Netherwood Lodge. Deep Thatch Cottage, Robin Hill studio and Sunnyside Cottage are close by Monk's House.

Bell and Grant are buried next to each other in simple graves beside a flinty stone wall in the churchyard of St Peter's in Firle. After so much artistic expression in life, their headstones are strikingly simple, reading only their names and their dates; Vanessa Bell 1879–1961 and Duncan Grant 1885–1978. Inside the church, a beautiful window inspired by William Blake's tree of life, designed by John Piper and made by David Wasley, features Downland sheep. The window is dedicated to the memory of Henry Gage, 6th Viscount Gage of Firle Place, a magnificent country house and estate open to the public.

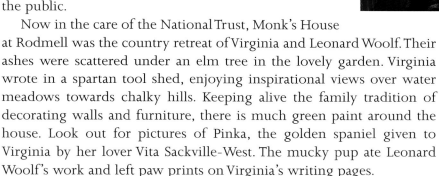

Now in the care of the National Trust, Monk's House at Rodmell was the country retreat of Virginia and Leonard Woolf. Their ashes were scattered under an elm tree in the lovely garden. Virginia wrote in a spartan tool shed, enjoying inspirational views over water meadows towards chalky hills. Keeping alive the family tradition of decorating walls and furniture, there is much green paint around the house. Look out for pictures of Pinka, the golden spaniel given to Virginia by her lover Vita Sackville-West. The mucky pup ate Leonard Woolf's work and left paw prints on Virginia's writing pages.

DOWNTIME

The sisters' houses are close to splendid walking on gentle hills along the South Downs Way, a hundred-mile path between Winchester and Eastbourne for walkers, cyclists and horse riders. From Charleston, a circular trail of around an hour leads to the top of Firle Beacon for huge views of the Sussex coast and inland; the route returns via a different path to the farmhouse.

...hungry and thirsty?

Middle Farm in Firle hosts the National Collection of Cider and Perry and there's a huge range to taste. You can also arrange to have your own fruit pressed for pure juice between late August and November; regulars book well ahead to deliver their harvest in any amount, from carrier bags to truckloads. Children enjoy farm animals on show and after a walk around the nature trail there's tasty home baking in the restaurant. The farm shop, butchery and bakery are excellent; look out for Sussex Slipcote cheese and Buttercup cheese made with unpasteurised milk from beautiful Jersey cows.

The Cricketers Arms in Berwick is a traditional flint cottage with a delightful beer garden. In Firle the Ram Inn hosts occasional exhibitions by the Firle Artists. The Abergavenny Arms is a freehouse in Rodmell with a reputation for good food and well-kept ales. Picnic in the grounds of Charleston farmhouse where the Outer Studio Café serves refreshments and afternoon tea.

41

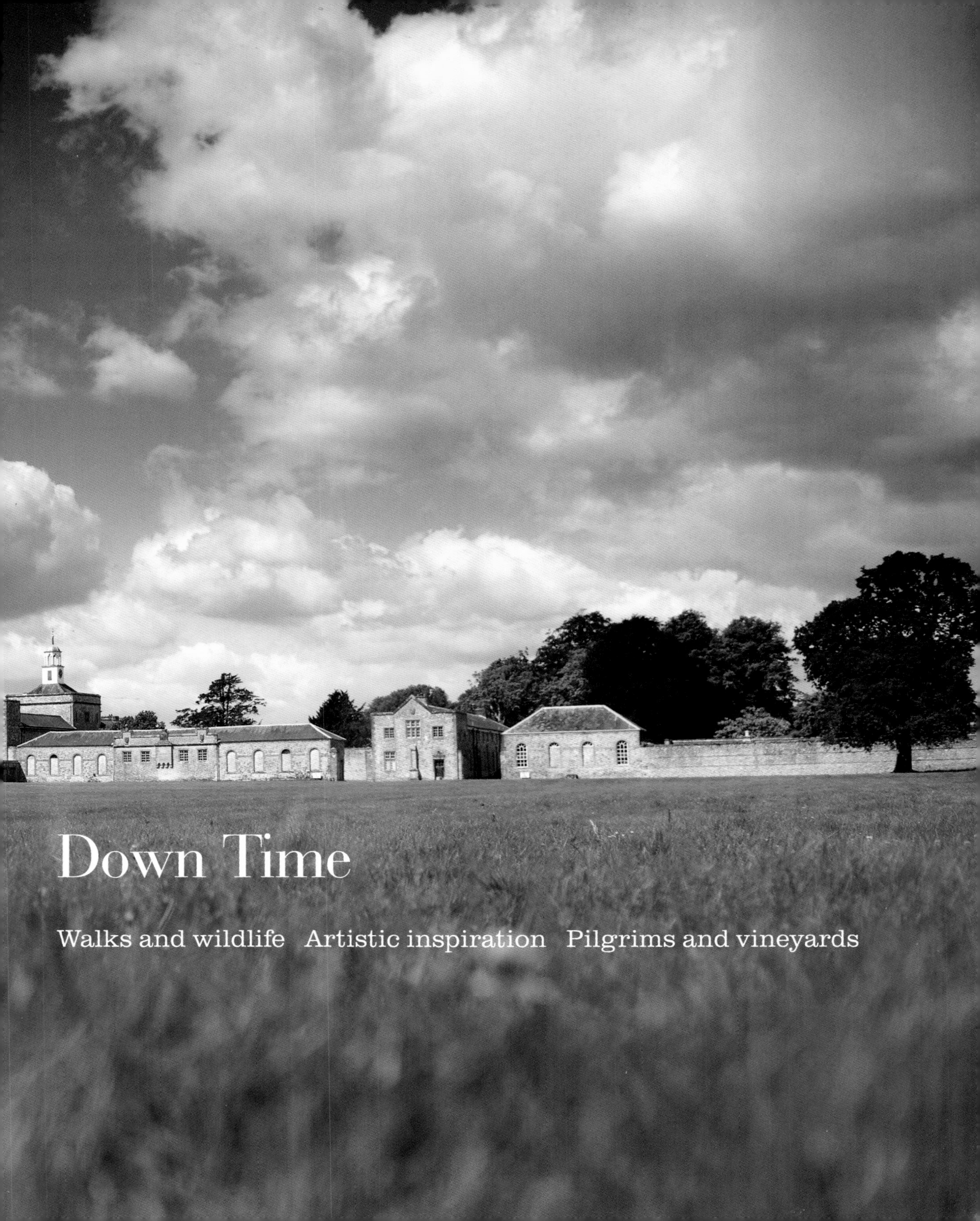

Down Time

Walks and wildlife   Artistic inspiration   Pilgrims and vineyards

Think of this weekend as a delicious hamper of English treats to enjoy in the chalky landscape of the South Downs (though you may not have time to do everything at the first attempt). Explore rolling hills with distant sea views, an Elizabethan manor house with a contemporary maze, a wildlife reserve with diverse and rare habitats, a vast museum in a chalk pit and an unexpected boutique vineyard.

The Pulborough Brooks Nature Reserve in the beautiful Arun Valley is one of the richest areas for wildlife in the entire UK, with farmland, woodland, heathland, river and wetland habitats. There's a warm welcome at the visitor centre and the opportunity to borrow powerful binoculars and observe wildlife from indoors. Two walking trails through wetland and heathland habitats make for easy exploration of an expansive landscape grazed by Highland cattle. From the reserve it's a short hop to Nutbourne Vineyard, where still and sparkling wines are produced on south-facing slopes. Feel free to wander through the vines and savour the flavours in an unusual tasting room within an 1840s windmill formerly used to grind grain. A glass of the vineyard's dry Sussex Reserve makes the perfect English aperitif.

Beautiful Parham House near Storrington is surrounded by elegant parkland. The 160-foot-long gallery of the Elizabethan home is breathtaking, with glorious views of the deer park and Downs. Allow plenty of time to appreciate an outstanding collection of needlework, paintings and furniture and to wander through romantic walled gardens. This landscape has long inspired the artistic community; Turner and Constable painted the South Downs and Eric Gill, a member of the Arts and Crafts movement, set up home in nearby Ditchling. Sir Arnold Bax, poet, composer and Master of the King's Musick,

...hungry and thirsty?

There are many country pubs in the area, most serving food for hungry walkers and cyclists. In Amberley there's the Black Horse in the village and the Bridge Inn by the river. Don't miss the village tearoom in a pretty courtyard; its home-made cream teas and elderflower cordial are scrumptious. After exploring the churches of Storrington, refuel at Vintage Rose bookshop and café. There are storybook readings for children every Saturday with coffee and croissants for parents. At Parham House there's a grassy picnic area in the shade of trees and a café in the Big Kitchen. Sit outside on the deck of the visitor centre café at Pulborough Brooks Nature Reserve, whose breakfast baps are a fitting reward for early risers.

lived at the White Horse pub in Storrington from 1941 to 1953. Writer and historian Hilaire Belloc noted the hostelry in his book *The Four Men*, which describes his walking tour through rural Sussex in 1902. The tale is a collection of musings and a celebration of the county, real ale and cheese.

Jesuit George Tyrrell, a leading Catholic theologian of the early 1900s, is buried in the churchyard of St Mary's in Storrington. His controversial views resulted in his excommunication. Buried in the Anglican churchyard, his headstone, carved by Eric Gill, features a chalice. The grave lies poignantly within sight of Our Lady of England Priory, home to a community of Roman Catholic Priests. The priory church serves as the parish church and contains the shrine of Our Lady of England. Pilgrims are welcome to visit the priory's peaceful woodland shrine near a small vineyard tended by the monks. Among artists and writers who have stayed at the priory are Hilaire Belloc and poet Francis Thompson,

If ever I become a rich man
Or if ever I grow to be old
I will build a house with deep thatch
To shelter me from the cold
And there shall the Sussex songs be sung
And the story of Sussex be told.

FROM 'THE SOUTH COUNTRY',
BY HILAIRE BELLOC

who wrote 'Ode to the Setting Sun', inspired by one of four special crosses there.

Backed by the wooded slopes of Amberley Mount and Rackham Mount, Amberley is a dreamy village worthy of a chocolate box. Historic cottages of the former agricultural community are situated on high land at the edge of the Wildbrooks floodplain, which provided reeds and withes for local people to use in their homes and for basket making. When the tidal Arun overflows water surges across the meadows, threatening the village. Near the duck pond, there's a floodwater marker on the walls of Amberley Castle, a fortified ecclesiastical manor house. Amberley's flinty church is a twelfth-century gem thought to be the work of French masons. There are colourful frescoes and in the country graveyard where raspberries and blackberries grow there's a memorial to Edwardian English illustrator Arthur Rackham. War artist and royal portrait painter Simon Elwes is buried here too. In a former United Reform Chapel, Amberley Village Pottery is a den of clay and glaze. The cheerful stripy and spotty dishes supplied to the village tearoom are on sale here.

At Houghton Bridge Wharf barges were loaded with chalk, hay, sand and gravel destined for London. Learn more about Downland industrial heritage at Amberley Museum and Heritage Centre, just across the car park of Amberley Station on the scenic Arun Valley Line, served by frequent trains from London Victoria and the south coast. Do not underestimate the amount of time required to fully explore the 36-acre site in a former chalk pit. If you seek quiet reflection, then visit the hamlet of North Stoke, where the airy and serene twelfth-century church of St Mary the Virgin in peaceful Downland farmland is a favourite stopping place for walkers and pilgrims.

...tired?

Amberley Castle Hotel is an exclusive retreat with modern fortifications; electric gates and CCTV deter casual visitors. The Thatched House bed and breakfast in Amberley village has superb views over the Wildbrooks nature reserve. For good food, great views and bed and breakfast, try the Sportsman pub in Rackham. At Slindon, four miles from Amberley, Gumber Bothy is in a converted traditional West Sussex barn owned by the National Trust. The White Horse in Storrington offers accommodation and a Sherpa service to transport cyclists' bags for them. The pub's Ebony bar is a homage to Steve McQueen.

WALKING AND CYCLING COUNTRY

The South Downs Way is a hundred-mile trail for walkers, horse riders and cyclists. Bikes are available to hire from South Downs Bikes in Storrington. They also organise regular Sunday morning rides. The Wey-South Path is an easy 36-mile route which ends near Amberley (beginning at Millmead Lock in Guildford). For a shorter walk of just a couple of hours, walk from Amberley village up the slope of Amberley Mount and across the level ridge to Rackham Mount, enjoying far-reaching views as you go. Descend through woodland into Rackham village, stopping for refreshments and more great views from the deck of the Sportsman pub. From here it's a gentle stroll back to Amberley.

ROCK
COTTAGE

42

Our Daily Bread

Artisan bakery   Grizzled skippers   Historic highways

Springtime is golden around the village of Long Crichel at the edge of Cranborne Chase in Dorset. The luminous bloom of acre upon acre of oilseed rape is extraordinary; King Midas would be right at home. While yellow fields illuminate the landscape, arable farms also grow barley for malt, peas for racing pigeons and wheat for bread.

At Long Crichel Bakery, delicious organic artisan bread is made with just four simple ingredients: flour, water, salt and occasionally yeast. The simple pleasure of a wholesome loaf is unbeatable; early morning visitors to the bread counter of the bakery's small country shop are rewarded with the appetising waft of warm crusty loaves and patisserie fresh from the oven just a few steps away.

Described proudly by his colleagues as 'the best baker in the world', Scott is passionate about a job that requires him to be at work from 1 a.m. until midday. 'I just love it,' he told me. 'I always have. It's something I've always wanted to do. I had a very sweet tooth from childhood so I trained to be a pastry chef and went on to become a baker.' Scott is a man on a mission; after a long, hot shift at work he returns home to bake more!

The oven at Long Crichel is wood-fired, fuelled by timber from local sustainable sources. Scott explained that bread in a wood-fired oven bakes at a falling temperature, making it crispy and easier to digest.

Across the lane from the bakery is the walled organic garden where Anni Sax grows fruit, flowers and vegetables biodynamically for use in bakery products and for sale in the shop. The lunar calendar and the moon's phases determine her work. She explained that 'the rhythm of root, fruit and leaf makes sure that everything is tended in turn; it's the best way to care for a large piece of land'.

Using clay from a local pit, Jonathan Garratt fires frostproof pots in an extraordinary wood kiln that he built in 1986 at Hare Lane Pottery. Once common throughout Europe, wood-fired earthenware is now rare, yet the results are beautiful; each piece takes on its own character. Tribal arts and prehistoric pottery influence Jonathan's slipware, planters and garden art installations. His courtyard sales area has the wow factor, an inspirational visual treat of exuberant plants and pots. Jonathan oversees the drama from his seat at the top of a ladder that catches the afternoon sun.

Observe grizzled skippers and green hairstreak butterflies on the wing at Martin Down, a precious landscape of chalk grassland, chalk heath, scrub and woodland that encompasses ancient earthworks and serves as a reminder of how Dorset, Hampshire and Wiltshire used to be. Now a protected National Nature Reserve, rare butterflies, day-flying moths, ground-nesting birds and meadow flowers are abundant. Look closely and the reserve is teeming with curious insect life too. There are several access points but if it's butterflies you're hoping to see, aim for the car park at the top of Sillens Lane in Martin village and from there walk west. In spring and summer glorious butterflies will be in flight over the wildflower meadow on your left. Find silver-

...tired?

In Cranborne, La Fosse restaurant with rooms uses local, fresh, seasonal produce and offers dinner, bed and breakfast. Cycle storage and packed lunches are available too.

washed fritillary and white admiral butterflies around Kitt's Grave.

Throughout the ages, humans have left their mark on this landscape, including the broad track of the Dorset Cursus, thought to be a Neolithic processional route that extended for six miles across Cranborne Chase. At Gussage Hill the Cursus skirts Neolithic long barrows and tumuli. Romans left their mark too; the straight raised highway of Ackling Dyke connected Vindocladia (Badbury Rings) with Sorviodunum (Old Sarum). And there are extraordinary works by medieval artists at the country chapel of Gussage St Andrew's. Repair works in the 1950s revealed wall paintings that illustrate Christ's Passion and death. The narrative begins with Christ before Pilate, or perhaps Herod, and includes an unusual scene of Judas hanging himself. The paintings were a perfect way to communicate the Bible to a congregation unable to read. The chapel is locked when not in use; anyone wishing to see the paintings can make contact via the website www.handleychurch.org.uk.

For me, the most dramatic local example of worlds colliding is Knowlton Rings, where the ruin of a small Norman church appears to have made a defiant stand in vain against the paganism of the immense Neolithic henge monument that surrounds it. The henge dwarfs the tiny flint chapel. In springtime the high banks of the earthwork are covered with cowslips and bluebells; it's an awe-inspiring picnic spot.

...hungry and thirsty?

Buy fresh bread and treats from Long Crichel Bakery and picnic at Knowlton Rings. While the splendid gardens of Cranborne Manor are open only on Wednesdays in spring, in summer the tearoom and adjacent walled garden centre, specialising in old roses, are open daily. The bakery hosts the monthly Long Crichel Supper Club; delicious food in unusual surroundings (reservation essential). Find an old bread oven, flagstone floors and a sunny beer garden at The Drovers Inn in Gussage All Saints. The Sheaf of Arrows in Cranborne is a friendly local pub with accommodation, and potter Jonathan Garratt recommends lunch at The Compasses Inn in Daneham.

43

Enchantment

Prehistory Ponies Tinners

Dartmoor National Park is a wild, natural landscape; vast bleak moors, lush river valleys, exposed granite tors, hut circles. standing stones and herds of roaming ponies are just part of the appeal.

While hundreds of hill ponies live on the moor, the registered Dartmoor Pony is a plain-coloured rare breed. Along with sheep and cattle, pony herds grazing the commons do have keepers, and the ability of hill farmers and commoners to continue grazing their livestock in this way is essential to the future conservation and maintenance of Dartmoor. To protect livestock, observe the 40mph speed limit on moorland roads and do not feed the ponies – it is illegal to do so. Should you come across an injured pony or a pony in distress, call the Dartmoor Commoners Council on 01822 618892.

On a hill above the River Teign, Chagford is a small town with a big personality and a favourite Dartmoor place. Visit in high summer and there's every chance of gridlock in the market square. At quieter times the town makes a great weekend base. At the heart of the Dartmoor tin industry, in 1305 Chagford became an official stannary town where refined tin was assessed, coined and sold. Celebrating this industrial heritage, Chagford holds an annual Tinners' Fair in May.

...hungry and thirsty?

There are four friendly pubs in Chagford, including the Globe, which hosts regular film nights. 22 Mill Street is a chic restaurant with rooms near Chagford's bowling green and Mill End Hotel is a great place for a special afternoon tea. There's smoked salmon tea, cheese tea, and traditional afternoon tea at the New Forge Café , delicious picnic ingredients for sale at Blacks Deli, Thomas's Bakery and Best Cellars, and the lovely Courtyard café and shop offers date and almond porridge with milk and honey for breakfast, the perfect start to a day on the moor.

Symbol of the National Park and an essential part of the tin mines' labour force, Dartmoor Ponies have been sold at Chagford's historic autumn pony fair and sales over hundreds of years. Today semi-feral ponies are 'drifted' (brought in) and selected weaned foals are auctioned. While spotted and coloured ponies are popular with buyers, plain ponies are, sadly, often overlooked. The Friends of the Dartmoor Hill Pony aim to prevent unsold animals meeting an unhappy end.

Chagford's weather-beaten Dartmoor granite market cross now serves as a war memorial in St Michael's churchyard. Inside the church you'll find a colourful medieval parclose screen and the tomb of Mary Whiddon. Leaving the church immediately after her wedding in 1641, Mary was shot and killed by a jealous suitor. Remembering the tragedy, Chagford brides leave their wedding bouquets upon her tomb. The drama of Mary Whiddon's death is believed to have inspired author RD Blackmore to write *Lorna Doone*.

Stone Lane Garden is extraordinary. In contrast to the mysterious windswept landscape of the moor, the sheltered hillside feels like an

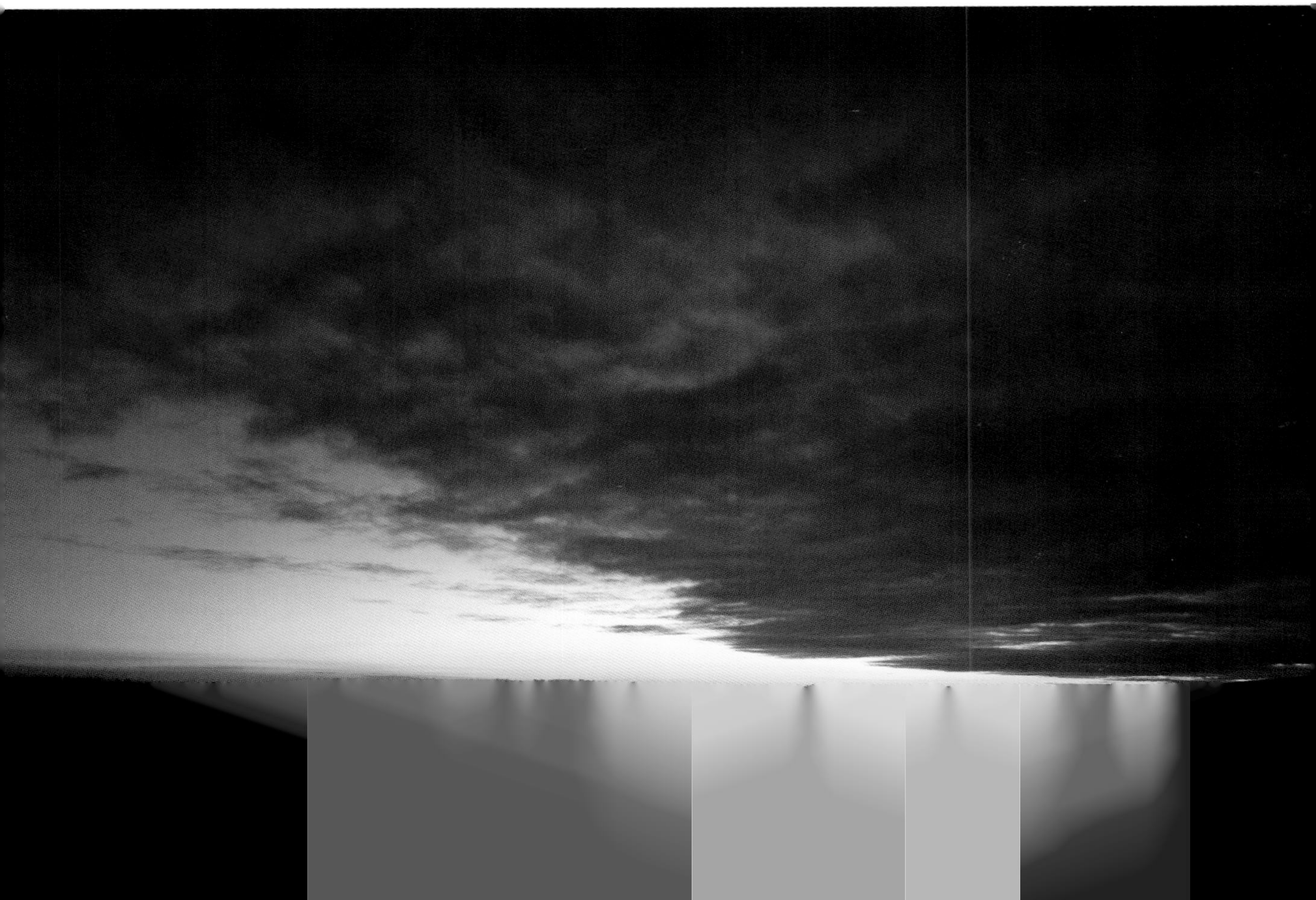

ethereal stage set where magic might happen at any moment. The five-acre arboretum created by June and Kenneth Ashburner hosts the national collection of mostly wild-origin birch and alder trees. In a ghostly glade, beautiful bark is all around; shiny, peeling and white. Paths wander informally, bridges criss-cross streams and curious woodland artworks invite you to approach from afar or reveal themselves at the last moment. The sensational experience is heightened as sunlight and breezes make their way through the trees, changing the mood as they go. One visit will never be enough.

Dartmoor contains the largest concentration of Bronze Age remains in Europe and there are further mysteries too; stone circles and standing stones are easily discovered with the aid of a good map. From Batworthy there are footpaths to Scorhill stone circle, the largest on Dartmoor, and to Shovel Down where a group of prehistoric monuments includes an avenue of stones. Fernworthy stone circle is hidden away at the end of the forestry track to Fernworthy Reservoir. Here the ring of stones is graduated in height and surrounded by trees, creating a different atmosphere from that of circles on the open moor.

Some of my favourite stones on Dartmoor are far from ancient; to discover them follow the riverbank from The Sandy Park Inn to a small island surrounded by natural granite boulders. In dappled sunlight beneath the trees a shapely split-granite boulder with a beautifully worked interior rests as the river rushes by. This inspirational work by Peter Randall-Page is a magnificent find.

CURIOUS

Chagford has much to explore. Neighbouring emporiums of Bowden & Son and Webber & Son stock everything you might require for life in the country. In Bowden's glorious warren there's even a museum. Few recycling centres are as much fun as Chagford's inspirational Proper Job. If you love bargain prices and a good rummage, then this bazaar is for you. Opened in the 1930s, Chagford's river-fed freshwater swimming pool is extraordinary. Open from May to September, this lovely pool was dug by hand by determined local residents!

...tired?

Surrounded by footpaths, including the Dartmoor Way and Two Moors Way, the Chagford area offers plenty of quality accommodation including Cyprian's Cot bed and breakfast in a sixteenth-century cottage with a pretty garden in town. Enjoy home-made cake and tea in the garden of Farleigh Cottage bed and breakfast, while at Heather Cottage in Thorn you can retreat to B&B in a garden chalet with a luxury steam room and wood-burner. Horse riders wishing to take their steeds on holiday can stable them at the self-catering Boldventure. Evelyn Waugh scribed *Brideshead Revisited* at Easton Court Hotel and for an indulgent experience you can't beat Gildleigh Park Hotel. The restaurant is outstanding; many of the ingredients are grown in the extensive grounds, which are lovely to explore. If you prefer to keep things simple, wild camping for one or two nights on the open land of Dartmoor is permitted. Choose your pitch with care – do not camp on farmland, moorland enclosed by walls, within 100 yards of a road, on flood plains or on archaeological sites. Leave no trace.

44

On the Right Track

Viaduct Victoriana Views

Take a ride or walk over an astonishing piece of Victorian engineering this weekend and explore ancient woodlands where a deep ravine conceals an elegant waterfall and a favourite Victorian beauty spot.

The Granite Way is an eleven-mile cycle ride or walkway linking Okehampton with Lydford Gorge via the towering Meldon Viaduct, one of only two wrought-iron truss-girder viaducts still standing in Britain (the other is the Bennerley Viaduct that spans the Erewash Valley between Awsworth and Ilkeston). The route begins at Okehampton Station on the scenic, seasonal Dartmoor Railway, which also connects Okehampton and Meldon Viaduct. Hire an all-terrain bike, tandem, trailer or tow along for the day from Adventure Okehampton, part of the Youth Hostel Association and based at the station yard, where a former Victorian railway goods shed has been skilfully converted into a modern hostel.

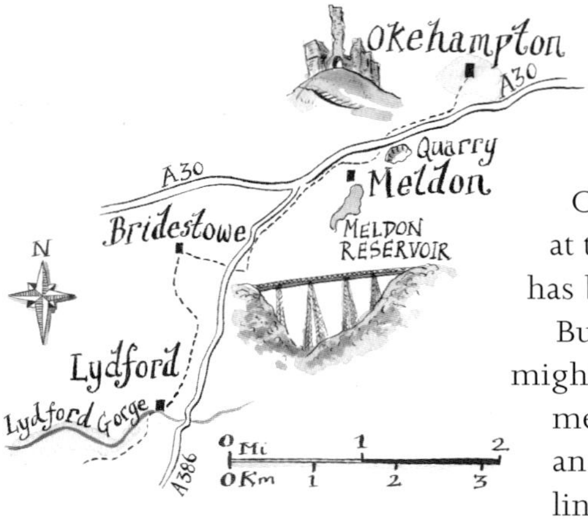

Built in 1874 for the London and South Western Railway, the mighty trusses of the Meldon Viaduct straddle the deep West Okement river valley. In 1878 the railway line was doubled and an almost duplicate viaduct built alongside the first. The down line travelled on the new section while the original viaduct carried the up line. To prevent sway as trains crossed, the structures were braced together. In 1968 rail services west of Okehampton were terminated but the viaduct continued to serve trains for Meldon Quarry

...hungry and thirsty?

Given the Victorian theme of the weekend, it's appropriate to pop into the Victorian Pantry Tearoom in a cobbled yard shared with the Museum of Dartmoor Life in Okehampton. On a sunny day owner Margaret serves tea outside at tables surrounded by pots and plants cared for by her brother Richard. The Pantry is part of Moffat's House, where Okehampton's great benefactor Sydney Simmons was born. Find pasties, preserves, local cheese and nest boxes at Okehampton's farmers' market in Fore Street on the third Saturday of every month.

Refuel at either end of the Granite Way, with a great pit stop at Meldon Viaduct too. Early birds enjoy breakfast at the old-fashioned Station Buffet tearoom at Okehampton Station then progress to the Buffet Car café at one end of the Meldon Viaduct. Enjoy splendid views from the terrace and an outdoor geology lesson among the exhibits of Rock Park, just a stone's throw away. At Lydford Gorge it's hard to resist the temptation of cream tea in the National Trust cafés at either end of the ravine.

and was used as a road crossing during the construction of nearby Meldon Reservoir. In 1990 the rails were finally lifted and six years later, after refurbishment, the viaduct reopened to walkers and cyclists. At 150 feet above the valley floor, the panoramic views are exhilarating.

Now in the care of the National Trust, Lydford Gorge is a beauty spot at the end of the Granite Way. At well over a mile long, the lush ravine is a challenge, suitable only for those with sturdy footwear and plenty of stamina. Paths are steep and narrow and the granite rock is slippery. Due to these hazards the gorge is not open all year round. Phone ahead of your visit to check, as even in summer it may be closed for safety. Maps and walking routes are available from the National Trust ticket office; allow up to three hours for the full tour of the gorge. At the southern end of the ravine the River Lyd from Dartmoor crashes over a sheer drop ninety feet high to create the elegant White Lady waterfall. In full torrent the cascade resembles the swishing skirts of a long dress. For thrill seekers the fury of the Devil's Cauldron whirlpool at the northern end of the gorge is unmissably scary.

The medieval riverside town of Okehampton is home to the Museum of Dartmoor Life, housed in a former agricultural mill. Thick stone walls and cobbled floors lend atmosphere to displays, which evoke Dartmoor life long gone. Step into a Bronze Age dwelling or a blacksmith's shop, look out for the uncomfortable metal slipper bath shared by five families in turn and, although not fit for purpose, a glass walking stick made in Meldon is a sheer work of art.

English Heritage cares for Okehampton castle, the largest in Devon. Founded around 1086, the fortress is beautifully situated, just a short walk from the town centre. An audio tour lends drama to the castle and picnic tables in the meadow make a great spot for lunch.

Sunlight streams through the glass roof of Okehampton's Victorian shopping arcade and a trio of metal pigs scamper around St James' Church on Fore Street, recalling the site of the pig pen. In medieval times swine were allowed to scavenge during daylight but had to be safely home by dusk. Okehampton native Sydney Simmons funded Simmons Park, opened in 1907 by William Treloar, Lord Mayor of London. Simmons named a park chalet in honour of Treloar. Recording the day in his diary, Treloar wrote, 'I declared the park open, at the request of Mr Simmons, who handed the deed to the Mayor and a silver key to me.'

...tired?

Fall out of bed, into your boots and onto the Granite Way from Okehampton Youth Hostel in the railway yard. The Lydford Caravan and Camping Park, affiliated to the Caravan Club, offers quiet pitches with views of Dartmoor's High Tors. Betty Cottles Inn has a camping and caravan park with a bunkhouse too. For a luxurious stay, the Dartmoor Inn is cosy, stylish and friendly with an excellent restaurant and a bijou shop.

45

Saints, strawberries and manure were all transported on this vital waterway

Quay to Quay

Ships Mines Siblings

This weekend explores the River Tamar, the border between Cornwall and Devon. For hundreds of years, while both counties were without a developed road network, the river provided transport. Saints, strawberries and manure were all transported on this vital waterway.

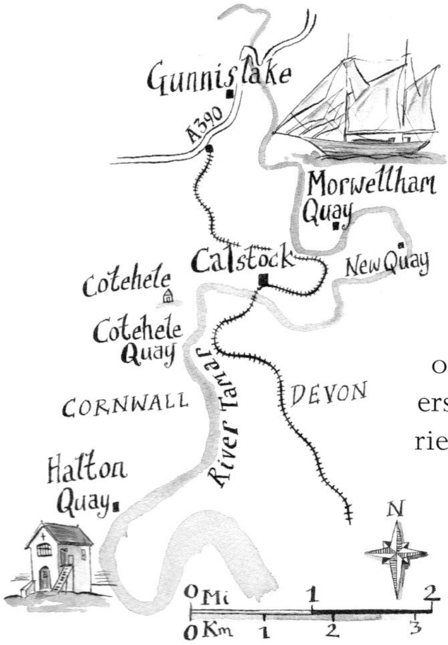

Today the river flows through a diverse landscape of tidal mudflats, fen, wet grassland, wildflower meadows and ancient woodlands. The historic industrial landscape of silver, copper and lead mines is largely overgrown, yet a string of small quays bear witness to boom times past when sailing barges populated the waterway. From Swansea came coal for steam engines, foundries and limekilns – to Swansea went copper for smelting. From Plymouth came limestone – to Plymouth went fruit, flowers and vegetables. Cider apple orchards flourished on both sides of the river, providing liquid refreshment for seafarers, and, thanks to the mild climate, early Tamar cherries, strawberries and daffodils attracted best market prices at London's Covent Garden market.

Atmospheric Halton Quay is where St Indract and his sister St Dominica landed from Ireland in 689. They established a religious settlement at a site now known as Chapel Farm. The medieval parish church of St Dominic is named after Dominica while a tiny white chapel at Halton shore is named after her brother. Formerly a shipping office over the store where Tamar fishermen kept seine-nets, the little chapel, consecrated in 1959, is among the smallest in Britain. St Indract's is open rarely but St Domi-

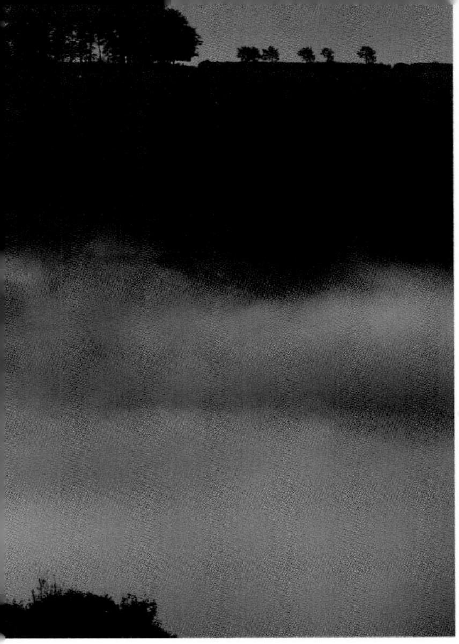

nic's welcomes visitors. Call in to see Tamar Valley strawberries in the Children's Window over the Lady Chapel altar, and the sibling saints with a Tamar salmon in the window above the west door.

Cotehele is one of my favourite National Trust estates. In the Cornish language the name means 'wood on the estuary'. Here the Edgcumbe family made full use of the river and prospered for 600 years. West Country barges constructed with timber grown on the estate sailed from Cotehele Quay laden with local produce, including copper, silver and lead. They returned with coal to fire quayside limekilns, which produced fertiliser for local farms. See the restored sailing barge *Shamrock*, built in 1899, berthed at Cotehele Quay from where it's just a ten-minute woodland walk to the water mill, which produced flour for the estate bakery. Flour is milled still on Tuesdays and Thursdays. Beyond the river, Cotehele's gallery, gardens and orchards make a fascinating visit.

...hungry and thirsty?

The curiously named Who'd Have Thought It Inn in St Dominick enjoys sweeping views over the Tamar from the conservatory. The Edgcumbe Arms on the river at Cotehele Quay is a great spot for lunch and afternoon tea; evening meals are served on Thursdays, Fridays and Saturdays in July. In a converted Methodist chapel Calstock Gallery bar is open on Friday nights for live music and entertainment. View the viaduct from the beer garden of the Tamar Inn. Try a pint of Betty Stogs Cornish Supreme Champion Ale in terraced gardens with valley views at the Rising Sun in Gunnislake. The Rifle Volunteer at St Ann's Chapel is a former mine captain's house with open fireplace, candlelit tables and beer garden. Look out for tables at garden gates along the roadside from where locals sell home-grown fruit, vegetables and flowers.

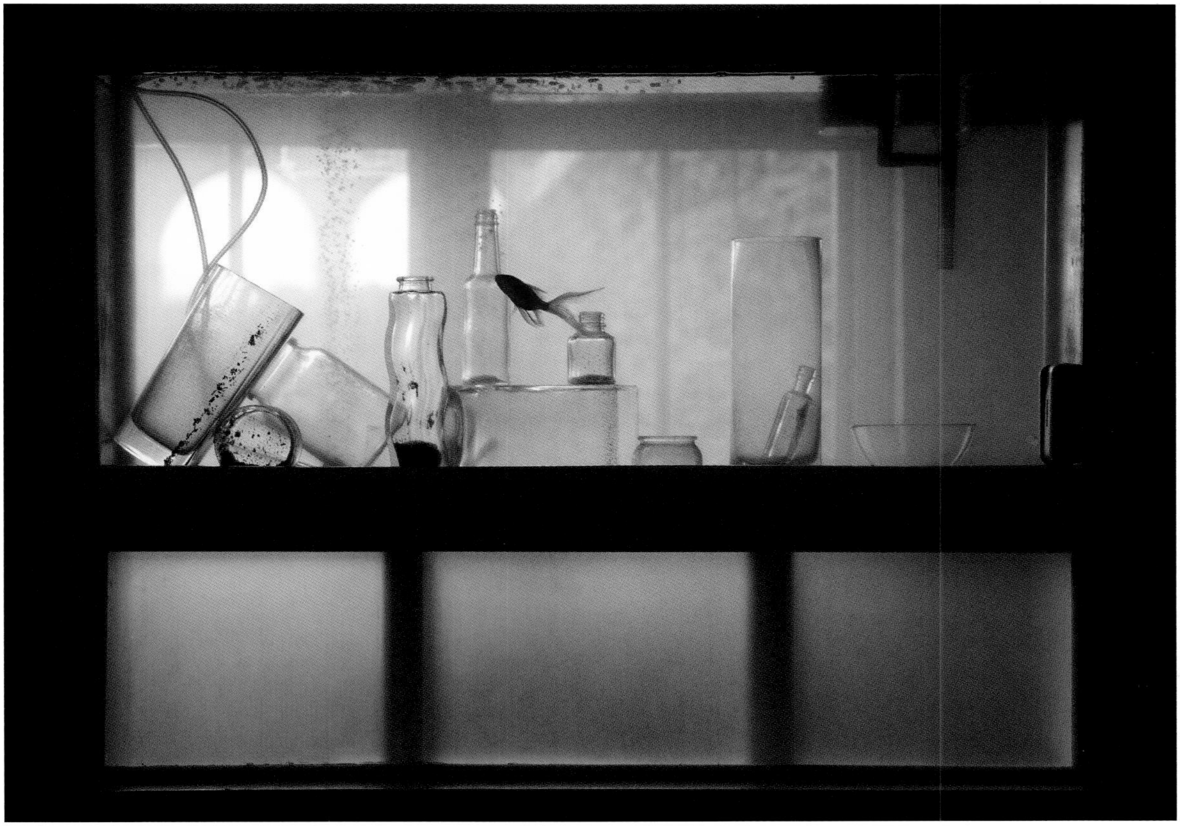

Beneath the statuesque Tamar Line railway viaduct, Calstock is a thriving community on a steeply terraced hillside. From the station high above the river, narrow lanes weave past village gardens overflowing with boats and canoes before ending at the slipway. Enjoy riverside walks through rustling reeds and the sight and sound of sky-high trains squeaking slowly across the single-track viaduct. Art inspired by the river can be found at the friendly Limekiln Gallery. Calstock's August regatta has been a highlight of the summer season for over a century.

Gunnislake is one of the Tamar's three ancient crossing places, along with Greystone and Horsebridge. In 1520 Sir Piers Edgcumbe of Cotehele commissioned the New Bridge to carry transport from Liskeard to Tavistock. Artist JMW Turner's painting Crossing the Brook shows the bridge in a serene landscape with children splashing through the water. The Tamar scene is now in the Tate collection.

...tired?

For bed and breakfast there's Higher Chapel Farm, not far from where the sibling saints landed at Halton Quay, and Willow Cottage, Calstock, which is surrounded by fields. The National Trust has eleven characterful self-catering cottages on the Cotehele Estate, including Engine Cottage, built to house the Cornish beam engine that pumped water out of Danescombe Valley mine. Take a tent or hire a timber camping pod at The Old Rectory family campsite in Gulsworthy.

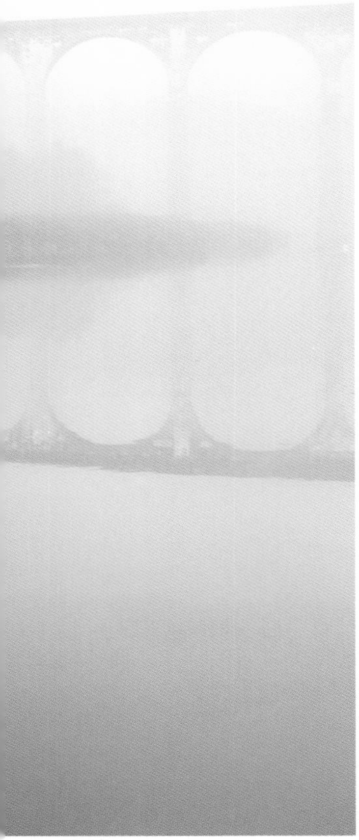

Become a time traveller at Morwellham Quay, the greatest copper ore port of Queen Victoria's empire. At its peak around the 1850s, when lead, copper, arsenic and manganese were mined in the surrounding hills, Morwellham's great dock was full of schooners, which sailed back and forth to Swansea. Departing with ore, they brought back coal for the steam engines and foundries of the Devonshire Great Consolidated Copper Mines. Do ride the train into the George and Charlotte copper mine. Wrap up warm; the cold air bites as the track travels deep into a subterranean world. Here hardy rock miners began their shift after taking an unpaid hour to descend terrifying ladders in the dark. With drills known as 'widow makers', it's little wonder that their life expectancy was about 40 years.

The settlement of New Quay came and went with the copper boom. Built to provide more access for shipping, by the time the last resident left in the 1950s the community was almost forgotten. Starting from Morwellham Quay car park, a half-hour walk through the woods high above the River Tamar leads to the deserted village, quay and limekilns.

TAKE TO THE WATER

Exploring the Tamar Valley from the water is a magical experience; keep your eyes peeled for kingfishers, otters and Salty the seal, a Calstock regular. Hire a canoe and join a three-hour river excursion between Morwellham and Cotehele with a pit stop at Calstock.

If you don't fancy paddling your own boat, a seasonal passenger ferry links Calstock and Cotehele. Allow forty-five minutes for a lovely mile and a half walk along the river past quays and through woods to your destination, then return afloat.

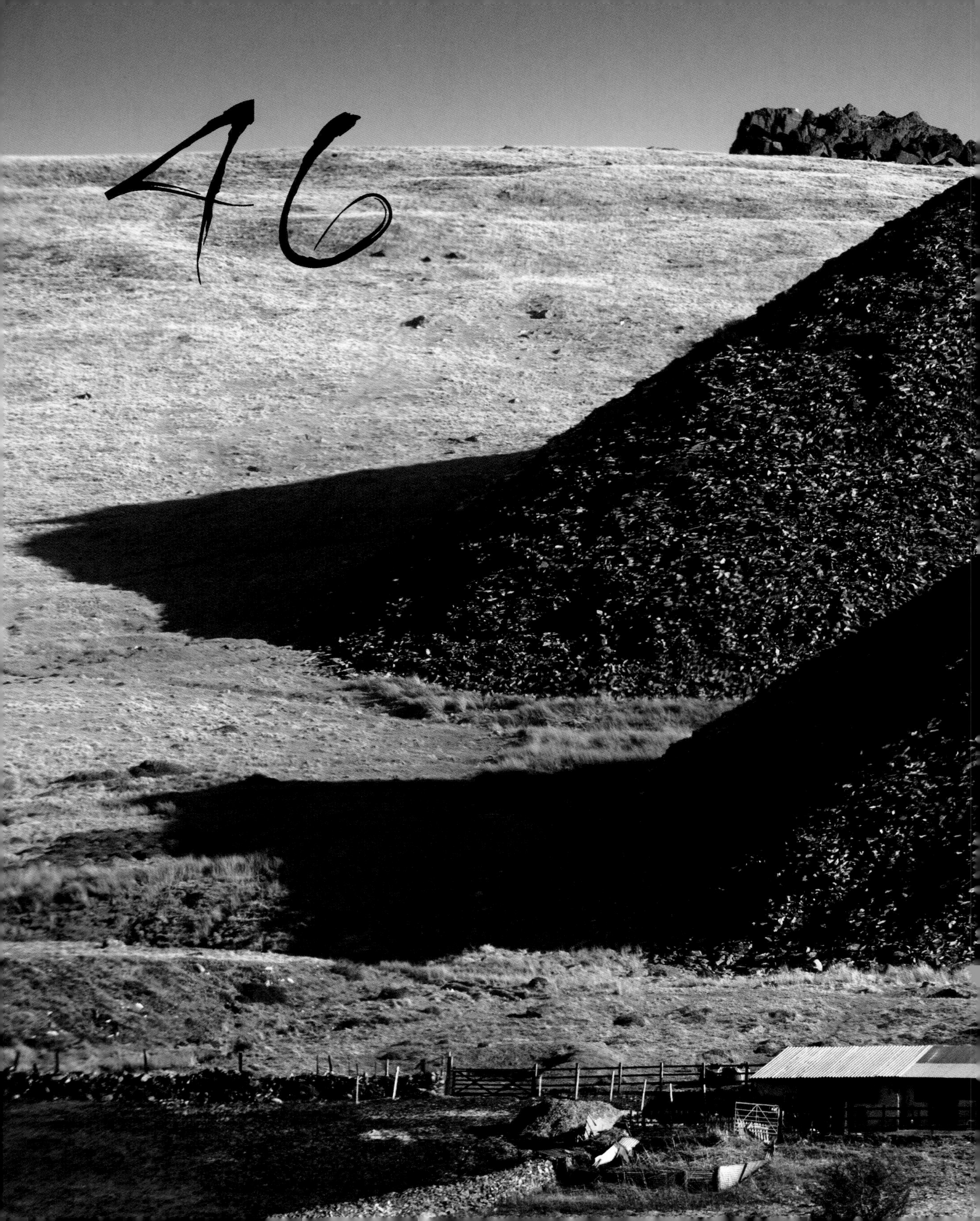
46

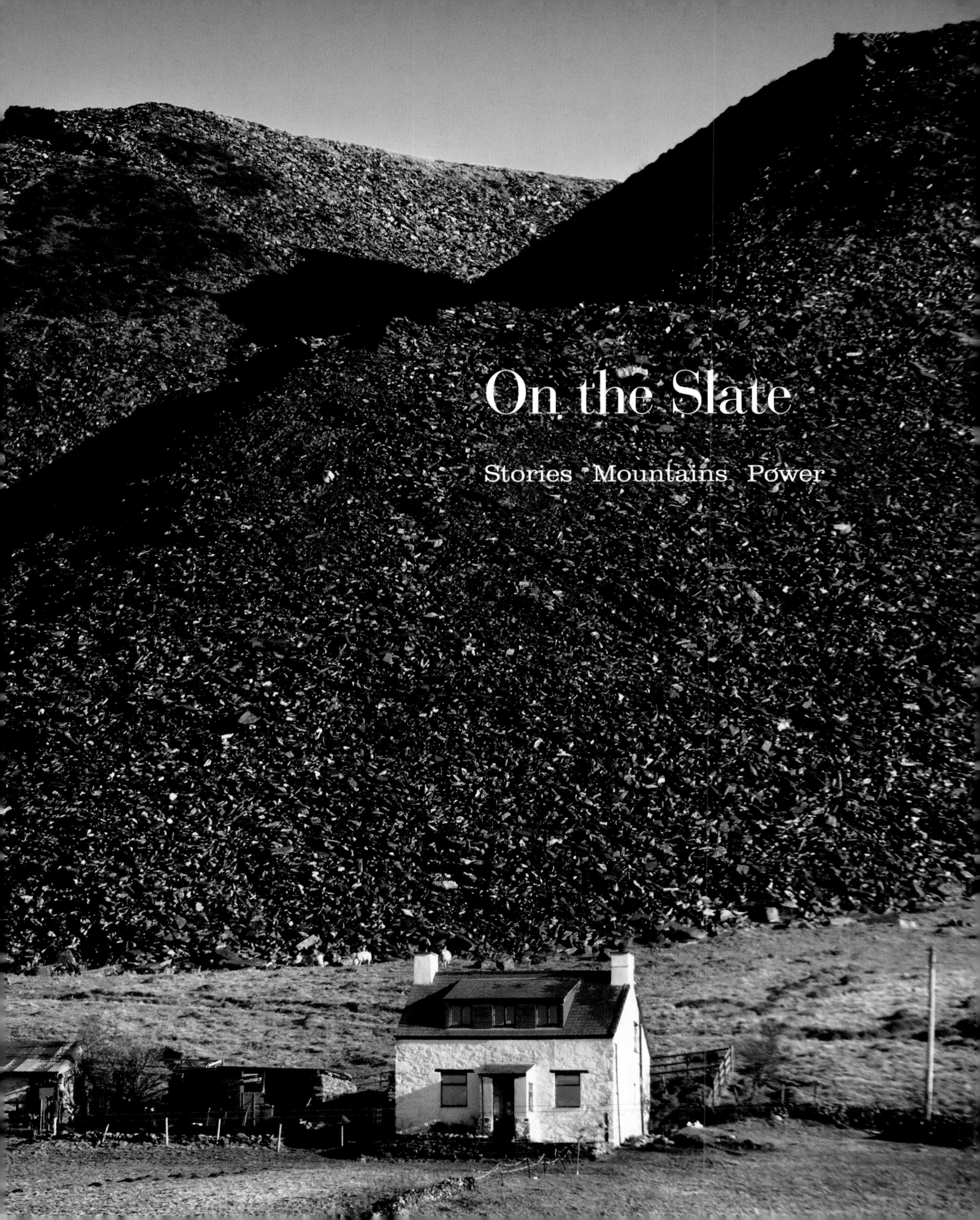

On the Slate

Stories Mountains Power

This weekend explores the Caernarfonshire mountain landscape beloved by Kate Roberts, quarryman's daughter, Plaid Cymru nationalist, journalist and Queen of Welsh literature. Regarded as the most distinguished twentieth-century writer of prose in Welsh, her stories of slate-quarrying communities are critically acclaimed. She is often described as the Welsh Chekhov.

Born in the mountain village of Rhosgadfan in 1891, Kate grew up in a tight-knit community where learning was valued. Her father was a quarryman and her mother managed their small-holding. In a simple windswept cottage the family read books of poetry and prose in Welsh and English. Kate viewed their mountain landscape as 'the most blessed place in the world'.

Kate's talent took her to Bangor University and after graduation she became a teacher. Having first written short stories, in 1927 she published a novel and in 1935, with her husband, she bought a printing works in Denbigh and began to self-publish. She wrote prolifically until 1976 and died at the age of ninety-four in 1985.

Kate's writing resonates with deep understanding of life on the mountain and in the valley. *Tea in the Heather* is among my favourites, capturing the bittersweet experience of country girls dreaming of glamour in London. Brazen Winni Ffinni Hadog persuades innocent Begw to escape their village with comic results. *The Awakening* follows the consequences of an extramarital affair in a small town where no

secret is safe and *The Loss* describes a couple's daytrip by bus to the mountains of their courtship. While Annie hopes to 'recapture something of the time of her wooing', Ted feels that life is complete when he sees his wife sitting knitting in the chair opposite him: 'It never occurred to him that there was a need to use the language of courtship after marriage.'

In the 1960s Kate's former family home, Cae'r Gors (Marsh Field), was in a poor state of repair and due for demolition. She bought it back and the stone cottage with dramatic views across the Foryd Estuary has since become the Kate Roberts Heritage Centre. Amid golden gorse, mauve heather and defunct grey slate quarries, Cae'r Gors is a great visit. A multimedia exhibition explores the Welsh writer's inspiration, and look out for enamel and glass artwork by Karen Jones. The cottage appears as if the family might have just stepped out for a walk. Photographs show Kate's grandmother in traditional Welsh dress. Thick stone walls contain the parents' bedroom, with a small window overlooking the hay barn. In the darkness of the crog loft the children slept like sardines under the eaves.

The hum of insects, gorse crackling, the murmur of heat and the velvet tones of the preacher, endlessly flowing. Were it not in the open air, most of the congregation would have been asleep.

FROM *FEET IN CHAINS* BY KATE ROBERTS, TRANSLATED BY JOHN IDRIS JONES

From Kate Roberts' mountain village, travel to the shores of Llyn Padarn and the National Slate Museum on the site of the Dinorwig Quarry complex where 3,000 men made slate tiles for roofs across the world. See the largest working waterwheel in mainland Britain and walk through workshops where blacksmiths produced, sharpened and

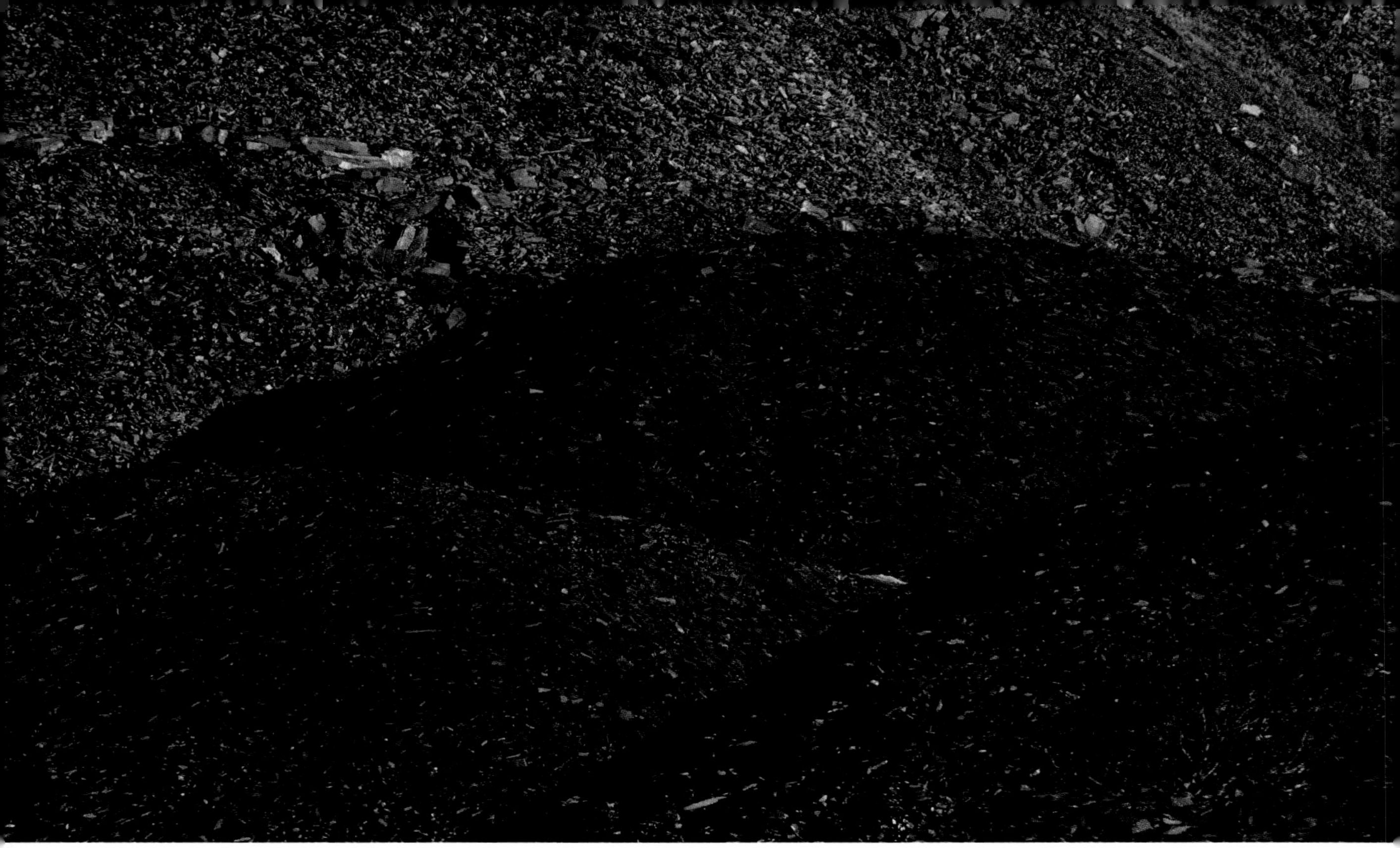

tempered tools for quarrymen. There's powerful machinery in the yard, including a steam crane used to unload coal from boats at Port Dinorwig. Four workers' cottages relocated from Tanygrisiau near Blaenau Ffestiniog reveal traditional interiors from different eras. When the quarry closed in 1969, attention turned to its neighbour, Elidir mountain.

In one of the world's greatest feats of engineering, ten miles of tunnels were blasted through Elidir to create Dinorwig hydro-electric power station, the second largest in the world. The Electric Mountain is also Europe's largest pump-stored power station. Dinorwig's duty is

...hungry and thirsty?

At Talysarn, birthplace of Welsh-language poet Robert Williams Parry, the Halfway Inn has mountain views and a cosy fire. Ty Mawr tearoom also offers bed and breakfast at the foot of Snowdon. Café Brynerefail and Café Pen y Pass have tasty food, the work of local artists and great views. Pete's Eats, a Llanberis landmark, has served pints of tea and generous portions to hungry climbers for decades. There are cafés at the Electric Mountain and Hafod Eryri too.

...tired?

This magnificent region of Wales offers a great range of places to stay. For campers there's Tal y Mignedd and Silver Birches at Bryn Gloch. Hafod y Llan National Trust campsite is ideally situated for the Watkin Path up Snowdon. The Snowdon Ranger Youth Hostel offers lake swimming from its own beach and the Jesse James bunkhouse is a favourite with climbers. Around Llanberis there's bed and breakfast at Betws Inn, Glyn Peris and plenty more. Further afield, Rhiwafallen restaurant has rooms and Ty n Rhos country house has a helipad! Sygun Fawr near Beddgelert enjoys views of Snowdonia and stylish Plas Dinas, nestling between the mountains and the Irish Sea, is a former Welsh gentleman's country residence with royal connections.

rapid response to enormous yet short-lived demands for electricity; as millions of kettles are switched on during televised football's half-time tea breaks, water thunders through the mountain and Dinorwig bursts into action. Following construction, the natural landscape of Snowdonia's National Park was expertly restored; from the outside you would never know that within the mass of rock lies a high-pressure tunnel taller than the Empire State Building. Don a hard hat and board the tour bus for a visit inside the cavernous belly of a mountain powerhouse that you will never forget.

Within a mile of the Electric Mountain are two extraordinary railways. Britain's highest rack railway, the Snowdon Mountain Railway, climbs through the clouds to Hafod Eryri (Summer Shelter) summit centre, where lines of verse by poet Gwyn Thomas are woven into the fabric of a weather-resilient stronghold. A fabulous wall of glass offers panoramic views across the mountain range to Ireland and the Isle of Man. For walkers there are six main routes to the summit of Yr Wyddfa (Snowdon), all illustrated clearly in car parks in Llanberis.

Locomotives once used to haul slate from Dinorwig Quarry now transport passengers on the Llanberis Lake Railway on the banks of Llyn Padarn. The lake and country park offer even more activity, from a five-mile circular walk around the shore to climbing, abseiling and sub-aqua diving in the spectacular Vivian Quarry Pool. There's fishing, bird watching and the Lon Las cycle track on the western shore and, to top it all, the dramatic ruins of Dolbadarn, a thirteenth-century castle built by Welsh princes to defend a treacherous mountainous trade route between Caernarfon and the Conwy Valley.

47

Something About Mary

Extraordinary journeys   Extraordinary churches

According to local legend, anyone who stays a night on the mountain wakes up either a poet or lunatic.

This weekend retraces the extraordinary walk of a young Welsh girl in 1800 in search of a Welsh bible. Mary Jones' 25-mile journey through the mountains of Gwynedd to buy a bible in Bala inspired the formation of the Bible Society, which aims to print bibles in all languages so that all may read it in their own tongue.

A spiritual revival swept across Wales in the 1790s, as preachers like Thomas Charles rode through remote countryside to share their message with rural communities, and families in isolated hamlets walked for miles to attend church. Welsh bibles were expensive, few families possessed one and those who did treated it with reverence.

Born in 1784 in the remote hamlet of Llanfihangel y Pennant at the foot of Cadair Idris mountain, Mary Jones attended a circulating church school where she learned to read. Every week for six years she walked two miles to a neighbour's farmhouse to pore over the bible in the parlour, determining that one day she would save enough money from the bees and chickens that she kept to afford a Welsh bible of her own. Aged fifteen she encountered Thomas Charles on horseback in a country lane – she explained the purpose of her journey to the neighbour's farmhouse, he was impressed and told Mary that if she could come to his home in Bala he was expecting a delivery of Welsh bibles from London. At the appointed time, Mary left her home to walk twenty-five miles across country with the cash for her bible and a bundle of bread and cheese.

On arrival the footsore child was disappointed to hear that the Reverend's delivery was delayed. He arranged for her to stay with a servant and when the bibles arrived she received three for the price of one. Inspired by her devotion, Reverend Charles established the British and Foreign Bible Society in 1804.

Mary's home at Llanfihangel y Pennant is an exquisite hideaway in the Snowdonia National Park, where the ruins of her cottage stand by a gurgling stream. From here the Pony Path climbs five miles up Cadair Idris, the easiest but longest ascent, taking around seven hours there and back. Locals used the route to reach the market at Dolgellau. In the vestry of St Michael's Church a small exhibition tells of the life of the hamlet's famous daughter. See also a three-dimensional map of the mountains, valleys and rivers of the Bro Dysynni area stitched by eighteen local people, a fantastic collective artwork that took two years to complete. Mary's parents are buried in the churchyard, surrounded by a multitude of Joneses from the valley.

From Mary's hamlet it's a short stroll to the ruins of Castell y Bere, a majestic mountain stronghold built by Prince Llywelyn the Great to

...hungry and thirsty?

Don't miss the Cross Foxes bar, restaurant and café with a beautiful terrace, slate floors, good food and luxurious rooms. Lakeside Ty n Cornel and Pen y Bont are perfect stops for tea or something stronger. Abergynolwyn café is a favourite with an outdoor terrace and the welcoming Railway Inn opposite. Sip coffee on a bench on the platform of Llanuwchllyn Station and sit indoors for traditional fish and chips in Bala at Y Badell Aur, the golden frying pan.

...tired?

For the wow factor choose stately Palé Hall, while for bed and breakfast with a private chapel and balcony views of Llyn Tegid visit Glan y Gro. Bala Backpackers is bright and cheery. Riverside guesthouse in a former quarrymaster's house offers motor caravanners a night stop. The Old Rectory bed and breakfast has awesome views of Tal y Llyn. Caravans and camping are welcome at Dolgamedd sheep farm with riverside walks and woodland paths.

secure the borders of his kingdom. The situation is spectacular; the castle dominates the Dysynni Valley, which features in *The Dark is Rising*, a five-volume fantasy for older children written by Susan Cooper. The landscape resounds to the bleating of sheep and the whistling of wind in the trees. Views to Cadair Idris are breathtaking but beware; according to local legend, anyone who stays a night on the mountain wakes up either a poet or lunatic. Before continuing Mary's journey you may wish to divert to her final resting place, in the churchyard of the Bethlehem Chapel in nearby Bryncrug. Look out for Craig yr Aderyn (Birds' Rock) en route – this haunt of choughs is a favourite with climbers when seasonal access is permitted. Until the eighteenth century the waters of the Dysynni Estuary washed around the base of the rock, yet since the land was drained the sea is over four miles away. Despite the water's retreat, a colony of cormorants breeds on the rock.

Lovely Abergynolwyn is the combination of two hamlets, Pant and Cwrt, which mushroomed with the success of the Bryneglwys Slate Quarry in the late nineteenth century. Now the quarry is closed and the community centre cum café and post office is at the heart of things. Nansi Hemming's sculpture in the village square evokes the water nymphs of the rivers meeting in the village, the Dysynni and Gwernol. The lake of Tal y Llyn is in idyllic mountain scenery; follow the bankside circular path to see brown-trout fishermen in bobbing boats, magical reflections in glassy water and, if you're lucky, playful resident otters.

The village of Brithdir conceals two treasures: the first is the spectacular Torrent Walk, a circular path of three miles through the mossy emerald gorge of the Clywedog River. The ravine, accessed from a small lay-by, is steep and good walking boots are essential. The second treasure is an astounding Arts and Crafts church concealed by an embankment of rhododendrons. St Mark's Church, designed by Liverpool-born architect Henry Wilson, is an exotic masterpiece in a most unlikely place.

Wilson is renowned for the immense bronze bas-relief doors he created for the cathedral of St John the Divine in New York. The doors of St Mark's are stylishly simple; a striking teak and ebony design is inlaid with abalone shell. There's no colour in the church windows yet the walls are sky blue and terracotta and the altar front is glowing copper. The metal panel depicts the Annunciation with angels and roses; on the right of the scene is chaplain Charles Tooth and his guardian angel. Tooth's wife Louisa Jeanette Richard, an heiress, built the church in his memory. The choir stalls are made of Spanish chestnut decorated with exquisite animal carvings. Someone with a sense of fun put the tortoise on one side of the church and the hare on the other, likewise an otter and fish. Look out for the kingfisher, owl, fawn, mice, and squirrel too. I'm certain that the protected lesser horseshoe bats roosting here feel right at home.

If travelling by car escape the main drag and follow the country road from Brithdir to see the Arts and Crafts lych gate at St Paul's Church in Bryncoedifor, where services are bilingual. Take the gated road towards Llety Wyn and return to the main road for a short distance before turning off to Llanuwchllyn. Entering the village you're greeted by the statues of OM Edwards, author and scholar, and his son Sir Ifan ab Owen Edwards, who established the Urdd or Welsh Language Youth Movement.

The village station is at the end of the Llyn Tegid, or Bala Lake, narrow-gauge railway, which opened in 1972; historic station buildings belie the line's youth, having been recycled from disbanded railways across Wales. From here you can ride a steam or diesel train alongside the lake into Bala.

The Bala building where Mary Jones received her bible has since become a Barclays Bank. On the opposite side of the road is another religious curiosity, a small parish church in a converted stable dedicated not to a Welsh saint, but to Our Lady of Fatima, another Mary. Seeking a church in the town for his scattered congregation, Father James Koenen, a Dutch Dominican priest, carried out the conversion in 1947. Recognising that many pilgrims are unable to travel to the Portuguese shrine of Our Lady of Fatima, where the Virgin Mary appeared to three children in 1917, the small Welsh church is the only one in the world outside Portugal to be dedicated to Our Lady of Fatima. Visitors are welcome at this Welsh chapel lined in slate, with a modern stained-glass window representing the miracle of the spinning sun in Fatima.

48

Largely undisturbed, this challenging and lonely hideaway is a place to be respected and explored with care.
Gaslight
Wilderness Drovers Chapels

There is an especially remote Welsh landscape in the Cambrian Mountains that inspires me. It is the wilderness of Elenydd, between Snowdonia and the Brecon Beacons, where few people venture. Largely undisturbed, this challenging and lonely hideaway is a place to be respected and explored with care.

Historically, hardy pobl mynydd (mountain people) inhabited the scattered farms of Elenydd. Few remain, although it is still a pastoral landscape dominated by sheep. Traditional mountain families were self-reliant, disconnected from the outside world for much of the year until the drovers arrived, bound for Kent and London with Welsh black cattle, pigs, sheep, geese and turkeys, bringing with them the latest news from Wales and abroad.

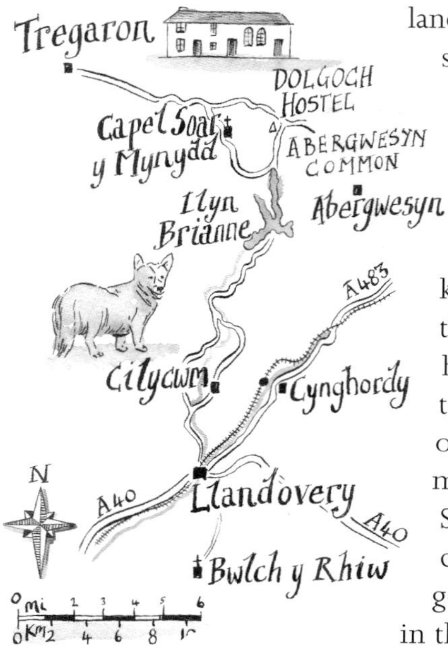

From the sixteenth century, as the breeding of stock animals boomed in Wales, skilled bilingual drovers with knowledge of mountain routes and animal husbandry escorted thousands of animals from Wales to southeast England. On horseback or on foot, they were assisted by corgi dogs, able to dash around larger animals' legs with ease. With the aim of selling fattened, healthy animals at high prices, the troupe moved at just two miles an hour, allowing the animals to graze. Serving the wider community, the drovers were paid to deliver correspondence to recipients along the way and to transport gold from the Dolaucothi Mine to London. The mine remains, in the care of the National Trust.

The Trust also owns Abergwesyn Common on the drovers' mountain road from Tregaron. Known as 'the rooftop of Wales', the vast 16,500-

...hungry and thirsty?

Atmospheric inns once frequented by the drovers are not in short supply, though food might be an issue. Buy essentials before heading to the hills. In Llandovery, Truly Scrumptious deli has ingredients for a luxury picnic and the West End café is legendary among motorbikers. For many the Royal Oak pub, village shop and tearoom at Rhandirmwyn are godsends. One of my favourite pubs on drovers' routes is the Neuadd Fawr Arms in Cilycwm, which serves good food too. Sit on the riverbank at the Towy Bridge Inn further along the river, or play killer pool with locals on Sunday afternoons in The Brunant Arms at Caeo. The Glanbran Arms in Cynghordy, formerly a meeting point for drovers from Cardiganshire, Pembrokeshire and Carmarthenshire, is now a cheery café and bistro owned by David and Sue White. Daily specials use local ingredients and David's home-made carrot cake is divine!

acre common was bought in memory of those who have died for the United Kingdom. The Trust is working to restore and protect the peat bog, which stores huge amounts of carbon, and to restrict the growth of dense purple moor grass, which prevents golden plover chicks from finding insect food.

To explore Elenydd, you need a map, compass and mountain clothing. Be sure to plan rations carefully; shops and cafés are few and far between. Cilycwm village in the Upper Towy Valley is a favourite place. Here drovers met at the smithy to shoe horses and cattle before heading east. Look out for cobbled gutters in the main street, used to water Welsh longhorn cattle retrieved from high pastures and destined for Smithfield Market in London.

Under blue skies the shimmering water and wooded hills of Llyn Brianne Reservoir justify the exotic local name of 'Little Switzerland'.

...tired?

Gaslight and starlight are among the main attractions of remote Dolgoch hostel in Elenydd. There's no electricity in thr former farmhouse and so atmospheric gas lamps illuminate the Welsh pews, slate foors and wood-burning stove. Step outside for starry skies undimmed by light pollution. There's camping by the Twyi at Rhindirmwyn and great food with a warm welcome at The Drovers stylish bed and breakfast in Llandovery. The New White Lion is another luxury bolthole in town. For panoramic views of the Black Mountain, Brecon Beacons and Cynghordy viaduct stay with the friendly Hadley family at Llanerchindda.

At 300 feet high the reservoir's huge dam and spillway are the tallest in Britain. The hydro-electric power station supplies the annual needs of 6,500 homes. In high summer the car park overflows with visitors. Beware – it may spoil your sense of isolation.

For Elenydd's mountain people chapel was a social occasion. Most farmers, shepherds and their families walked or rode miles on horseback to attend. Among Elenydd's many lovely churches, these are favourites. Built in 1822 in the middle of nowhere, Capel Soar Mynydd is the most remote church in Wales. The visitors' book bears witness to a great sense of peace, yet I like to imagine the Sunday bustle of the congregation tethering up to seventy horses in the stables and yard before piling indoors to squeeze into twenty-five neat wooden compartments with their working dogs. Often saddle-sore, the visiting minister would preach from the simple pulpit with his back to the Towy River (Afon Twyi), his eyes upon his flock and the hills behind.

The church of St Michael in Cilycwm is said to be the first Methodist chapel in Wales; check out the skeleton wall painting. Memento mori! Off the main street Capel y Groes, a Welsh independent chapel, is painted vibrant pink.

Whitewashed tiny Bwlchyrhiw in the Cothi Valley is one of the prettiest, oldest Non-conformist chapels in Wales. Look out for the deep baptismal pool with sluice gates in the mountain stream where Baptist converts were fully immersed in water to emerge as a new person in Christ. Red-painted Gosen Calvinistic Methodist Chapel is spectacularly situated beneath the eighteen arches of Cynghordy Viaduct. Time has erased the names and dates on small twin gravestones by the doorway.

Look out for the statue of a drover near the friendly information centre in the historic market town of Llandovery. This is a good place to pick up detailed maps and walking routes. Formerly a strategic military centre from where the Romans controlled the Towy Valley, Llandovery is built around four rivers, the Bawddwr, Gwydderig, Bran and Tywi. It seems strange to find the ruins of a Norman castle in the car park; many travellers must pass through without ever seeing it, or the magnificent glinting statue of Llywelyn ap Gruffydd Fychan of Caeo, who was brutally hung, drawn and quartered by Henry IV in 1401 for refusing to betray Welsh liberation leader Owain Glyndwr to the English. A plaque in the market square denotes the exact spot of his gruesome execution.

On a lighter note, for inspired decorative arts visit Han Made, a cleverly named little shop of treasures where talented designer Hannah Madden has created a simply beautiful range of hand-printed cards, fabric and notebooks.

49
CRICKHOWELL NEWS
810468
Lloyds TSB
ROTARY
INTERNATIONAL
SERVICE ABOVE SELF
Clarence Hall
1891

Top Table

Caves Locks Tramroad

A weekend around the handsome Georgian town of Crug Hywel (Crickhowell), which takes its name from the mountain that rises above it, is a great introduction to the Brecon Beacons National Park, the Black Mountains and the Monmouthshire and Brecon Canal.

The annual Crickhowell Walking Festival takes place over a fortnight in early spring, with around seventy guided walks for all ages and abilities; this is a sociable way to blow away the winter cobwebs. A favourite easy walk for families is the four-mile ascent from Llanbedr village to the flattish top of Crug Hywel, known as Table Mountain. After a couple of hours in the hills, ramblers reward themselves with refreshment at the Red Lion village pub.

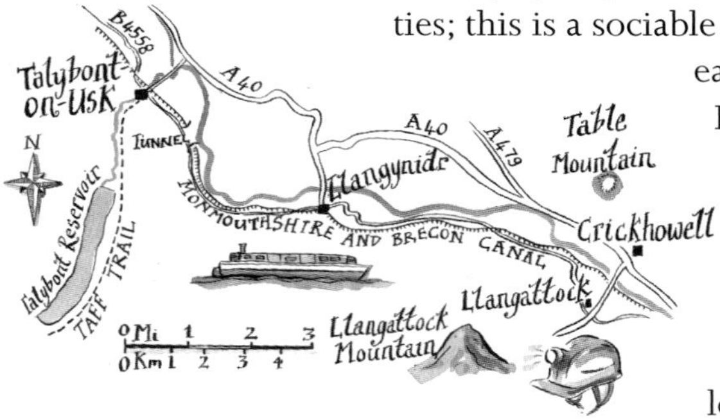

Two of my favourite places in town are the vibrant Oriel Cric Gallery, showcasing work by local artists, and Book-ish, an inviting den of great reads and lovely toys. Crickhowell's Resource and Information Centre stocks a wide range of local walking routes, including the town trail, which visits the ruined Norman castle and curiously elegant stone bridge that spans the River Usk. Allow around an hour for this.

Rising above Crickhowell, Llangattock Mountain is a hot spot for international cavers in pursuit of deep vast chambers, corkscrew squeezes and underground rivers. Above ground there's more leisurely

...hungry and thirsty?

To make a change from cooking in the galley of their boat, canal folk pile into the Talybont Stores and Café for good coffee and tasty food. All-day porridge is a big hit with energetic walkers, cyclists and cavers. Crickhowell's Number 18 Bistro is a local favourite, along with the Courtroom Café. Thomsett's traditional fish and chip shop comes highly recommended by local college students. Crickhowell market days are Friday and Saturday; traders sell from stalls around Tuscan columns in the attractive Market Hall. Near Crickhowell the Nantyffin Cider Mill Inn is extra special – the former drovers' inn serves home-made lemonade in summer, elderberry cordial in autumn and mulled cider in winter. On the menu is locally sourced seasonal food, including wild game.

In Crickhowell the cobbled yard of the Bear Inn reveals its past as a coaching inn. The Dragon Inn is pretty in pink and benches outside the Bridgend Inn overlook the stone bridge and River Usk. While international rugby matchdays are something special at the Horseshoe Inn, Llangattock, you can watch canal boats in the lock at Llangynidr from the garden of the Coach and Horses pub.

pleasure on the Monmouthshire and Brecon Canal, which meanders for thirty-five miles through the Usk Valley to link Brecon in the north with Pontypool in the south. Stroll along the towpath of the 'Mon and Brec', one of Britain's most scenic waterways, and you'll encounter black and white lift bridges, gaily painted barges and wandering canalside sheep. Cavers will feel right at home in the Ashford Tunnel, between Llangynidr and Talybont-on-Usk; headroom is limited and whoever takes the rudder must bend down for a safe passage through this dark, narrow channel.

While much of the canal is now deeply rural, the early-nineteenth-century Brinore Tramroad, which connects with the canal behind the White Hart Inn at Talybont-on-Usk, recalls the canal's industrial past. Horse-drawn trams loaded with limestone rock from local quarries descended precariously by gravity from the hills to canalside limekilns. The resulting quicklime was loaded onto barges for sale as fertiliser and for use in the building trade. Today the eight-mile route is a bridleway popular with riders, walkers and cyclists.

Taith Taff, or the Taff Trail, on the National Cycle Network also connects with Talybont.

Crossing a canal lift bridge, the route takes cyclists, walkers and horse riders to the dam at Talybont Reservoir. For spectacular views across the reservoir, hills and forests, daredevils should follow the winding, steep and narrow road that crosses canal bridge number 142 and climbs into the hills, where the Beacons Way long-distance path crosses the rolling landscape.

...tired?

Characterful pubs in Talybont-on-Usk back on to the canal, making the village a great base for exploration. There are rooms at the Traveller's Rest and the Star Inn, which has a pretty canalside garden, and a bunkhouse at the White Hart. Popular with larger groups, Danywenallt Youth Hostel, a converted farmhouse, is close to the reservoir. For tents and caravans there's Talybont Farm and Pencelli Castle Campsite. Llandetty Hall Farm offers bed and breakfast in a Grade II listed seventeenth-century farmhouse, or there's Ty Gwyn in Crickhowell where rooms are inspired by Welsh writers. Alternatively, hire a boat from Cambrian for a good night's sleep afloat.

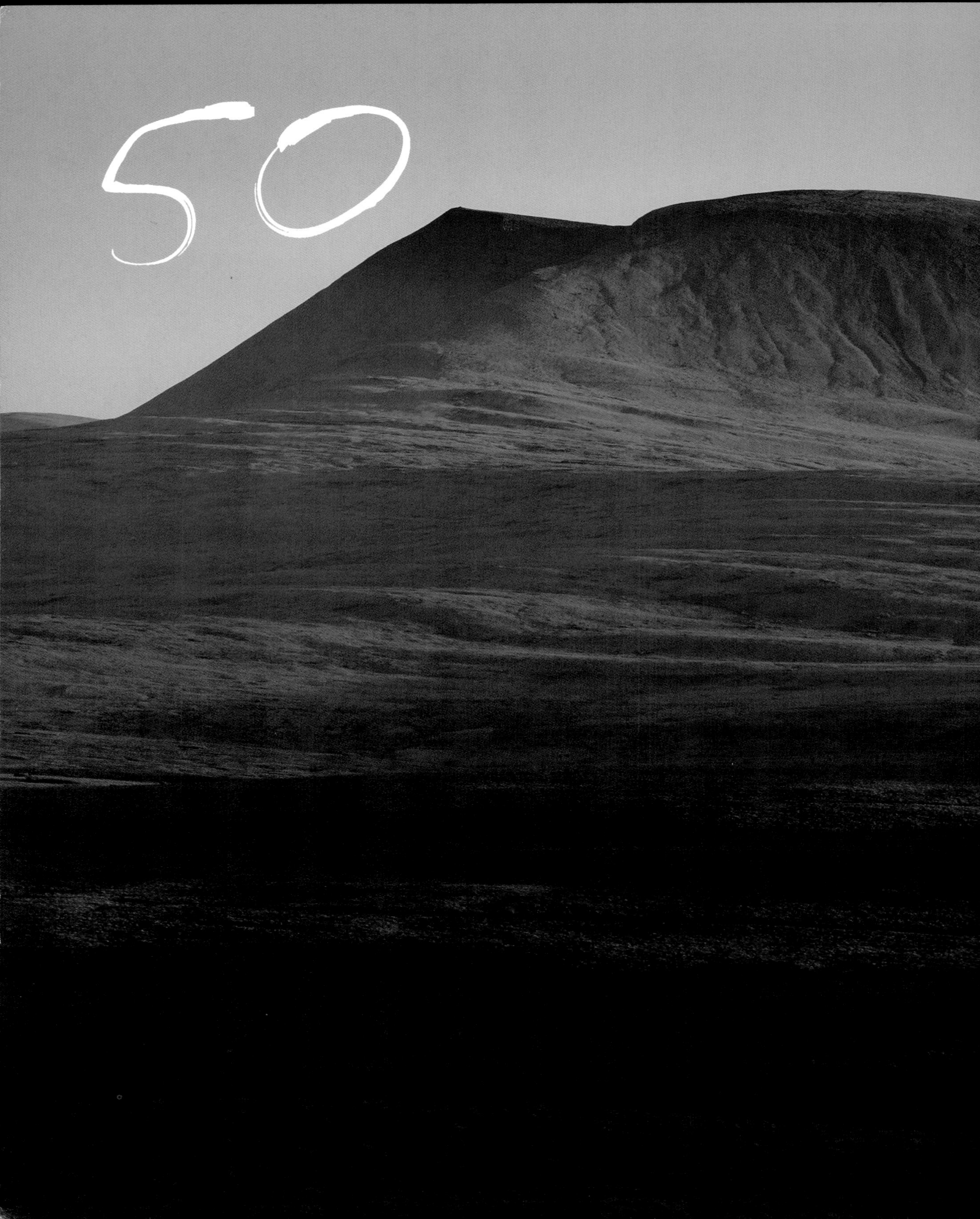
50

Black Mountain Red Kite

Drama Mystery Magic

Escape to Y Myndd Du – the Black Mountain – a remote landscape between the valleys of the Twyi and Tawe rivers. Rolling up and downhill, deep lanes criss-cross the countryside. Without a map you'll soon be lost. Here the majestic red kite is king and the sight of these graceful hunters patrolling their wild territory is inspirational. See them soar high above herds of ponies and glide effortlessly over the ruins of dramatic Welsh castles.

The abandoned workings of Herbert's Quarry offer panoramic views of the Towy Valley, spread like a patchwork picnic blanket at your feet. In fierce winds limestone spoilheaps and ruined quarry buildings on the hill offer shelter to the mountain's ponies. In less severe weather, walkers, cavers, climbers and paragliders abound.

Defiant on a mighty mound high above Cennen Gorge, the location of Carreg Cennen Castle is spectacular. Few fortresses dominate the landscape with such aplomb. To reach the stronghold, visitors must first negotiate hens, cattle and tractors in the farmyard below. From here it's a steep scramble to the ramparts with views across the valley to the Bronze Age burial cairns of Tair Carn Uchaf and Tair Carn Isaf. Take a torch to explore the deep dark cave beneath the castle, dwelling place of long-gone Neolithic residents.

Dinefwr Castle was a seat of the kings and princes of southwest Wales until their defeat by Edward I. Combine exploration of the for-

tress and its parkland (enhanced in 1775 by 'Capability' Brown) with a visit to nearby Newton House, restored and furnished in the Edwardian style. Both are National Trust properties.

The streets of colourful Llandeilo slope steeply on a hill above a bend in the Towy River. Pick up a town trail leaflet from shops and hotels to discover diverse architecture and the vast open space of Penlan Park, gifted to the locals by Lord Dynevor in 1908. There's a lovely gentle walk of around a mile through the bluebells of Castle Woods and along the Towy River to Dinefwr Castle; park at Llandeilo Bridge and follow the waymarked path.

...tired?

Perfectly situated for a magical lake walk, Llanddeusant Youth Hostel, formerly the Red Lion Inn, backs onto the church of St Simon and St Jude, which has an impressive oak barrel ceiling. Observe clear starry skies and the red kite feeding station next to the Black Mountain Caravan and Camping Park or savour creature comforts at the Cawdor hotel in Llandeilo. Surrounded by ancient woodland and spring bluebells, Ty Cefyn Tregib is a beautifully situated bed and breakfast with further accommodation in a yurt and Airstream caravan. In Llandeilo, Fronlas bed and breakfast combines chic with eco, using organic bedlinen and mattresses.

Local legend tells of the emergence of a beautiful and mysterious woman from the waters of Llyn y Fan in the twelfth century. She married a local shepherd but tragically he fulfilled her prophecy that he would unwittingly beat her three times, causing her to return to the lake, leaving him and their three sons, Cadwgan, Gruffydd, and Einion. The boys' knowledge of herbal remedies, handed down to them by their mother, brought them great fame as the Physicians of Myddfai. On a clear day walks from Llyn y Fan Fach to the remote ridges of the Black Mountain are magnificent. Take a map and follow signs to the lake from Llanddeusant village. A narrow lane gives way to a stony track that climbs beside the lake and on into the hills. The time and length of the walk depend on weather conditions, your route and your fitness!

SOUVENIR

In Llandeilo, check out distinctive design at special prices at the UK's only Toast archive store. See the work of sixty local craftspeople at Crafts Alive co-operative, from traditional Welsh love spoons to Jane Davies' extraordinary Metier Mosaics, created from recycled urinals and figurines. Buy *On the Black Hill*, Bruce Chatwin's brilliant and evocative tale of country life in this deeply Welsh landscape.

...hungry and thirsty?

Try warming Welsh cawl, a traditional vegetable broth, at Carreg Cennen Castle barn café, where huge windows overlook the beautiful valley. There are hand-made chocolates and home-made ice cream at Heavenly in Llandeilo. Pop into the Angel pub next door for a coffee and ask for a glimpse of the fantastically painted ceiling of the function room, a true labour of love. Pick up tasty picnic ingredients, including local cheese, from the deli counters at Barita and the Olive Branch.

Llangadog was an important meeting place for travellers and local people. Coaching inns and hostelries, including the blue-painted Goose and Cuckoo, and the Red Lion Inn, surround the small village square. In Llandeilo there are comfy leather sofas, open fires and slate floors in the relaxed bar of the Cawdor Hotel.

Nefol
Hufen Iâ
Siocled
a
Melysfwyd
Heavenly
Ice Cream
Chocolate
&
Sweets
heavenlychocs.com
PUDDINGS / PWDIN
Desserts made to order by our very own pastry chefs. Ask an Angel customer for a reference!
Gwneir ein pwdinau gan ein cogydd teisennau. Gofynnwch i un o gwsmeriaid yr Angel amdanynt!
heavenlychocs.com
GELATO / HUFEN IÂ
We make artisan ice cream & sorbet here on the premises, come and watch. Any flavour made to order!
Rydym yn cynhyrchu hufen iâ ar y safle, dewch i weld. Gellir archebu unrhyw flas ar y pryd!
heavenlychocs.com
CHOCOLATE / SIOC
A vast range
delicious chocola
and traditional swe
including diabetic,
gluten & sugar free.
Ystod eang o siocledi
blasus losin traddodiadol
gan gynnwys rhai diab
neu'n rhydd o glwten a

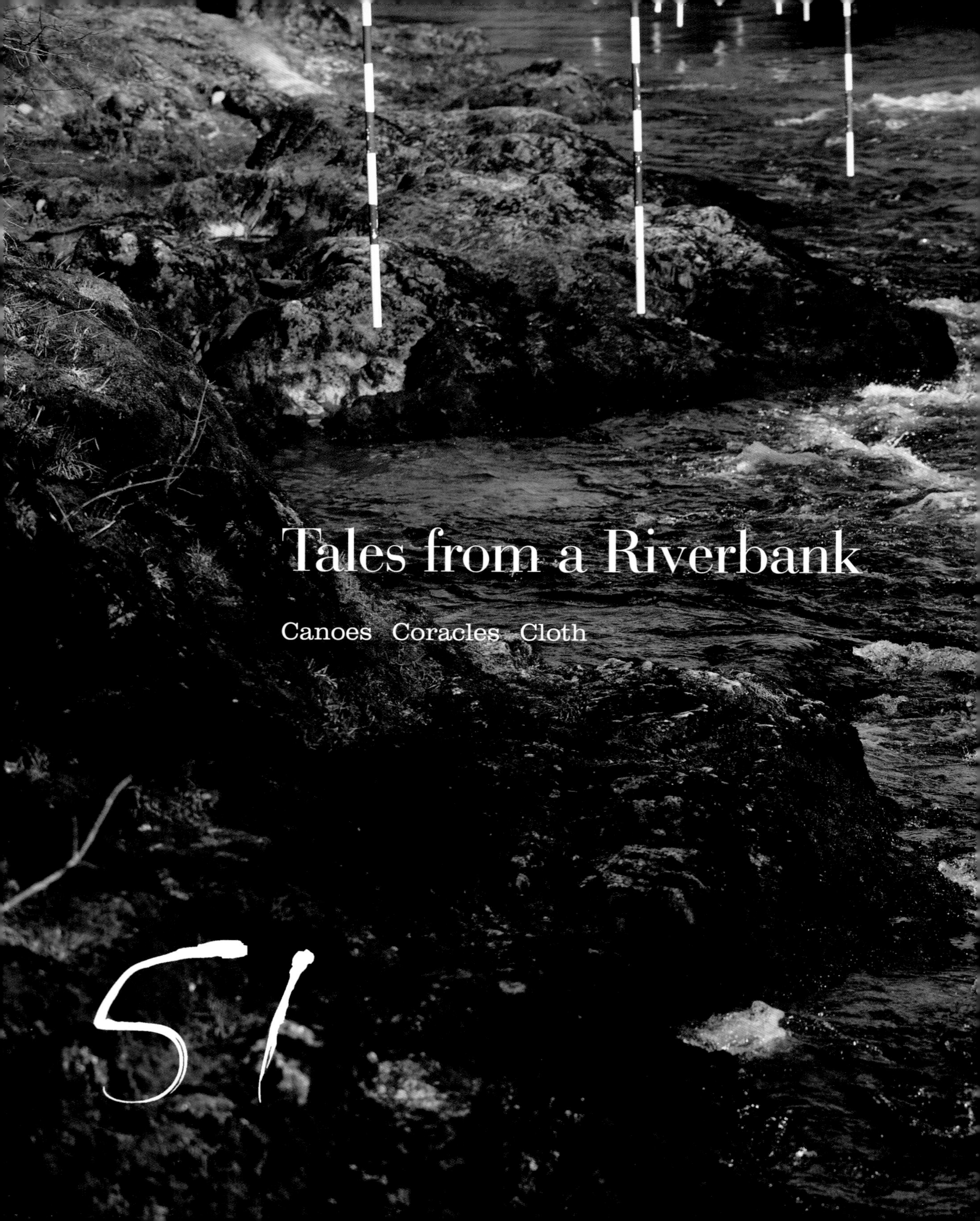

Tales from a Riverbank

Canoes Coracles Cloth

51

The Teifi has many moods around Llandysul; white-water narrows, pools twenty feet deep, tree-lined glides and sparkling shallows.

From the Cambrian Mountains to Cardigan Bay, the River Teifi flows for seventy-five miles, traversing Welsh moorland, peat bog and deep gorges before reaching the west coast. Here seasonal high tides flush migratory Atlantic salmon and sewin, or sea trout, into the spate river. To achieve their mission and spawn upstream they must face the Teifi's challenge of fierce rapids and waterfalls. This weekend explores part of their journey.

For much of its journey, the River Teifi serves as a county boundary line; the stone bridge straddling the river at Cenarth is partly in Carmarthenshire and partly in Ceredigion. At this Teifi beauty spot tourists marvel at dramatic waterfalls and the determination of salmon and sewin summoning all their strength to leap through the torrent from one deep pool to the next. The best runs of salmon are between May and October, and between May and August for sea trout.

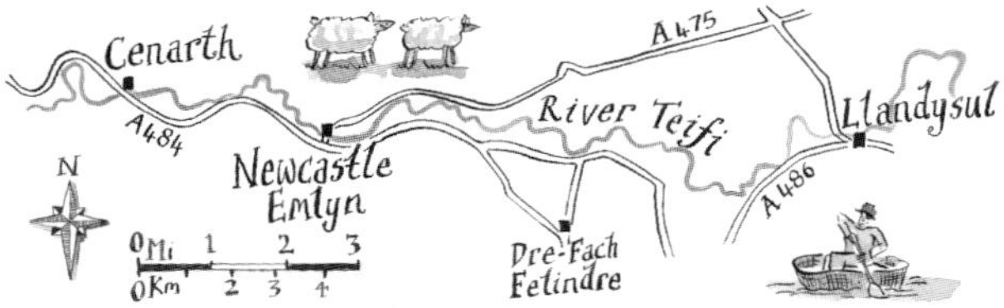

At Cenarth farmers used the waters of the Teifi to soften the fleece of their flock before sheering. Sheep were cajoled into the water and guided by coracles to the other side, where they were sent back across the bridge to return to their starting point. The process was repeated three times. The National Coracle Centre at Cenarth is fascinating; Martin Fowler's collection of basket boats reveals their worldwide use. See how Iraq's huge flat-bottomed coracles known as guffas were used to transport horses on the Euphrates and Tigris. Each river has different conditions and so coracles vary in style. The wood used to build them reflects what was most readily available. In Wales, Carmarthen coracles are made from ash and St Clears coracles from applewood. A pair of Teifi fisherman, each with a coracle or gwrwgl on his back, would walk up to ten miles along the river before taking to the water and drifting with the current to catch just one fish at a time in the net strung between them.

Legend claims that the last dragon in Wales was slain at Newcastle Emlyn, where ruins of a thirteenth-century castle survey the Teifi. Today a mighty golden dragon sculpture guards the entrance to the castle mound. More friendly than ferocious, he welcomes visitors to picnic, walk the dog and enjoy the view.

Visit the superb National Wool Museum in a working mill at Drefach Felindre. Wool is the most versatile textile fabric – warm in winter and cool in summer – and wool-gathering (gwlana) is an old Welsh

...tired?

In the hills above the Teifi, Nant Gwyn Faen is a beautifully situated organic-farm bed and breakfast. The friendly welcome, hand-made furniture, log fires and home-made food – including sausages – are all good reasons to stay with Amanda. Enjoy a stylish stay with breakfast and dinner at the Pink House in the market town of Newcastle Emlyn or sleep as close as possible to the Teifi at Argoed Meadows camping site in Cenarth. Sign up for a day course with Llandysul Paddlers and stay at their riverside bunkhouse.

...hungry and thirsty?

There's good food and wine at The Daffodil at Penrhiwllan, not far from Nant Gwyn Faen Farm. Y Gorlan, or the Fold, café at the National Wool Museum is bright and airy and Buon Appetito in Llandysul is a friendly coffee shop and deli favoured by hungry canoeists. The beauty spot of Cenarth boasts two pubs and a café with a model village. The village store sells award-winning Caws Cenarth cheese. Enjoy Te Prynhawn (afternoon tea) in the riverside beer garden of the Nags Head Inn at Abercych, a characterful pub. For good coffee in Newcastle Emlyn, visit Pachamama close by Bag-age, a pretty shop selling recycled and hand-made work. There's fine dining at Ludo's in the Cooper's Arms and rich Welsh steak and kidney pies to take away at Ty Croeso deli.

custom. Teams of women followed drovers and shearers through the country collecting scraps of fleece to be washed and spun by hand at home. The Teifi Valley's weavers sold their flannel at local fairs until the arrival of industrial mills in the valley.

At Dre-fach Felindre the story of wool comes alive in the working environment of Melin Teifi. The free visit is a sensory experience; from the clickety-clack of machinery in the weaving shed to the strangely comforting smell of wool and the feel of the finished product in the shop where beautiful fabric is on sale.

While the Teifi has been one of Britain's finest game-fishing rivers for centuries, there are now dramatic new sports: slalom, freestyle, surf and Canadian canoeing are hugely popular on this river where coracles once reigned supreme. The hillside town of Llandysul has become an important centre for watersports including canoeing, kayaking and river swimming, and Llandysul Paddlers offer day courses on the river. The Teifi has many moods around Llandysul; white-water narrows, pools twenty feet deep, tree-lined glides and sparkling shallows. Fishermen and sports enthusiasts find them irresistible; however shared use of this wonderful Welsh river requires respect and negotiation.

52

Good Vibrations

Relax Unwind Indulge

It's time for delicious food, stylish accommodation and inspired retail therapy in Narberth, the creative capital of West Wales. Relax, unwind and indulge.

Allow yourself plenty of time to discover 'Arberth' as it is known in Welsh; to hurry would be a terrible shame. The small Pembrokeshire market town has been a convivial meeting place for centuries; travellers on coaching routes from Caernarfon to Haverford West and Tenby to Cardigan alighted here for rest and refreshment. Traders, locals and drovers gathered at traditional country markets; the High Street was formerly Pig Market Street and St James Street was Sheep Street. There's still a lively influx of locals and visitors, many of whom arrive at the handsome Victorian railway station.

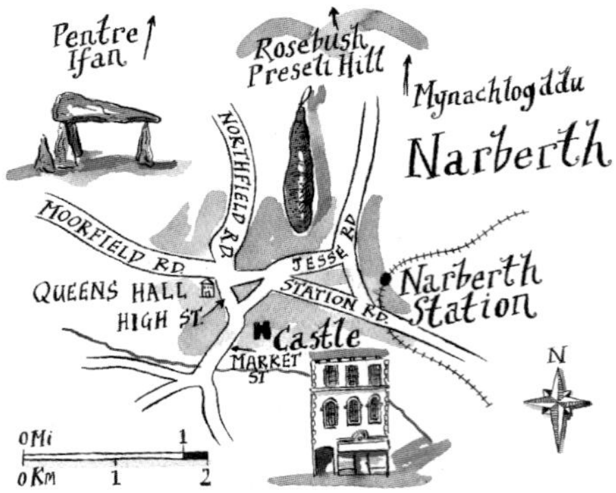

Strolling around Narberth is a delight. Distinctive independent stores have much character, and you'll often find the owners behind the counter, passionate about their products and happy to chat; it's a long way from the identikit high street experience of many modern towns. Among my favourite Narberth stores is Fay Phillips' den of vintage clothes and interiors. Step into a world of throwbacks, where fun is part of the scene. Who knows what you might find? Little black dresses, egg

COFIO (REMEMBERING)

Before the sun has left the sky, one small minute,
One dear minute before the journeying night,
To call to mind the things that are forgotten
Now in the dust of ages lost from sight.

Like foam of a wave on a lonely seacoast breaking,
Like the wind's song where there's no ear to mind,
I know they're calling, calling to us vainly–
Old unremembered things of humankind.

Exploit and skill of early generations,
From tiny cottages or mighty hall,
Fine tales that centuries ago were scattered,
The gods that nobody knows now at all.

Little words of old, fugitive languages
That were sprightly on the lips of men
And pretty to the ear in the prattle of children–
But no one's tongue will call on them again.

Oh, generations on the earth unnumbered,
Their divine dreams, fragile divinity–
Is only silence left to the hearts' affections
That once rejoiced and grieved as much as we?

Often when I'm alone and it's near nightfall,
I yearn to acknowledge you and know each one.
Is there no way fond memory can keep you,
Forgotten ancient things of the family of man?

WALDO WILLIAMS, TRANSLATED BY TONY CONRAN

coddlers, boxy handbags with clasps that clunk, antique knitting patterns and groovy winkle-pickers. There's more vintage inspiration at Giddy Aunt, where you can select a tune on the jukebox and sing your head off while perusing rails of colourful hand-made clothes.

The Welsh Farmhouse Company caters for Welsh country life outdoors and in; find shooting jackets, hip flasks, seriously stylish boots,

...hungry and thirsty?

You won't go hungry; there are plenty of good places to eat in Narberth, including Ultracomida, where you can warm up with a café carajillo, combining a long shot of espresso with a slug of Spanish brandy. Dinner reservations are essential at the weekend. Enjoy organic, Fair Trade and local food at Plum Vanilla and exquisite hand-made chocolates at Fredericks Chocolaterie. For cocktails go to Diablos. The relaxed atmosphere of Café Bar Monti makes it family-friendly and Sospan Fach café is a popular local rendezvous.

There are several pubs in town, or slightly further afield at Rosebush in the Preseli Hills there's the The Old Post Office and the weirdly wonderful Tarn Sinc, highest hostelry in Pembrokeshire. Built from corrugated iron, the pub was intended to be a temporary watering hole and hotel on the railway line serving slate quarries in the Preseli Hills. However, the odd charm of the place ensured its longevity. There's sawdust on the floor, ghost trains and spooky waxwork dummies on the disused station platform. It's enough to give you the shivers. Don't miss it!

good reads and designer homeware. Damson and Slate is a breath of Welsh air; treasures here are made in Wales, from hand-knitted hats and socks, hand-made teddy bears with characterful faces, hand-spun and hand-woven Herdwick yarn rugs hand-dyed with plant extracts, stoneware serving dishes and woven Welsh blankets to stave off winter's chill. I can't sew to save my life but Canvas and Cloth makes me wish I could. Stuffed with soft wool felt, delicate silk scraps, unusual ribbons and buttons, this is dreamland for the nimble-fingered. The friendly team at Good Life is passionate about renewable energy, so be inspired by their knowledge, experience and intriguing stock, from wind turbines and water diviners to forward-thinking books.

There are many artists and craftspeople in this vibrant town; see their work at the Jelly Egg gallery, Oriel Q in Queens Hall and at the Golden Sheaf, a beautiful store over two floors of a Georgian building, where contemporary art is comfortably at home with clothing, jewellery and inspirational books. At Narberth Pottery Simon Rich applies zinc crystalline glaze to porcelain and fires it up to 1270 degrees Celsius.

When you're feeling peckish, there are plenty of friendly

cafés; a favourite is Ultracomida café and deli, serving food and drink from artisan producers in Spain. I defy you to leave empty-handed; the quality of the olives, ham, saffron, chocolate, cheese, rice and almonds is superb and the range of paella pans is impressive. If you can't carry all the treats home, there's always the online store. In September the town hosts the family-friendly Gwyl Fwyd – Food Festival – with demonstrations and talks from passionate chefs and producers.

Tear yourself away from the shops to visit the romantic ruins of Narberth Castle, a sunny, sheltered picnic spot on the edge of town. Beyond are the mysterious Preseli Hills, or Mynydd Preseli, rich in Celtic legend. The Golden Road is an ancient ridgeway, and Gors Fawr (the Great Marsh) is a sacred circle of small standing stones. Curiously, blue stones of spotted dolerite from these hills form the inner circle of Stonehenge. For a three-hour circular walk into the hills from the village of Mynachlog-ddu visit www.pembrokeshirecoast.org.uk.

Further afield, Pentre Ifan is regarded as Wales' most impressive megalith monument. Watching the setting sun sink slowly into a distant sea from this hilltop burial chamber is a magical end to a special day; you can understand how the distant voices of this mysterious landscape inspired Waldo Williams, pacifist and poet, to write '*Cofio*' ('Remembering').

...tired?

Spoil yourself and stay somewhere really special. My favourites are Plas Farmhouse bed and breakfast, a historic ochre building in the heart of town, and the Grove Hotel with contemporary artwork on the walls and a beautiful walled garden.

Directory

1. Go with the Flow
Royal Society for the Protection of Birds (RSPB)
Tel: 01767 680551
rspb.org.uk

Caravan Club Grummore
Lairg IV27 4UE
Tel: 01549 411226
caravanclub.co.uk

The Forsinard Hotel
Forsinard KW13 6YT
Tel: 01641 571221

Corn Mill Bunkhouse
Achumore KW13 6YT
Tel: 01641 571219
achumore.co.uk

Altnaharra Hotel
Altnaharra IV27 4UF
Tel: 01549 411222
altnaharra.com

The Altnaharra B&B
Altnaharra IV27 4UG
Tel: 01549 411258
altnaharra.net

Strathnaver Museum
Bettyhill KW14 7SS
Tel: 01641 521418
strathnavermuseum.org.uk

2. Leap of Faith
Sutherland Sporting Co.
Lairg IV27 4DB
Tel: 01549 402229
scottishtweeds.co.uk

Rogart Station
Rogart IV28 3XA
Tel: 01408 641343
sleeperzzz.com

Park House B&B
Lairg IV27 4AU
Tel: 01549 402208
parkhousesporting.com

Woodend Camping and Caravan Park
Lairg IV27 4DN
Tel: 01549 402248

Pier Café
Lairg IV27 4EG
Tel 07970767361

Lairg Spar Shop
Lairg IV27 4XF
Tel: 01847 611202

The Overscaig House Hotel
Loch Shin IV27 4NY
Tel:01549 431203
overscaighotel.co.uk

Rosehall Craft Shop
Lairg IV27 4XF

Falls of Shin
Lairg IV27 4EE
Tel: 01549 402231
fallsofshin.co.uk

3. A Road Less Travelled
Loch Ness Riding in Dores
Dores IV2 6TX
Tel: 07973 815208
lochnessriding.co.uk

Loch Ness Marathon
Tel: 0844 875 1411
lochnessmarathon.com

Rockness
rockness.co.uk

Loch Ness Film Festival
lochnessfilmfestival.co.uk

Rohan B&B
Gorthleck IV2 6YP
Tel: 01456 486495
stayrohan.co.uk

Pottery House
Dores IV2 6TR
Tel: 01463 751267
potteryhouse.co.uk

Craigdarroch House Hotel
Loch Ness IV2 6XU
Tel: 01456 486400
hotel-loch-ness.co.uk

Dores Inn
Inverness IV1 2TR
Tel: 01463 751203
thedoresinn.co.uk

Foyers Village Store
Inverness IV2 6XU
Tel: 01456 486233

Schoolroom Café & Brin Herb Nursery
Flichity IV2 6XD
Tel: 01808 521288
brinherbnursery.co.uk

Whitebridge Hotel
Stratherrick IV2 6UN
Tel: 01456 486226
whitebridgehotel.co.uk

The Steadings
Strathnairn IV2 6XD
Tel: 01808 521314
steadingshotel.co.uk

4. The Angels' Share
Speyside Cooperage
Craigellachie AB3 89RS
Tel: 01340 871108
speysidecooperage.co.uk

The Macallan Distillery
Craigellachie AB38 9RX
Tel: 01340 871471
themacallan.com

Keith and Dufftown Railway
Dufftown AB55 4BA
Tel: 01340 821181
keith-dufftown-railway.co.uk

Glenfiddich Distillery
Dufftown AB55 4DH
Tel: 01340 820 373
glenfiddich.com

Strathmill Distillery
Keith AB55 5DQ
Tel: 01542 882295

Strathisla Distillery
Keith AB55 3BS
Tel: 01542 783044

Glenlivet Estate
Ballindalloch AB37 9EX
Tel: 01807 580799
glenlivetestate.co.uk

Speyside Way Visitor Centre
Aberlour AB38 9QP
Tel: 01340 881266

Aberlour distillery
Aberlour AB38 9PJ
Tel: 01340 881249
aberlour.com

Glenfarclas Distillery
Ballindalloch AB37 9BD
Tel: 01807 500257
glenfarclas.co.uk

Cardhu Distillery
Aberlour AB38 7RY
Tel: 01479 874635

The Glenlivet Distillery
Ballindalloch AB37 9DB
Tel: 01340 821720
theglenlivet.com

The Dowans Hotel
Aberlour AB38 9LS
Tel: 01340 871488
dowanshotel.com

The Mash Tun
Aberlour AB38 9QP
Tel: 01340 881771
mashtun-aberlour.com

Castleview B&B
Auchindoun AB55 4DY
Tel: 01340 820941
castleviewdufftown.co.uk

Laggan Farmhouse B&B
Dufftown AB55 4DS
Tel: 01340 820392
lagganfarmdufftown.co.uk

Aberlour Gardens
Aberlour AB38 9LD
Tel: 01340 871586
aberlourgardens.co.uk

Glenlivet Public Hall
Ballindalloch AB37 9BX
Tel: 01807 590486
glenlivethall.org.uk

Tomintoul Youth Hostel
Tomintoul AB37 9EX
Tel: 01807 580364
syha.org.uk

The Spey Larder
Aberlour AB38 9QA
Tel: 01340 871243
speylarder.com

Walkers Shortbread Ltd
Aberlour AB38 9LD
Tel: 01340 871555
walkersshortbread.com

5. Waterworld
Great Glen Way
greatglenway.com

Caledonian Canal Visitor Centre
Fort Augustus PH32 4BA
Tel: 01320 366493

The Lovat Hotel
Fort Augustus PH32 4DU
Tel: 01456 490000
thelovat.com

Caledonian Hotel
Fort Augustus PH32 4BQ
Tel: 01320 366256
caledonian-hotel.co.uk

Lock Inn
Fort Augustus PH32 4AU
Tel: 01320 366302

The Boathouse
Fort Augustus PH32 4BD
Tel: 01320 366682
lochnessboathouse.co.uk

The Eagle Barge
South Laggan PH34 9EA
Tel: 01320 340210

6. Night Train
Corrour Estate
Inverness PH30 4AA
Tel: 01397 732200
corrour.co.uk

Loch Ossian Youth Hostel
Corrour PH30 4AA
Tel: 01397 732207
syha.org.uk

The Crianlarich Hotel
Crianlarich FK20 8RW
Tel: 01838 300272
crianlarich-hotel.co.uk

Caledonian Sleeper
scotrail.co.uk

7. Bonnie Lassie, Will Ye Go?
Cluny House
Aberfeldy PH15 2JT
Tel: 01887 820795
clunyhousegardens.com

Bolfracks Garden
Aberfeldy PH15 2EX
Tel: 01887 820207
bolfracks.com

Loch Tay Boating Centre
Kenmore PH15 2HG
Tel : 01887 830291
loch-tay.co.uk

Scottish Crannog Centre
Kenmore PH15 2HY
Tel: 01887 830583
crannog.co.uk

Castle Menzies
Weem PH15 2JD
Tel: 01887 820982
menzies.org

National Kayak School
Tel: 01631 565310
nationalkayakschool.com

Freespirits
Grandtully
PH9 0PL
Tel: 01887 840400
freespirits-online.co.uk

Splash Whitewater Rafting
Aberfeldy PH15 2AQ
Tel: 01887 829706
rafting.co.uk

Beyond Adventure
Aberfeldy PH15 2BW
Tel: 01887 829202
beyondadventure.co.uk

Aberfeldy Golf Club
Aberfeldy PH15 2BH
Tel: 01887 820535
aberfeldy-golfclub.co.uk

Kenmore Hotel
Kenmore PH15 2NU
Tel: 01887 830205
kenmorehotel.com

The Inn on the Tay
Grandtully PH9 0PL
Tel: 01887 840760
theinnonthetay.co.uk

Fernbank House
Aberfeldy PH15 2BL
Tel: 01887 820486
fernbankhouse.co.uk

Rose Cottage B&B
Aberfeldy PH15 2BH
Tel: 01887 820533

Scottish Canoe Association
Grandtully PH15 2QY
Tel: 0131 317 7314
canoescotland.org

Bunkhouse & Glassie Farm
Aberfeldy PH15 2JN
Tel: 01887 820265
thebunkhouse.co.uk

The Watermill & Homer
Aberfeldy PH15 2BG
Tel: 01887 822896
aberfeldywatermill.com

Ailean Chraggan Hotel
Weem PH15 2LD
Tel: 01887 820346
aileanchraggan.co.uk

House of Menzies
Aberfeldy PH15 2JD
Tel: 01887 829666
houseofmenzies.com

Courtyard at Kenmore
Kenmore PH15 2HN
Tel: 01887 830763
thecourtyard-restaurant.co.uk

Weem Hotel
Weem PH15 2LD
Tel: 01887 820381
weemhotel.com

Dewar's World of Whisky
Aberfeldy PH15 2EB
01887 822010
dewarswow.com

Aberfeldy Distillery
Aberfeldy PH15 2EB
01887 822010

Legends of Grandtully
Grandtully PH9 0PL
Tel. 01887 840775
legendsofgrandtully.com

8. Neverland

JM Barrie's Birthplace
Kirriemuir DD8 4BX
Tel. 0844 493 2142
nts.org.uk

Kirriemuir Museum
Kirriemuir DD8 4BB
Tel: 01575 575479

Glen Clova Hotel
Glen Clova DD8 4QS
Tel: 01575 550350
clova.com

The Bothy Clachnabrain
Glen Clova DD8 4QU
Tel: 01575 540330

Cortachy House B&B
Cortachy DD8 4LX
Tel: 01575 540229
cortachyhouse.co.uk

Muirhouses Farmhouse B&B
Kirriemuir DD8 4QG
Tel: 01575 573128
muirhousesfarm.co.uk

Drumshademuir
Roundyhill DD8 1QT
Tel: 01575 573284
drumshademuir.com

Prosen Hostel
Kirriemuir DD8 4SA
Tel: 01575 540238
prosenhostel.co.uk

Airlie Arms
Kirriemuir DD8 4HB
Tel: 01575 572847
theairliearms.co.uk

Thrums Hotel
Kirriemuir DD8 4BE
Tel: 01575 572758
thrumshotel.co.uk

88 Degrees Café
Kirriemuir DD8 4EY
Tel: 01575 570888

Auld Surgery
Kirriemuir DD8 4BE
Tel: 07840 392005
theauldsurgery.co.uk

Angus Fine Art & Tea Rooms
Kirriemuir DD8 4EG
Tel: 01575 572447

The Steeple
Kirriemuir DD8 4BB
Tel: 01575 572697

The Star Rock Shop
Kirriemuir DD8 4EZ
Tel: 08714 333000

McLaren's Bakers
Kirriemuir DD8 4EY
Tel 01575 572964
thebridieshop.co.uk

9. Walk This Way

The John Buchan Story at the Chambers Institution
Peebles EH45 8AJ
Tel: 01721 724820

Cornice Museum of Ornamental Plasterwork
Peebles EH45 8BA
Tel: 01721 720212

Tontine Hotel
Peebles EH4 8AJ
Tel: 01721 720 892
tontinehotel.com

Castlehill Knowe B&B
Peebles EH45 9JN
Tel: 01721 740218
castlehill-knowe.co.uk

Skirling House
Skirling ML12 6HD
Tel: 01898 860 274
skirlinghouse.com

The Laurel Bank Tea Room
Biggar ML12 6HF
Tel: 01899 830462
laurelbanktearoom.co.uk

Oven Door Tearoom
Peebles EH45 8SF
Tel: 01721 723456

Dawyck Botanic Garden
Peebles EH45 9JU
Tel: 01721 760 254
rbge.org.uk

10.Treasure Hunt

Museum of Lead Mining
Wanlockhead ML12 6UT
Tel: 01659 74387
leadminingmuseum.co.uk

Tolbooth Museum
Sanquhar DG4 6BN
Tel: 01659 50186

Crawfordjohn Heritage Venture
Crawfordjohn ML12 6SU
Tel: 01864 504206
crawfordjohn.org

Wanlockhead Inn
Biggar ML12 6YE
Tel: 01659 74424

Lettershaws Farm
Biggar ML12 6TA
Tel: 01864 502369

Craigend Cottage B&B
Westoun ML11 0NH
Tel: 01555 820898
craigendbandb.co.uk

Blackaddie House Hotel
Sanquhar DG4 6JJ
Tel: 01659 50270
blackaddiehotel.co.uk

Harvey's Café
Sanquhar DG4 6DP
Tel: 01659 50955

11. Siege Mentality

Threave Garden & Estate
Castle Douglas DG7 1RX
Tel: 01556 502575
nts.org.uk
historic-scotland.gov.uk

Castle Douglas Food Town
cd-foodtown.org

Albion House B&B
Castle Douglas DG7 1LD
Tel: 01556 502360
albionhousecastledouglas.co.uk

Lochside Caravan Park
Castle Douglas DG7 1EZ
Tel: 01556 502949

Designs Gallery
Castle Douglas DG7 1DZ
Tel: 01556 504552
designsgallery.co.uk

Sulwath Brewers Ltd
Castle Douglas DG7 1DT
Tel: 01556 504525
sulwathbrewers.co.uk

12. Starstruck

Glentrool Visitor Centre
Newton Stewart DG8 6SZ
Tel: 01671 840302
forestry.gov.uk

7stanes Mountain Biking
7stanesmountainbiking.com

The Breakpad Bike Shop
Newton Street DG8 7BE
Tel: 01671 401303
thebreakpad.com

HDI Bike Hire
Newton Street DG8 6DB
Tel: 01671 404002
hdi-online.biz

Newton Stewart Walkfest
newtonstewartwalkfest.co.uk

Elmlea Plants
Newton Stewart DG8 6PX
Tel: 01671 402514

Galloway Forest Observatory Astronomical Society
wigtownshire-astro.org.uk

Flowerbank Guest House
Newton Stewart DG8 6PJ
Tel: 01671 402629
flowerbankgh.com

Kirroughtree Hotel
Newton Stewart DG8 6AN
Tel: 01671 402141
mcmillanhotels.co.uk

Minnigaff Youth Hostel
Newton Stewart DG8 6PL
Tel: 01671 402211
syha.org.uk

The House o' Hill Hotel
Bargrennan DG8 6RN
Tel: 01671 840243
houseohill.co.uk

Café Cree
Newton Stewart DG8 6BT
Tel: 01671 404203
cafecree.co.uk

Cinnamon Shop & Café
Newton Stewart DG8 6NL
Tel: 01671 404440
cinnamon-online.co.uk

13. Theatre of War

Tourist Information Centre
Rothbury NE65 7UP
Tel: 01669 620887

Cragside
Rothbury NE65 7PX
Tel: 01669 620333
nationaltrust.org.uk

Barrowburn Farmhouse
Morpeth NE65 7BP
Tel: 01669 621176
barrowburn.com

Rose and Thistle Inn
Morpeth NE65 7BQ
Tel: 01669 650226
roseandthistlealwinton.com

The Potting Shed
Harbottle NE65 7DG
Tel: 01669 650407
thepottingshedharbottle.co.uk

Tosson Tower Farm
Morpeth NE65 7NW
Tel: 01669 620228
tossontowerfarm.com

Tomlinson's
Morpeth NE65 7SF
Tel: 01669 621979
tomlinsonsrothbury.co.uk

Orchard House
Rothbury NE65 7TL
Tel: 01669 620684
orchardhouserothbury.com

Star Inn
Harbottle NE65 7DG
Tel: 01669 650221

Harley's Tearoom
Rothbury NE65 0XA
Tel: 01669 620240
harleystearoom.co.uk

The Congregational
Rothbury NE65 7TL
Tel: 01669 621900
thecongregational.org.uk

Tully's Deli & Tea Room
Rothbury NE65 7TB
Tel: 01669 620574

Rothbury Family Butchers
Rothbury NE65 7SS
Tel: 01669 620744

14. Empire Building

National Park Centre
Bardon Mill NE47 7AN
Tel: 01434 344396

Once Brewed Youth Hostel
Bardon Mill NE47 7AN
Tel: 0845 371 9753
yha.org.uk

Roman Army Museum
Brampton CA8 7JB
Tel: 01697 747485
vindolanda.com

Allen Banks & Staward Gorge
Hexham NE47 7BU
Tel: 01434 344218
nationaltrust.org.uk

Hadrian's Wall Bus: AD122
traveline.info

Reading Rooms B&B
Haydon Bridge NE47 6JQ
Tel: 01434 688802
thereadingroomshaydon
bridge.co.uk

The Old Repeater Station
Grindon NE47 6NQ
Tel: 01434 688668
hadrians-wall-bedandbreak
fast.co.uk

Demesne Farm
Bellingham NE48 2BS
Tel: 01434 220258
demesnefarmcampsite.co.uk

The Garden Station
Langley NE47 5LA
Tel: 01434 684391
thegardenstation.co.uk

Slack House Farm
Gilsland CA8 7DB
Tel: 01697 747351
slackhousefarm.co.uk

Lanercost Tea Room
Lanercost CA8 2HQ
Tel: 01697 741267
lanercosttearoom.co.uk

Ye Olde Forge Tea Rooms
Greenhead CA8 7HE
Tel: 01697 747174

The Twice Brewed Inn
Bardon Mill NE47 7AN
Tel: 01434 344534
twicebrewedinn.co.uk

15. Tranquillity

Tourist Information Centre
Middleton-in-Teesdale
DL12 0QG
Tel: 01833 641001

Langdon Beck Youth Hostel
Barnard Castle DL12 0XN
Tel: 0845 371 9027
yha.org.uk

The Old Barn B&B
Middleton-in-Teesdale
DL12 0QG
Tel: 01833 640258
theoldbarn-teesdale.co.uk

Teesdale Hotel
Middleton-in-Teesdale
DL12 OQG
Tel: 01833 640264
teesdalehotel.co.uk

Brunswick House
Middleton-in-Teesdale
DL12 0QH
Tel: 01833 640393
brunswickhouse.net

Holwick Camping Barn
Low Way Farm
Barnard Castle DL12 0NJ
Tel: 0800 0191 700
yha.org.uk

The Farmhouse Kitchen
Low Way Farm
Barnard Castle DL12 0NJ
Tel: 01833 640506

Forresters Hotel
Middleton-in-Teesdale
DL12 0QH
Tel: 01833 641435
forrestersmiddleton.co.uk

Café 1618
Middleton-in-Teesdale
DL12 0QG
Tel: 01833 640300
cafe1618.com

The Café Caramel
Middleton-in-Teesdale
DL12 0QG
Tel: 01833 640924
cafecaramel.co.uk

The Conduit Tea Rooms
Middleton-in-Teesdale
DL12 0QG
Tel: 01833 640717

Strathmore Arms
Holwick DL12 0NJ
Tel: 01833 640362
strathmorearms.co.uk

Langdon Beck Hotel
Forest-in-Teesdale DL12 0XP
Tel: 01833 622267
langdonbeckhotel.com

16. Return to Eden

Settle–Carlisle railway line
settle-carlisle.co.uk

Bells of Lazonby
Lazonby CA10 1BG
Tel: 01768 898437
bellsoflazonby.co.uk

Lazonby Pool & Campsite
Lazonby CA10 1BL
Tel: 01768 898346
lazonbypool.co.uk

Midland Hotel
Lazonby CA10 1BG
Tel: 01768 898901

Mains Farm
Kirkoswald CA10 1DH
Tel: 01768 89834

Staffield Hall
Kirkoswald CA10 1EU
Tel: 07976 619222
staffieldhall.co.uk

The Watermill
Little Salkeld CA10 1NN
Tel: 01768 881523
organicmill.co.uk

Highland Drove Inn
Carleton Village CA11 8TP
Tel: 01768 865588
kyloes.co.uk

Fetherston Arms
Kirkoswald CA10 1DQ
Tel: 01768 898284
fetherstonarms.co.uk

Crown Inn at Kirkoswald
Kirkoswald CA10 1DQ
Tel: 01768 870435

17. From High Fell to Gentle Shore

Mirehouse
Bassenthwaite CA12 4QE
Tel: 01768 772287
mirehouse.com

Skiddaw House Youth Hostel
Bassenthwaite CA12 4QX
Tel: 07747 174293
yha.org.uk

Traffords Caravan Site
Bassenthwaite CA12 4QH
Tel: 01768 776298

Bassenthwaite Parish Room
Bassenthwaite CA12 4QP
Tel:017687 76393
bassenthwaitevillage.co.uk

Ravenstone Hotel
Bassenthwaite CA12 4QG
Tel: 0800 163983
ravenstonemanor.co.uk

Castle Inn Hotel
Bassenthwaite CA12 4RG
Tel: 01768 776401
castleinncumbria.co.uk

Armathwaite Hall
Bassenthwaite CA12 4RE
Tel: 01768 776551
armathwaite-hall.com

Old Sawmill Tearoom
Mirehouse CA12 4QE
Tel: 01768 774317
theoldsawmill.co.uk

The Sun Inn
Bassenthwaite CA12 4QP
Tel: 01768 776439
thesunatbassenthwaite.co.uk

The Pheasant Inn
Bassenthwaite CA13 9YE
Tel: 01768 776234
the-pheasant.co.uk

Keswick Museum & Gallery
Keswick CA12 4NF
Tel: 01768 773263
keswickmuseum.webs.com

The Pheasant Inn
Bassenthwaite
CA13 9YE
Tel: 01768 776234
the-pheasant.co.uk

18. Show and Shine

King George IV Inn
Eskdale Green CA19 1TS
Tel: 01946 723470
kinggeorge-eskdale.co.uk

Ravenglass & Eskdale
Railway
ravenglass-railway.co.uk
Eskdale Mill
Boot CA19 1TG
Tel: 01946 723335
eskdalemill.co.uk

Rainors Farm B&B
Gosforth CA20 1ER
Tel: 01946 725934
wasdaleyurt.co.uk

Murt Camping Barm
Murt CA20 1ET
Tel: 01687 74301
campingbarns.co.uk

Fisherground Campsite
Eskdale CA19 1TF
Tel: 01946 723349
fishergroundcampsite.co.uk

Shepherds Views Holidays
Holmrook CA19 1XU
Tel: 01946 729907
shepherdsviews.co.uk

Low Wood Hall Hotel
Nether Wasdale CA20 1ET
Tel: 01946 726100
lowwoodhall.co.uk

Lingmell House
Wasdale CA20 1EX
Tel: 01946 726261
lingmellhouse.co.uk

Burnthwaite & Penny Hill
Wallthwaite CA12 4QP
Tel: 01768 779445

Bowderdale Farm
Wasdale Head
Tel: 01943 726113
bowderdale.co.uk

Hermon's Hill
Gosforth CA20 1ER
Tel: 01946 725008
hermonshill.co.uk

Stanley House B&B
Eskdale CA19 1TF
Tel: 01946 723327
stanleyghyll-eskdale.co.uk

Wastwater Youth Hostel
Wasdale CA20 1ET
Tel: 0845 371 9350
yha.org.uk

Eskdale Youth Hostel
Boot CA19 1TH
Tel: 0845 371 9317
yha.org.uk

The Woolpack Inn
Eskdale CA19 1TH
Tel: 01946 723230
woolpack.co.uk

Wasdale Head Inn
Wasdale Head CA20 1EX
Tel: 01946 726229
wasdale.com

The Strands Hotel
Wasdale CA20 1ET
Tel: 0871 951 1000
strandshotel.com

The Bower House Inn
Eskdale CA19 1TD
Tel: 01946 723244
bowerhouseinn.co.uk

Woodlands Tearoom
Santon Bridge CA19 1UY
Tel: 01946 726281
santonbridge.co.uk

19. Night at the Museum

Swaledale Museum
Reeth DL11 6QT
Tel: 01748 884118
swaledalemuseum.org

Garden House Pottery
Reeth DL11 6QT
Tel: 01748 884188
gardenhousepottery.co.uk

Punch Bowl Inn
Low Row DL11 6PF
Tel: 01748 886233
pbinn.co.uk

The Burgoyne Hotel
Reeth DL11 6SN
Tel: 01748 884292
theburgoyne.co.uk

Springfield House
Reeth DL11 6UY
Tel: 01748 884634
springfield-house.co.uk

Dales Bike Centre
Fremington DL11 6AW
Tel: 01748 884908
dalesbikecentre.co.uk

Hoggarth's Farm Campsite
Keld DL11 6LT
Tel: 01748 886335
swaledalecamping.co.uk

Scabba Wath Campsite
Low Row DL11 6NT
Tel: 01748 884601

Park House Campsite
Keld DL11 6DZ
Tel: 01748 886549
keldbunkhouse.com

Usha Gap Campsite
Muker DL11 6QG
Tel: 01748 886214
ushagap.btinternet.co.uk

The Farmers Arms
Muker DL11 6QG
Tel: 01748 886297
farmersarmsmuker.co.uk

The CB Inn
Arkengarthdale DL11 6EN
Tel: 01748 884567
cbinn.co.uk
Keld Lodge
Keld DL11 6LL
Tel: 01748 886259
keldlodge.com

Tan Hill Inn
Reeth DL11 6ED
Tel: 01833 628246
tanhillinn.co.uk

Overton House Café
Reeth DL11 6SY
Tel: 01748 884332
overtonhousecafe.co.uk

Ice Cream Parlour
Reeth DL11 6TE
Tel: 01748 884929
reethicecreamparlour.co.uk

The Village Stores
Muker DL11 6QG
Tel: 01748 886409

20. Less is Moor
Lidmoor Farm
Bransdale YO62 7JL
Tel: 01751 430335
lidmoor.co.uk

Bitchagreen Cottage B&B
Farndale East Y062 7LB
Tel: 01751 433250
farndalecottage.co.uk

Feversham Arms Hotel
Helmsley YO62 5AG
Tel: 01439 770 766
fevershamarmshotel.com

The Royal Oak Inn
Gillamoor YO62 7HX
Tel: 01751 431414
theroyaloakgillamoor.co.uk

21. Grand Designs
Malton Museum
Malton YO17 7LP
Tel: 01653 695136
maltonmuseum.co.uk

Eden Camp
Malton YO17 6RT
Tel: 01653 697777
edencamp.co.uk

Scampston Hall
Malton YO17 8NG
Tel: 01944 759111
scampston.co.uk

Castle Howard
York YO60 7DA
Tel: 01653 648333
castlehoward.co.uk

Wharram Percy
Malton YO17 9TW
Tel: 0870 333 1181
english-heritage.org.uk

G. Woodall and Son Ltd
Malton YO17 7LP
Tel: 01653 692086
gwoodall.com
The Old Lodge Hotel
Malton YO17 7EG
Tel: 01653 690570
theoldlodgemalton.co.uk

Kingfisher Café & Bookshop
Malton YO17 7LL
Tel: 01653 695265
kingfishercafe-bookshop.co.uk

The Hidden Monkey
Malton YO17 7LW
Tel: 01653 694982
hiddenmonkeytearooms.co.uk

The Spotted Cow
Malton YO17 7JN
Tel: 01653 697568

The Blue Ball Inn
Malton YO17 7JF
Tel: 01653 690692

22. Well Versed
Polkadot Lane
Hebden Bridge HX7 8AH
Tel: 07789 077338
polkadotlane.co.uk

Jules China
Hebden Bridge HX7 8AQ
Tel: 01422 845714
juleschina.co.uk

Pot Stop
Hebden Bridge HX7 8ER
Tel: 01422 844543

Ribbon Circus
Hebden Bridge HX7 8AH
Tel: 01422 847803
ribboncircus.com

Spirals
Hebden Bridge HX7 6EU
Tel: 01422 847462
spiralsfairtrade.co.uk

Radiance Lighting
Hebden Bridge HX7 6AA
Tel: 01422 845764
radiancelighting.co.uk

Hebden Bridge Bookshop
Hebden Bridge HX7 8EL
Tel: 01422 843686
hbbooks.co.uk

Picture House & Trades Club
Hebden Bridge HX7 8EE
Tel: 01422 845 265
thetradesclub.com

Visitor and Canal Centre
Hebden Bridge HX7 8AF
Tel: 01422 843831

Hardcastle Crags
Tel: 01422 844518
nationaltrust.org.uk

Calderdale Festival
walkandridefestival.co.uk
The Ted Hughes Festival & Ted's House
Mytholmroyd HX7 5QN
theelmettrust.co.uk

Holme House B&B
Hebden Bridge HX7 8AD
Tel: 01422 847588
holmehousehebdenbridge.co.uk

Angeldale Guesthouse
Hebden Bridge HX7 7DD
Tel: 01422 847321
angeldale.co.uk

Croft Mill Apartment Hotel
Hebden Bridge HX7 8AB
Tel: 01422 846836
croftmill.com

Rambles B&B
Hedben Bridge HX7 7JP
Tel: 07921 500090
rambles.me.uk

Hebden Bridge Hostel
Hebden Bridge HX7 8DG
Tel: 01422843183
hebdenbridgehostel.co.uk

Mankinholes Youth Hostel
Todmorden OL14 6HR
Tel: 0845 371 9751
yha.org.uk

Hebden Bridge Camping
Hebden Bridge HX7 7HT
Tel: 01422 844334
hebdenbridgecamping.co.uk

Towngate Tea room
Heptonstall HX7 7LW
Tel: 07989 321931
towngatetearoom.vpweb.co.uk

The Stubbing Wharf
Hebden Bridge HX7 6LU
Tel: 01422 844107
stubbingwharf.com

The Packhorse Inn
Hebden Bridge HX7 7AT
Tel: 01422 842803
thepackhorse.org

Innovation Café
Bridge Mill
Hebden Bridge HX7 8ET

Greens Vegetarian Café
Hebden Bridge HX7 8AH
Tel: 01422 843587
greensvegetariancafe.co.uk

Organic House Café Bar
Hebden Bridge HX7 6AA
Tel: 01422 843429
organic-house.co.uk

Saker Bakery
Hebden Bridge HX7 6AA
Tel: 01706 818189

Pennine Provisions
Hebden Bridge HX7 8EH
Tel: 01422 844945

Station Café
Hebden Bridge HX7 6JE
Tel: 01422 844743

23. Tunnel Vision
Marsden Moor Estate
Huddersfield HD7 6DH
Tel: 01484 847016
nationaltrust.org.uk

Weirside B&B
Weirside HD7 6BU
Tel: 01484 840601
marsdenbedandbreakfast.com

The Shippon
Delph OL3 5RL
Tel: 01457 872357
the-shippon.co.uk

Titanic Spa
Linthwaite HD7 5UN
Tel: 01484 843544
titanicspa.com

Standedge Tunnel
Marsden HD7 6NQ
Tel: 01484 844298
standedge.co.uk

Mozzarellas
Marsden HD7 6BW
Tel: 01484 845511
mozzarellas.uk.com

Riverhead Brewery Tap
Marsden HD7 6BR
Tel: 01484 841270

A Month of Sundaes
Marsden HD7 6BR
Tel: 01484 845868
amonthofsundaes.com

The Olive Branch
Marsden HD7 6LU
Tel: 01484 844487
olivebranch.uk.com

The Railway Hotel
Marsden HD7 6AX
Tel: 0871 951 1000

Hey Green Country House
Marsden HD7 6NG
Tel: 01484 848000
heygreen.com

Shakespeare Inn
Marsden HD7 6BW
Tel: 01484 844818

Marsden Jazz Festival
marsdenjazzfestival.com

24. Bewitched
Clitheroe Castle Museum
Clitheroe BB7 1BA
Tel: 01200 424568

Cycle Adventure
cycle-adventure.co.uk
Off the Rails
offtherails.org.uk

Pedal Power Clitheroe
Clitheroe BB7 2HJ
Tel: 01200 422066
pedalpowerclitheroe.co.uk

The Inn at Whitewell
Clitheroe BB7 3AT
Tel: 01200 448222
innatwhitewell.com

Bashall Barn
Clitheroe BB7 3LQ
Tel: 01200 428964
bashallbarn.co.uk

The Bowland Beer Company
Clitheroe BB7 3LQ
Tel: 01200 443592
bowlandbrewery.com

Leagram Organic Dairy
Chipping PR3 2QT
Tel: 01995 61532

Waddington Arms
Clitheroe BB7 3HP
Tel: 01200 423262
waddingtonarms.co.uk

Clark House Farm
Chipping PR3 2GQ
Tel: 01995 61209
clarkhousefarm.com

King's House Youth Hostel
Slaidburn BB7 3ER
Tel: 0845 371 9343
yha.org.uk

Red Pump Inn
Clitheroe BB7 3DA
Tel: 01254 826227
theredpumpinn.co.uk

The Parkers Arms
Newton in Bowland
BB7 3DY
Tel: 01200 446236
parkersarms.co.uk

Cheesie Tchaikovsky
Clitheroe BB7 2BX
Tel: 01200 428366

D Byrne & Co.
Clitheroe BB7 2EP
Tel: 01200 423152
dbyrne-finewines.co.uk

Exchange Coffee Company
Clitheroe BB7 2DP
Tel: 01200 442270
caffeine-rush.co.uk

Mansell's Coffee Shop
Clitheroe BB7 2DQ
Tel: 01200 425129

Taste @ Clitheroe
Clitheroe BB7 2DQ
Tel: 01200 442006

Cowmans Famous Sausage Shop
Clitheroe BB7 2BT
Tel: 01200 423842
cowmans.co.uk

Harrison and Kerr
Clitheroe BB7 2EU
Tel: 01200 423253

Emporium
Clitheroe BB7 1BE
Tel: 01200 444 174
theemporiumclitheroe.co.uk

25. Watersmeet
Heritage Centre
New Mills SK22 3BN
Tel: 01663 746904
newmillsheritage.com

Torrs Hydro New Mills
New Mills SK22 4AA
Tel: 01663 898070
torrshydro.org

New Mills Golf Club
Shaw Marsh SK22 4QE
Tel: 01663 743485
newmillsgolfclub.co.uk

Twiggys B&B
New Mills SK22 3AR
Tel:01663 745036
twiggys-bandb.co.uk

The Waltzing Weasel Inn
Birch Vale SK22 1BT
Tel: 01663 743402
waltzingweasel.co.uk

The Beehive Inn
High Peak SK22 3EY
Tel: 01663 742 087

W. Potts and Son
New Mills SK22 3EL
Tel: 01663 744389

Llamedos Café
New Mills SK22 4AE
Tel: 01663 747770

Rosie's Tea & Coffee Room
Hayfield SK22 2HS
Tel: 01663 745597
rosiesinhayfield.com

26. A River Runs Through It
Lathkill Dale Campsite
Bakewell DE45 1JG
Tel: 07971 038702
lathkilldalecampsite.co.uk

Knotlow Farmhouse B&B
Flagg SK17 9QP
Tel: 01298 85313
knotlowfarm.co.uk

Mandale House
Bakewell DE45 1JF
Tel: 01629 812416
mandalehouse.co.uk

Sheldon's Luxury Retreat
Sheldon DE45 1QS
Tel: 01629 812180
sheldonsluxuryretreat.co.uk

Meadow Cottage
Youlgrave DE45 1UT
Tel: 01629 636523
meadowcottagebe-dandbreakfast.co.uk

Youlgrave Youth Hostel
Youlgrave DE45 1UR
Tel: 0845 371 9151
yha.org.uk

Castle Farm
Middleton DE45 1LS
Tel: 01629 636746
castlefarmmiddleton.co.uk

Haddon Grove Farm
Bakewell DE45 1JF
Tel: 01629 812343
haddongrovefarmcottages.co.uk

The Lathkil Hotel
Over Haddon DE45 1JE
Tel: 01629 812501
lathkil.co.uk

The Cock and Pullet
Sheldon DE45 1QS
Tel: 01629 814292

Bulls Head Inn
Monyash DE45 1JH
Tel: 01629 812372
thebullsheadmonyash.co.uk

The Bulls Head
Youlgrave DE45 1UR
01629 636307

The Old Smithy
Monyash DE45 1JH
Tel: 01629 810190
oldsmithymonyash.co.uk

Farmyard Inn
Youlgrave DE45 1UW
Tel: 01629 636221
farmyardinn.co.uk

Hollands Butchers
Youlgrave DE45 1WL
Tel: 01629 636234

Edge Close Farm Tea Rooms
Flagg SK17 9QT
Tel: 01298 85144
edgeclosefarmtearooms.net

Uncle Geoff's Diner
Over Haddon DE45 1JE
Tel: 01629 812555

Haddon House Stables
Over Haddon DE45 1HZ
Tel: 01629 813723
haddonhousestables.co.uk

27. Rest and Repose
Woodhall Spa Pool
Woodhall Spa LN10 6QH
Tel: 01526 352448
woodhallspa.org

Woodhall Spa Golf Club
Woodhall Spa LN10 6PU
Tel:01526 352511
woodhallspagolf.com

The Petwood Hotel
Woodhall Spa LN10 6QG
Tel:01526 352411
petwood.co.uk

Kinema in the Woods
Woodhall Spa LN10 6QD
Tel: 01526 352166
thekinemainthewoods.co.uk

Woodhall Spa Cottage Museum
Woodhall Spa LN10 6SH
Tel: 01526 353070
cottagemuseum.co.uk

Bardney Station
Lincoln LN3 5UF
Tel: 01526 397299
bardneyheritage.com

Rose Cottage B&B
Woodhall Spa LN10 6YW
Tel: 01526 354932
rosecottagebandb.net

Janet's Tearoom
Woodhall Spa LN10 6QL
Tel: 07910 4241571

The Book Fayre
Woodhall Spa LN10 6RW
Tel: 01526 354501

Woodhall Spa Bakery
Woodhall Spa LN10 6ST
Tel: 01526 352183

28. Hooked!
Normanton Church Museum
Rutland Water LE15 8RP
Tel: 01780 686800

Rutland Water Fly Fishers
rwff.org.uk

Rob Waddington
Rutland Fly Fishing & B&B
Tel: 01572 722422
rutlandwaterflyfishing.co.uk
thelodgebarnsdale.co.uk

Rutland Watersports Centre
Whitwell LE15 8BL
Tel: 01780 460154

Rutland Water Cruises
Wymondham LE14 2BA
Tel: 01572 787630
rutlandwatercruises.com

Lyndon Nature Reserve & Visitor Centre
Lyndon LE15 8TU
Tel: 01572 737378

Anglian Water Bird Watching
Egleton LE15 8BT
Tel: 01572 737378
rutlandwater.org.uk

Rutland Cycling
rutlandcycling.com

Rutland County Museum
Oakham LE15 6HP
Tel: 01572 758440

Oakham Castle
Oakham LE15 6DT
Tel: 01572 758440

Artdejardin
Wingwell LE15 8SE
Tel: 01572 737727
artdejardin.co.uk

Barnsdale Gardens
Exton LE15 8AH
Tel: 01572 813200
barnsdalegardens.co.uk

Number 17 Northgate B&B
Oakham LE15 6QR
Tel: 01572 759271
17northgate.co.uk

Broccoli Bottom B&B
Manton LE15 8SZ
Tel: 07702 437102
broccolibottom-rutland.co.uk

Lyndon Top Campsite
Rutland Water LE15 8RN
Tel: 01539 431222

Hambleton Bakery
Exton LE15 8AN
Tel: 01572 812995
hambletonbakery.co.uk

Wing Hall
Wing LE15 8RY
Tel: 01572 737090
winghall.co.uk

Rutland Caravanning and Camping Park
Oakham LE15 7NX
Tel: 01572 813520

Hambleton Hall
Hambleton LE15 8TH
Tel: 01572 756991
hambletonhall.com

Barnsdale Lodge
Exton LE15 8AH
Tel: 01572 724678
barnsdalelodge.co.uk

Barnsdale Hall
Oakham LE15 8AB
Tel: 01572 757901
barnsdalehotel.co.uk

Rutland County Golf Club
Great Casterton PE9 4AQ
Tel: 01780 460330
rutlandcountygolf.co.uk

Normanton Park Hotel
Rutland Water LE15 8RP
Tel:01780 720315
normantonpark.co.uk

Olive Branch Pub
Clipsham LE15 7SH
Tel: 01780 410355
theolivebranchpub.com

Lake Isle Hotel
Uppingham LE15 9PZ
Tel: 01572 822951
lakeisle.co.uk

Blue Ball Inn
Braunston LE15 8QS
Tel: 01572 722135
theblueballbraunston.co.uk

King's Arms Inn
Wing LE15 8SE
Tel: 01572 737634
thekingsarms-wing.co.uk

The Crown Inn
Uppingham LE15 9PY
Tel: 01572 822 302
thecrownrutland.co.uk

The Finch's Arms
Hambleton LE15 8TL
Tel: 01572 756575
finchsarms.co.uk

The Castle Cottage Café
Oakham LE15 6DT
Tel: 01572 757 952
castlecottagecafe.co.uk

29. Along for the Ride
Shropshire Steamboat
Ellesmere SY12 0PA
Tel: 01691 623126

The Boat Inn
Erbistock LL13 0DL
Tel: 01978 780666
boatondee.com

The Garden House
Erbistock LL13 0DL
Tel: 01978 781149
simonwingett.com

Cross Foxes
Erbistock LL13 0DR
Tel: 01978 780380
crossfoxes-erbistock.co.uk

Bangor On Dee Racecourse
Wrexham LL13 0DA
Tel: 01978 782323
bangorondeeraces.co.uk

Mereside Farm B&B
Mereside SY12 0PA
Tel: 01691 622404
meresidefarm.co.uk

The Grange B&B
Ellesmere SY12 9DE
Tel: 01691 623495
thegrange.uk.com

Teal Cottage
Ellesmere SY12 0EU
Tel: 01691 622782

Yew Tree House B&B
Lower Frankton SY11 4PB
Tel: 01691 622126
yewtreebandb.co.uk

The Garden House B&B
Erbistock LL13 0DL
Tel: 01978 781149
simonwingett.com

Stableyard Hotel
Bangor-on-Dee
Tel: 01978 780642
stableyard.co.uk

The Boathouse Restaurant
Ellesmere SY12 0PA
Tel: 01691 623852

Corner House Café
Ellesmere SY12 0EP
Tel: 01691 263478

Talgarth Tearooms
Ellesmere SY12 0DG
Tel: 01691 624440
talgarthtearooms.co.uk

The White Hart Inn
Ellesmere SY12 0ET
Tel: 01691 622333

La Belle Vie
Ellesmere SY12 0EP
Tel: 01691 624835
labellevie-ellesmere.co.uk

Coco Coffee Bar
Ellesmere SY12 0ED
Tel: 07976 822658

The Black Lion Hotel
Ellesmere SY12 0EG
Tel: 01691 622418
theblacklionhotel.co.uk

The White Horse Inn
Overton LL13 0DT
Tel: 01978 710111
thewhitehorseoverton.co.uk

Woodlands of Erbistock
Eyton LL13 0SP
Tel: 01978 781048
woodlands-ice-cream.co.uk

Buck House Hotel
Bangor-on-Dee LL13 0BU
Tel: 01978 780336
buckhousehotel.co.uk

30. Deep Purple
Shropshire Walks
shropshirewalking.co.uk

Long Mynd Bridleways
longmyndbridleways.com

Plush Hill Cycles
Church Stretton SY6 6DA
Tel: 01694 720133
plushhillcycles.co.uk

Church Stretton Golf Club
Church Stretton SY6 6JH
Tel: 01694 722281
churchstrettongolfclub.co.uk

Mary Webb Society
marywebbsociety.co.uk

Bog Visitor Centre
Stiperstones SY5 0NG
Tel: 01743 792484
bogcentre.co.uk

Visitor Information Centre
Church Stretton SY6 6EY
Tel: 01694 723133

Shropshire Hills Shuttle Bus
shropshirehillsaonb.co.uk

Midland Gliding Club
Tel: 01588 650206
longmynd.com

Stable Cottage
Church Stretton SY6 6PX

Brow Farm Campsite
Ratlinghope SY5 0SR
Tel: 01588 650641
browfarmcampsite.co.uk

Small Batch Campsite
Small Batch SY6 6PW
Tel: 01694 723358
smallbatch-camping.co.uk

Long Mynd Hotel
Church Stretton SY6 6AG
Tel: 01694 722244
longmynd.co.uk

Belvedere Guest House
Church Stretton SY6 6DP
Tel: 01694 722232
belvedereguesthouse.co.uk

Highlands B&B
Church Stretton SY6 7AF
Tel: 01694 723737
highlandsbandb.co.uk

Jinlye B&B
Castle Hill SY6 6JP
Tel : 01694 723243
jinlye.co.uk

Mynd House B&B
Ludlow Road SY6 6RB
Tel: 01694 722212
myndhouse.com

Victoria House B&B
Church Stretton SY6 6BX
Tel: 01694 723823
bedandbreakfast-shropshire.co.uk

Lawley House B&B
Smethcott SY6 6NX
Tel: 01694 751236
lawleyhouse.co.uk

All Stretton Bunkhouse
Meadow Green SY6 6JW
Tel: 01694 722593
allstrettonbunkhouse.co.uk

Bridges Youth Hostel
Ratlinghope SY5 0SP
Tel: 01588 650656
yha.org.uk

The Buck's Head
Church Stretton SY6 6BX
Tel: 01694 722898
the-bucks-head.co.uk

Stiperstones Inn
Stiperstones SY5 0LZ
Tel: 01743 791327
stiperstonesinn.co.uk

The Crown Inn
Wentnor SY9 5EE
Tel: 01588 650613

The Ragleth Inn
Little Stretton SY6 6RB
Tel: 01694 722711
theraglethinn.co.uk

The Green Dragon Inn
Little Stretton SY6 6RE
Tel: 01694 722925

The Studio Restaurant
Church Stretton SY6 6BY
Tel: 01694 722672
thestudiorestaurant.net

Van Doesburg's Deli
Church Stretton SY6 6BU
Tel: 01694 722867
vandoesburgs.co.uk

Berry's Coffee House
Church Stretton SY6 6BU
Tel: 01694 724452
berryscoffeehouse.co.uk

Acorn Wholefood Cafe
Church Stretton SY6 6BW
Tel: 01694 722495
wholefoodcafe.co.uk

Mr Bun the Baker
Church Stretton SY6 6BW
Tel: 01694 723018

Entertaining Elephants
Church Stretton SY6 6BX
Tel: 01694 723922

Stretton Antiques Market
Church Stretton SY6 6BH
Tel: 01694 723718

Chalet Pavilion Tearoom
Church Stretton SY6 6JG
Tel: 01694 723068

31. After Apple Picking
Mortimers Cross Water Mill
Near Leominster HR6 9PE
english-heritage.org.uk

Croft Castle
Croft HR6 9PW
Tel: 01568 780246
nationaltrust.org.uk

Brook Farm Cider
Wigmore HR6 9UJ
Tel: 01568 770562
brookfarmcider.co.uk

Dunkerton's Cider Company
Pembridge HR6 9ED
Tel: 01544 388653
dunkertons.co.uk

The Old Rectory
Pembridge HR6 9EU
Tel: 01544 387968
theoldrectorypembridge.co.uk

Lowe Farm B&B
Pembridge HR6 9JD
Tel: 01544 388395
bedandbreakfastlowefarm.co.uk

Townsend Farm
Pembridge HR6 9HB
Tel: 01544 388527
townsend-farm.co.uk

Pear Tree Farm
Wigmore HR6 9UR
Tel: 01568 770140
peartree-farm.co.uk

The Old House B&B
Kingsland HR6 9QS
Tel: 01568 709120
teacosy.nl

The Riverside Inn
Leominster HR6 9ST
Tel: 01568 708440
theriversideinn.org

Westonbury Mill
Kington HR6 9HZ
Tel: 01544 388650
westonburymillwatergardens.com

Sally's Pantry
Pembridge
Tel: 01544 388187

The Garden Tea Rooms
Stoneleigh HR6 9QS
Tel: 01568 709142

The Kings House Inn
Pembridge HR6 9HB
Tel: 01544 388029
kingshouseinn.co.uk
Eardisland Community Shop
Eardisland HR6 9BN
Tel: 01544 388984

Mortimer Country Stores
Wigmore HR6 9UJ
Tel: 01568 770307

Wigmore Castle
Wigmore HR6
Tel: 0870 333 1181
english-heritage.org.uk

32. Avon Calling
Pershore Abbey
Pershore WR10 1DT
Tel: 01386 552071
pershoreabbey.org.uk

Swan Inn
Birlingham WR10 3AQ
Tel: 01386 750485
theswaninn.co.uk

Rye Cottage B&B
Elmley Castle
WR10 3JF
Tel: 01386 710838

Pensham Fields B&B
Pensham WR10 3HE
Tel: 01386 552004
penshamfields.co.uk

Harrowfields B&B
Eckington WR10 3BA
Tel: 01386 751053
harrowfields.co.uk

Myrtle Cottage
Eckington WR10 3AS
Tel: 01386 750893
myrtle-cottage.com

Eckington Manor
Pershore WR10 3BH
Tel: 01386 751600
eckingtonmanorcookeryschool.co.uk

The Barn B&B
Pensham WR10 3HA
Tel: 01386 555270
pensham-barn.co.uk

Defford Arms
Defford WR8 9BD
Tel: 01386 750378

Quintessence Deli
Pershore WR10 1DU
Tel: 01386 553689

Belle House Restaurant
Pershore WR10 1AJ
Tel: 01386 555 055
belle-house.co.uk

Revills Farm Shop
Defford WR8 9BS
Tel: 01386 750466
revillsfarmshop.co.uk

Pershore Plum Fayre
pershoreplumfestival.org.uk

The Plant Centre
Pershore WR10 3JP
Tel: 01386 551149
warwickshire.ac.uk

33. Fentastic!
Burwell Museum
Burwell CB25 0HL
Tel: 01638 605544
burwellmuseum.org.uk

Wicken Fen
Ely CB7 5XP
Tel: 01353 720274
nationaltrust.org.uk

Wicken Fen Vision
wicken.org.uk

Anglesey Abbey
Cambridge CB25 9EJ
Tel: 01223 810080
nationaltrust.org.uk

Fen Paddle Company
fenpaddle.co.uk

Dragonfly Cottage
Wicken CB7 5XP
Tel: 01353 727054
dragonflycottage.co.uk

Meadow View Campsite
Wicken CB7 5XH
Tel: 077652 48267

The Old Vicarage
Isleham CB7 5RX
Tel: 01638 780095
old-vicarage-isleham.com

The Meadow House B&B
Burwell CB25 0HB
Tel: 01638 741926
themeadowhouse.co.uk

Chestnut House
Burwell CB25 0HB
Tel: 01638 742996

By Jove! Tearoom
Burwell CB25 0HD
Tel: 01638 602086
byjovetearooms.co.uk

Five Bells Pub
Burwell CB5 0HD
Tel: 01638 741404

The Fox
Burwell CB25 0BA
Tel: 01638 741267
thefoxburwell.co.uk

Five Miles from Anywhere
No Hurry Inn
Wicken CB7 5YQ
Tel: 01353 721654
fivemilesinn.com

Dyke's End Pub
Reach CB25 0JD
Tel: 01638 743816
dykesend.co.uk

Maid's Head
Wicken CB7 5XR
Tel: 01353 720727
maidsheadwicken.com

34. Broadly Speaking
Damselfly Boat
Tel: 01603 270479

Broads Authority
Norwich NR3 1UB
Tel: 01603 610734
broads-authority.gov.uk

Old Hall Farm
South Walsham NR13 6DS
Tel: 01502 730414
oldhallfarm.co.uk

Oak Farm B&B
South Walsham NR13 6DD
Tel: 07920884505

Leeward B&B
South Walsham NR13 6EE
Tel: 01603 270491
leewardbedandbreakfast.co.uk

Fairhaven Gardens
South Walsham NR13 6DZ
Tel: 01603 270449
fairhavengarden.co.uk

Granary Stores
Farm Lane NR13 6HY
Tel: 01603 270432

The Ship
South Walsham NR13 6DQ
Tel: 01603 270049
theshipsouthwalsham.co.uk

Kings Arms Pub
Walsham NR13 6DY
Tel: 01603 270039
broadlandchinese.com

The Maltsters Pub
Ranworth NR13 6AB
Tel: 01603 270900
themaltsters.com

The Fur and Feather Inn
Woodbastwick NR13 6HQ
Tel: 01603 720003
thefurandfeatherinn.co.uk

Woodforde's Brewery
Woodbastwick NR13 6SW
Tel: 01603 720353
woodfordes.co.uk

Salhouse Broad
Salhouse NR13 6HE
Tel: 01603 722775
salhousebroad.org.uk

Norfolk Wherry Trust
wherryalbion.com
Wherry Yacht Charter
wherryyachtcharter.org

35. Dyed in the Wool
Clare Castle Country Park
Clare CO10 8NW
Tel: 01787 277491

Clare Priory
Clare CO10 8NX
Tel: 01787 277326
clarepriory.org.uk

Clare Ancient House
Clare CO10 8NY
Tel: 01787 277572
clare-ancient-house-museum.co.uk

The Guildhall
Lavenham CO10 9QZ
Tel: 01787 247646
nationaltrust.org.uk

Little Hall
Lavenham CO10 9QZ
Tel: 01787 247019
littlehall.org.uk

Lavenham Pharmacy
Lavenham CO10 9PX
Tel: 01787 247284

The Wildlife Art Gallery
Lavenham CO10 9PZ
Tel: 01787 248562
wildlifeartgallery.com

Ship Stores B&B
Clare CO10 8PX
Tel: 01787 277834
ship-stores.co.uk

Cobbles B&B
Clare CO10 8NP
Tel: 01787 277539
cobblesclare.co.uk

The Grain House
Halstead CO9 4AH
Tel: 01440 785552
thegrainhouse.co.uk

School Barn Farm
Sudbury CO10 7JN
Tel: 01787 282556
schoolbarnfarm.co.uk

The Swan Hotel
Lavenham CO10 9QA
Tel:01787 247477
theswanatlavenham.co.uk

Lavenham Priory B&B
Lavenham CO10 9RW
Tel: 01787 247404
lavenhampriory.co.uk

Number One Deli & Café
Clare CO10 8NY
Tel: 01787 278932
numberonedeli.co.uk

Café Clare
Clare CO10 8NH
Tel: 01787 278148
cafeclare.co.uk

Cavendish Tea Room
Cavendish CO10 8AS
Tel: 01787 259000
cavendishtearoom.co.uk

The George
Cavendish CO10 8BA
Tel: 01787 280248
thecavendishgeorge.co.uk

Great House
Lavenham CO10 9QZ
Tel: 01787 247431
greathouse.co.uk

Sweetmeats Tea Room
Lavenham CO10 9RW
Tel: 01787 248442
goodfoodarmy.co.uk

The Greyhound Pub
Lavenham CO10 9PZ
Tel: 01787 247475
thegreyhound-lavenham.com

36. 'Not on one strand are all life's jewels strung ...'
Buscot Park
Faringdon SN7 8BU
Tel:0845 345 3387
nationaltrust.org.uk

Coleshill Village Tea Shop
Swindon SN6 7PT
Tel: 01793 763619

Kelmscott Manor
Kelmscott GL7 3HJ
Tel: 01367 253348
kelmscottmanor.co.uk

Buscot Manor B&B
Buscot SN7 8DA
Tel: 01367 252225
buscotmanor.co.uk

The Trout Inn
Lechlade GL7 3HA
Tel: 01367 252313
thetroutinn.com

The Swan Hotel
Radcot-on-Thames
OX18 2SX
Tel: 01367 810220
swanhotelradcot.co.uk

The Plough Inn
Wheatley OX33 1JH
Tel: 01865 874159
ploughkelmscott.com

The Riverside
Lechlade GL7 3AQ
Tel: 01367 252229
riverside-lechlade.com

Colleys Lechlade
Lechlade GL7 3AE
Tel: 01367 252218
colleyslechlade.co.uk

The Crown Inn
Lechlade GL7 3AE
Tel: 01367 252198
crownlechlade.co.uk

The Trout at Tadpole Bridge
Buckland Marsh SN7 8RF
Tel: 01367 870382
trout-inn.co.uk

Cotswolds Boat Hire
Lechlade GL7 3HA
Tel: 01793 727083
cotswoldboat.co.uk

Cotswold Canoes
Lechlade GL7 3AQ
Tel: 07900 154 098

37. Standing on Ceremony
Alexander Keiller Museum
Avebury SN8 1RF
Tel: 01672 539250
nationaltrust.org.uk
english-heritage.org.uk

Avebury Manor
Avebury SN8 1RF
Tel: 01672 539250
nationaltrust.org.uk

The Lodge
Avebury SN8 1RQ
Tel: 01672 539023
averburylodge.co.uk

Isobel Cottage
Fishlock's Cottage
nationaltrustcottages.co.uk

The Old Forge B&B
East Kennet SN8 4 EY
Tel: 01672 861686
theoldforge-avebury.co.uk

Circle Restaurant
Avebury SN8 1RF
Tel: 01672 539514
nationaltrust.org.uk

Divine Café
Cherhill SN11 8UU
Tel: 01249 815979
divinecafe.biz

Goddard Arms & YHA
Clyffe Pypard SN4 7PY
Tel: 01793 731386
yha.org.uk

New Inn
Avebury SN4 9NW
Tel: 01672 539240
thenewinn.net

38. The Hills Are Alive
Music at Woodhouse
Holmbury St Mary
RH5 6NL
Tel: 01306 730956
woodhousesounds.com

Pedal and Spoke
Peaslake GU5 9RR
Tel: 01306 731639
pedalandspoke.co.uk

Peaslake School
Colmans Hill GU5 9ST
Tel: 01306 730411
peaslakeschool.com

Taste of Surrey
Peaslake GU5 9RG
Tel: 01306 730991
tasteofsurrey.com

The Hannah Peschar
Sculpture Garden
Ockley RH5 5QR
Tel: 01306 627 269
hannahpescharsculpture.
com

Holmbury St Mary YHA
Dorking RH5 6NW
Tel: 0845 371 9323
yha.org.uk

Henman Basecamp
Tel: 01306 712711
nationaltrust.org.uk

Tumblers B&B
Forest Green RH5 5SG
Tel: 01306 621411
tumblersforestgreen.co.uk

Hurtwood Park Polo Club
Ewhurst GU6 7SW
Tel: 01483 272828
hurtwoodparkpolo.co.uk

Gatton Manor
Ockley RH5 5PQ
Tel: 01306 627555
gattonmanor.co.uk

The Inn on the Green
Ockley RH5 5TD
Tel: 01306 711032
thegreenrooms.com

The Scarlett Arms
Walliswood RH5 5RD
Tel: 01306 627243
scarlettarms.com

The Kings Head
Holmbury St Mary RH5 6NP
Tel: 01306 730282
kingsheadholmbury.co.uk

The Royal Oak
Holmbury St Mary RH5 6PF
Tel: 01306 730120

Butchers Hall
Forest Green RH5 5RZ
Tel: 01306 621188
thebutchershall.co.uk

The Parrot Inn
Shalford GU4 8DW
Tel: 01483 561400
parrotinn.co.uk

Village Stores
Peaslake GU5 9RL
Tel: 01306 730474
peaslakevillagestores.com

Leith Hill & The Servery
RH5 6LY
Tel:01306 712711
nationaltrust.org.uk

39. Blooming Marvellous
Tenterden Folk Festival
tenterdenfolkfestival.org.uk

Colonel Stephens Museum
Tenterden TN30 6HE
Tel: 01580 765155
hfstephens-museum.org.uk

Bodiam Castle
Robertsbridge TN32 5UA
Tel: 01580 830196
nationaltrust.org.uk

Great Dixter
Rye TN31 6PH
Tel: 01797 252878
greatdixter.co.uk

Bodiam Ferry Co.
Newenden TN18 5PP
Tel: 01797 253838
bodiam-ferry.co.uk

Kent Motorhome Rental
Sittingbourne ME10 3DN
Tel: 01795 519492
kentmotorhomerental.co.uk

The White Hart
Godalming GU8 5PH
Tel: 01428 683695

Spring Farm B&B
Northlands TN32 5UX
Tel: 01580 831222
bedandbreakfastbodiam.co.uk

Wellington House B&B
Northiam TN31 6LB
Tel: 01797 253449
wellingtonhousebandb.co.uk

The Tower House B&B
Tenterden TN30 6LL
Tel: 01580 761920
tower-house.biz

The Curlew Restaurant
Bodiam TN32 5UY
Tel: 01580 861394
thecurlewrestaurant.co.uk

Biddenden Vineyard
Biddenden TN27 8DF
Tel: 01580 291726
biddendenvineyards.com

Sedlescombe Organic
Vineyard
Sedlescombe TN32 5SA
Tel: 01580 830715
englishorganicwine.co.uk

Chapel Down Vinery
Tenterden TN30 7NG
Tel: 01580 763033
chapeldown.com

The Nutmeg Delicatessen
Tenterden TN30 6BW
Tel: 01580 764125

40. Friends and Lovers
Charleston House
Lewes BN8 6LL
Tel: 01323 811265
charleston.org.uk

Firle Place
Lewes BN8 6LP
Tel: 01273 858307
firle.com

Monk's House
Lewes BN7 3HF
Tel:01323 870001
nationaltrust.org.uk

The Ram Inn
Firle BN8 6NS
Tel: 01273 858222
raminn.co.uk

Dairy Farmhouse B&B
Firle BN8 6NB
Tel: 01273 858280
dairyfarmbandb.co.uk

Netherwood Lodge B&B
Chiddingly BN8 6HS
Tel: 01825 872512
netherwoodlodge.co.uk

Deep Thatch Cottage
Rodmell BN7 3HF
Tel: 01273 477086
deepthatchcottage.co.uk

Robin Hill Studio B&B
Rodmell BN7 3HS
Tel: 01273 476715

Sunnyside Cottages B&B
Rodmell BN7 3HA
Tel: 01273 476876

Middle Farm
Firle BN8 6LJ
Tel: 01323 811411
middlefarm.com

The Cricketers Arms
Berwick Village BN26 6SP
Tel: 01323 870469
cricketersberwick.co.uk

The Abergavenny Arms
Rodmell BN7 3HE
Tel: 01273 472416
abergavennyarms.com

41.Down Time
Nutbourne Vineyard
Pulborough RH20 2HH
Tel: 01798 815196
nutbournevineyards.com

Parham House and Gardens
Parham RH20 4HS
Tel: 01903 742021
parhaminsussex.co.uk

White Horse Hotel
Pulborough RH20 4DJ
Tel: 01903 745831
whitehorsestorrington.com

Our Lady of England Priory
Storrington RH20 4LN
Tel: 01903 742150
norbertines.co.uk

Amberley Village Pottery
Amberley BN18 9ND
Telephone: 01798 831876
amberleypottery.co.uk

Amberley Museum
Amberley BN18 9LT
Tel: 01798 831370
amberleymuseum.co.uk

Arun Valley Line
arunrail.com

South Downs Bikes Ltd
Storrington RH20 4EE
Tel: 01903 745534
southdownsbikes.com

The Sportsman Inn
Amberley BN18 9NR
Tel: 01798 831787
thesportsmaninn.org.uk

Amberley Castle Hotel
Amberley BN18 9LT
Tel: 01798 831992
amberleycastle.co.uk

The Thatched House B&B
Amberley BN18 9NQ
Tel: 01798 831329
thatchedhouseamberley.
co.uk

Gumber Bothy
Slindon BN18 0RN
Tel: 01243 814484
nationaltrust.org.uk

Black Horse
Amberley BN18 9NL
Tel: 01798 831700

The Bridge Inn
Amberley BN18 9LR
Tel: 01798 831619
bridgeinnamberley.com

Amberley Village Tearoom
Amberley BN18 9SR
Tel: 01798 839196
amberleyvillagetearoom.
co.uk

Vintage Rose Book Shop
Pulborough RH20 4NA
Tel: 01903 744100

42. Our Daily Bread
Long Crichel Bakery
Wimborne BH21 5JU
Tel: 01258 830852
longcrichelbakery.co.uk

Hare Lane Pottery
Cranborne BH21 5QT
Tel: 01725 517700
jonathangarratt.com

La Fosse
Cranborne BH21 5PR
Tel: 01725 517604
la-fosse.com

Cranborne Estate
Cranborne BH21 5PS
Tel: 01725 517289
cranborne.co.uk

The Drovers Inn
Wimbourne BH21 5ET
Tel: 01258 840084
drovers-inn.co.uk

Sheaf of Arrows
Wimborne BH21 5PR
Tel: 01725 517456
sheafofarrows.co.uk

The Compasses Inn
Tisbury SP3 6NB
Tel:01722 714318
thecompassesinn.com

43. Enchantment
The Dartmoor Hill Pony
Association
Tel: 07734 785644
dartmoorhillpony.com.

Stone Lane Gardens
Chagford TQ13 8JU
Tel: 01647 231311
stonelanegardens.com

Sandy Park Inn
Chagford TQ13 8JW
Tel: 01647 433267
sandyparkinn.co.uk

James Bowden and Son
Chagford TQ13 8AH
Tel: 01647 433271

Webber and Son
Chagford TQ13 8AQ
Tel: 01647 432 213

Proper Job
Chagford TQ13 8DR
Tel: 01647 432985
proper-job.typepad.com

Chagford Swimming Pool
Chagford TQ13 8DA
Tel: 01647 432929

Cyprian's Cot B&B
Chagford TQ13 8BB
Tel: 01647 432256
cyprianscot.co.uk

Farleigh Cottage B&B
Chagford TQ13 8AZ
Tel: 01647 432600
farleighcottage.co.uk

Heather Cottage B&B
Chagford TQ13 8EX
Tel: 07734 915626
thegreatdevonescape.co.uk

Boldventure
Chagford TQ13 8EX
Tel: 01647 433664
boldventuresouth.co.uk

Easton Court
Chagford TQ13 8JL
Tel: 01647 433654
easton.co.uk

Gildleigh Park Hotel
Gidleigh Park TQ13 8HH
Tel: 01647 432367
gidleigh.com

The Globe Inn
Chagford TQ13 8AJ
Tel: 01647 433485
theglobeinnchagford.co.uk

22 Mill Street
Chagford TQ13 8AW
Tel: 01647 432244
22millst.com

Mill End Hotel
Chagford TQ13 8JN
Tel: 01647 432282
millendhotel.com

The New Forge Café
Chagford TQ13 8AB
Tel: 01647 433226
thenewforge.co.uk

Blacks Delicatessen
Chagford TQ13 8AB
Tel: 01647 433545
blacks-deli.com

Thomas of Chagford
Chagford TQ13 8AA
Tel: 01647 433199

Best Cellars Ltd
Chagford TQ13 8AH
Tel: 01647 432262
bestcellars.co.uk

Courtyard Café and Whole-food Shop
Chagford TQ13 8AE
Tel: 01647 432 571

44. On the Right Track
Dartmoor Railway
Okehampton EX20 1EJ
Tel: 01837 55164
dartmoor-railway.co.uk

Okehampton Youth Hostel
Okehampton EX20 1EW
Tel: 01837 53916
adventureokehampton.com
yha.org.uk

Museum of Dartmoor Life
Okehampton EX20 1HQ
Tel: 01837 52295
museumofdartmoorlife.eclipse.co.uk

Okehampton Castle
Okehampton EX20 1JA
Tel: 01837 52844
english-heritage.org.uk

Lydford Caravan Park
Lydford EX20 4BE
Tel: 01822 820497
lydfordsite.co.uk

Betty Cottles Inn
Okehampton EX20 4LR
Tel: 01837 55339
bettycottles.co.uk

Dartmoor Inn
Lydford EX20 4AY
Tel: 01822 820221
dartmoorinn.com

The Victorian Pantry
Okehampton EX20 1HQ
Tel: 01837 53988

45. Quay to Quay
Cotehele & Edgcumbe Arms
St Dominik PL12 6TA
Tel: 01579 351346
nationaltrust.org.uk

Limekiln Gallery
Callington PL18 9QT
Tel: 01822 834654
limekilngallery.com

Calstock Regatta
calstockrowingclub.co.uk

Morwellham Quay
Tavistock PL19 8JL
Tel: 01822 832766
morwellham-quay.co.uk

Higher Chapel Farm B&B
Halton Quay PL12 6SL
Tel: 01579 350894
higherchapel.co.uk

Willow Cottage B&B
Calstock
Tel: 01822 832291

Hall Court
Cotehele PL12 6TA
nationaltrustcottages.co.uk

The Old Rectory
Tavistock PL19 8JA
Tel: 01822 832927
tamarvalleycamping.co.uk

Who'd Have Thought It
St Dominik PL12 6TG
Tel: 01579 350214
whodhavethoughtitinn.co.uk

Calstock Gallery Bar
Calstock PL18 9QX
Tel: 01822 833183
calstockarts.org

Tamar Inn
Calstock PL18 9QA
Tel: 01822 832487
tamarinn.co.uk

The Rising Sun Inn
Gunnislake PL18 9BX
Tel: 01822 832201
rising-sun-inn.co.uk

The Rifle Volunteer
Gunnislake PL18 9HL
Tel: 01822 833038

Canoe Tamar
Tel: 01822 833409
canoetamar.co.uk

Calstock Ferry
Calstock PL18 9QE
Tel: 01822 833331
calstockferry.co.uk

46. On the Slate
Kate Roberts Centre
Rhosgadfan LL54 7EY
Tel: 01286 831715
caergors.org

National Slate Museum
Llanberis LL55 4TY
Tel: 01286 870630
museumwales.ac.uk

Electric Mountain
Llanberis LL55 4UR
Tel: 01286 870636
fhc.co.uk

Snowdonia Mountain Railway
Llanberis LL55 4TY
Tel: 0844 493 8120
snowdonrailway.co.uk

Llanberis Lake Railway
Llanberis LL55 4TY
Tel: 01286 870549
lake-railway.co.uk

Silver Birches Campsite
Betws Garmon LL54 7YR
Tel: 01286 650707
silver-birches.org.uk

Hafod Y Llan
Beddgelert LL55 4NQ
Tel: 01766 510129
nationaltrust.org.uk
Snowdon Ranger Hostel
Rhyd Ddu LL54 7YS
Tel: 0845 371 9659
yha.org.uk

Jesse James Bunkhouse
Penisarwaun LL55 3DA
Tel: 01286 870521
jessejamesbunkhouse.co.uk

Betws Inn
Betws Garmon LL54 7YY
Tel: 01286 650324
betws-inn.co.uk

Glyn Peris Guest House
Llanberis LL55 4EL
Tel: 01286 872711
glynperisguesthouse.com

Rhiwafallen Restaurant
Llandwrog LL54 5SW
Tel: 01286 830172
rhiwafallen.co.uk

Sygun Fawr Country House
Beddgelert LL55 4NE
Tel: 01766 890258
wsygunfawr.co.uk

Plas Dinas Country House
Bontnewydd LL54 7YF
Tel: 01286 830214
plasdinas.co.uk

The Halfway Inn
Talysarn LL54 6HG
Tel:01286 880433

Ty Mawr B&B
Rhyd Ddu LL54 6TL
Tel: 01766 890837
snowdonaccommodation.co.uk

Café Brynrefail
Brynrefail LL55 3NR
Tel: 01286 685500
caban-cyf.org

Pete's Eats
Llanberis LL55 4EU
Tel: 01286 870117
petes-eats.co.uk

47. Something about Mary
Palé Hall
Llandderfel LL23 7PS
Tel: 01678 530285
palehall.co.uk

Glan y Gro B&B
Bala LL23 7BT
Tel: 01678 521009
glan-y-gro.co.uk

Bala Backpackers
Bala LL23 7EL
Tel: 01678 521700
bala-backpackers.co.uk

Riverside House
Abergynolwyn LL36 9YR
Tel: 01654 782235
riverside-wales.co.uk

The Old Rectory B&B
Tal-y-Llyn LL36 9AJ
Tel: 01654 782225
rectoryonthelake.co.uk

Dolgamedd Caravan Park
Dolgamedd LL40 2DG
Tel: 01341 450221

Cross Foxes Hotel
Brithdir LL40 2SG
Tel: 01341 421001
crossfoxes.co.uk

Pen y Bont
Bala LL23 7PH
Tel: 01678 520549
penybont-bala.co.uk

Railway Inn
Abergynolwyn LL36 9YW
Tel: 01654 782279

Y Badell Aur
Bala LL23 7AF
Tel: 01678 520310

48. Gaslight
Han Made
7 Kings Road
Llandovery SA20 0AW

Dolgoch Bunkhouse
Tregaron SY25 6NR
Tel: 01974 298 680
elenydd-hostels.co.uk

Rhandirmwyn
Rhandirmwyn SA20 0NT
Tel: 01550 760257
campingandcaravanningclub.co.uk

The New White Lion Hotel
Llandovery SA20 0BZ
Tel: 01550 720685
newwhitelion.co.uk

Llanerchindda Farm
Cynghordy SA20 0NB
Tel: 01550 750274
cambrianway.com

Just So Scrumptious
Llandovery SA20 0AW
Tel: 01550 720824
justsoscrumptious.co.uk

The Royal Oak Inn
Rhandirmwyn SA20 0NY
Tel: 01550 760201
theroyaloakinn.co.uk

Neuadd Fawr Arms
Llandovery SA20 0ST
Tel: 01550 721644

The Towy Bridge Inn
Rhandirmwyn SA20 0PE
Tel: 01550 760370

The Brunant Arms
Caio SA19 8RD
Tel: 01558 650483

49. Top Table
Crickhowell Walking Festival
crickhowellfestival.com

Red Lion
Llanbedr NP8 1SR
Tel: 01873 810754

Book-ish
Crickhowell NP8 1BD
Tel: 01873 811256
book-ish.co.uk

White Hart Inn
Talybont-on-Usk LD3 7JD
Tel: 01874 676227
breconbunkhouse.co.uk

Traveller's Rest
Talybont-on-Usk LD3 7YP
Tel: 01874 676233
travellersrestinn.com

The Star Inn
Talybont-on-Usk LD3 7YX
Tel: 01874 676635
starinntalybont.co.uk

Danywenalt Youth Hostel
Talybont-on-Usk LD3 7YS
Tel: 0845 371 9548
yha.org.uk

Talybont Farm & Campsite
Brecon LD3 7LX
Tel: 01874 665451
pencelli-castle.com

Llandetty Hall Farm
Talybont LD3 7YR
Tel: 01874 676415

Ty Gwyn B&B
Crickhowell NP8 1DG
Tel: 01873 811625
tygwyn.com

Cambrian Cruisers
Ty Newydd LD3 7LJ
Tel: 01874 665315
cambriancruisers.co.uk

Talybont Stores
Talybont-on-Usk LD3 7YJ
Tel: 01874 676663
talybontstores.co.uk

No. 18 Brasserie
Crickhowell NP8 1BD
Tel: 01873 810337
black-mountain.com

Court Room Café
Crickhowell NP8 1BD
Tel: 01873 812497

Nantyffin Cider Mill Inn
Crickhowell NP8 1SG
Tel: 01873 810775
cidermill.co.uk

Bear Hotel
Crickhowell NP8 1BW
Tel: 01873 810408
bearhotel.co.uk

Dragon Inn
Crickhowell NP8 1BE
Tel: 01873 810362
dragoncrickhowell.co.uk

Bridge End Inn
Powys NP8 1AR
Tel: 01873 810338
thebridgeendinn.com

The Horseshoe Inn
Llangattock NP8 1PA
Tel: 01873 810393

Coach and Horses
Llangynidr NP8 1LS
Tel: 01874 730245
coachandhorses.org

50. Black Mountain Red Kite
Carreg Cennen Castle
Llandeilo SA19 6UA
Tel: 01558 822291
carregcennencastle.com

Dinefwr & Newton Park
Llandeilo SA19 6RT
Tel: 01558 823902
nationaltrust.org.uk

Llanddeusant Youth Hostel
Llangadog SA19 9UL
Tel: 0845 371 9750
yha.org.uk

Black Mountain Caravan Park
Llanddeusant SA19 9YG
Tel: 01550 740217
blackmountainholidays.co.uk

Cawdor Hotel
Llandeilo SA19 6EN
Tel: 01558 823500
thecawdor.com

Ty Cefn Tregib B&B
Llandeilo SA19 6TD
Tel: 01558 823942
tregib.co.uk

Fronlas B&B
Llandeilo SA19 6LB
Tel: 01558 824733
fronlas.com

Heavenly Chocolate
Llandeilo SA19 6EN
Tel: 01558 822800
heavenlychoc.co.uk

Angel Inn
Llandeilo SA19 6EN
Tel: 01558 822765
angelbistro.co.uk

Barita Delicatessen
Llandeilo SA19 6EN
Tel: 01558 823444

Olive Branch Delicatessen
Llandeilo SA19 6AH
Tel: 01558 823030

Goose and Cuckoo
Llangadog SA19 7EE
Tel: 01550 777359
gooseandcuckoo-llangadog.com

The Red Lion
Llangadog SA19 9AA
Tel: 01550 777357
redlioncoachinginn.co.uk

Toast
Llandeilo SA19 6BA
Tel: 01558 824330
toast.co.uk

Crafts Alive
Llandeilo SA19 6EN
Tel: 01558 822010
crafts-alive.co.uk

51. Tales from a River Bank
National Coracle Centre
Newcastle Emlyn SA38 9JL
Tel: 01239 710980
coraclemuseum.co.uk

National Wool Museum
Clyngwyn SA44 5UP
Tel: 01559 370929
museumwales.ac.uk

Melin Teifi
Drefach SA44 5UP
Tel: 01559 371003
melinteifi.com

Llandysul Paddlers
Llandysul SA44 4AA
Tel: 01559 363209
llandysul-paddlers.org.uk

Nantygwynfan Organic Farm
Llandysul SA44
Tel: 01239 851914
organicfarmwales.co.uk

Pink House B&B
Newcastle Emlyn SA38 9BQ
Tel: 01239 712882
the-pink-house.co.uk

Argoed Meadow Campsite
Argoed SA38 9JL
Tel: 01239 710690
cenarthcampsite.co.uk

The Daffodil at Penrhiwllan
Tremyfoel SA44 5NN
Tel: 01559 370 343
daffodilinn.co.uk

Buon Appetito
Llandysul SA44 4BD
Tel: 01559 363608
buonappetitowales.co.uk

Caws Cenarth Welsh Cheese
Glyneithinog SA37 0LH
Tel: 01239 710432
cawscenarth.co.uk

The Nags Head Inn
Boncath SA37 0HJ
Tel: 01239 841200

Pachamama Bistro
Newcastle Emlyn SA38 9AE
Tel: 01239 711334

BagAge
Newcastle Emlyn SA38 9AE
Tel: 01239 712835
bagage-fairtrade.co.uk

Ludo's The Coopers Inn
Newcastle Emlyn SA38 9EH
Tel: 01239 639088

Ty Croeso Delicatessen
Newcastle Emlyn SA38 9AJ
Tel: 01239 710343

Fay Phillips' Vintage
Narberth
SA67 7AA
Tel: O1834 861151
fayphillipsvintage.co.uk

Giddy Aunt Clothes
Narberth SA67 7AU
Tel: 01834 869223
giddyauntclothes.co.uk

Welsh Farmhouse Company
Narberth SA67 7AS
Tel: 01834 861123
welshfarmhousecompany.com

Damson and Slate
Narberth SA67 7AS
Tel: 01834 862877
damsonandslate.co.uk

Canvas and Cloth
Narberth SA67 7DB
Tel: 01834 860 119
canvasandcloth.co.uk

Good Life
Narberth SA67 7DB
Tel: 01834 811476
goodlifeincorporated.com

Jellyegg
Narberth SA67 7AR
Tel: 01834 860061
jellyegg.com

Oriel Queen's Hall Gallery
Narberth SA67 7AS
Tel: 01834 869454
orielqueenshallgallery.org.uk

The Golden Sheaf Gallery
Narberth SA67 7AR
Tel: 01834 860407
thegoldensheaf-gallery.co.uk

52. Good Vibrations
Narberth Pottery
Narberth SA67 7AX
Tel: 01834 860732
simonrich-narberthpottery.co.uk

Ultracomida Delicatessen
Narberth SA67 7AR
Tel: 01834 861491
ultracomida.co.uk

Plas Farmhouse B&B
Narberth SA67 7BH
Tel: 01834869089
plasfarmhousenarberth.co.uk

Plum Vanilla
Narberth SA67 7DB
Tel: 01834 862762
plumvanilla.com

Fredericks Chocolaterie
Narberth SA67 7DB
Tel: 01834 862838

Sospan-Fach Café
Narberth SA67 7AS
Tel: 01834 862767
sospan-fach.co.uk

Tafarn Sinc
Rosebush SA66 7QU
Tel: 01437 532214
tafarnsinc.co.uk

The Old Post Office
Rosebush SA66 7QU
Tel: 01437 532205

List of Photographs

Acknowledgements

Thank you to everyone involved in the making of the 52 *Weekends in the Country*. Without Muriel and Michael it would never have been possible. It's been a privilege to work again with inspired designer David Rowley and map ace Michael Hill. Thanks for the care taken by the production, media and marketing teams at Virgin, for Sheila Crowley's enthusiasm, Hannah Knowles' overview and Yvonne Jacob's attention to detail. To all the special people along the way, thanks and see you soon.

> *'Why, one day in the country*
> *Is worth a month in town'*

From 'Summer' by CHRISTINA ROSSETTI